*f*P

UNDER THE KNIFE

HOW A WEALTHY NEGRO SURGEON
WIELDED POWER IN
THE JIM CROW SOUTH

HUGH PEARSON

THE FREE PRESS

THE FREE PRESS
A Division of Simon & Schuster, Inc.
1230 Avenue of the Americas
New York, NY 10020

THE FREE PRESS and colophon are trademarks
of Simon & Schuster, Inc.

Designed by Maura Fadden Rosenthal/Mspace

Manufactured in the United States of America

10 9 8 7 6 5 4 3 2 1

Library of Congress Cataloging-in-Publication Data

Pearson, Hugh.
Under the knife : how a wealthy Negro surgeon wielded
power in the Jim Crow South / Hugh Pearson.
       p.   cm.
    1. Griffin, Joseph Howard, 1888–   . 2. Bainbridge
(Ga.)—Race relations.   3. Afro–American surgeons—Georgia
—Bainbridge Biography.   4. Bainbridge (Ga.) Biography.
5. Afro–Americans—Civil rights—Georgia—History—20th
century.   6. Georgia—Race relations.   7. Pearson family.
I. Title.
F294.B35P43   2000
617´.092—dc21
[B]   99-39636
                                                              CIP
ISBN 0-684-84651-9

FOR NANCY, JORDAN, FRANCESCA, AND NATHANIEL,
AND THE AFRO-AMERICAN MEN AND WOMEN
IN THE FIELD OF MEDICINE.

PROLOGUE

Growing up in Fort Wayne, Indiana, always left me with a feeling of regret. In the winter it was cold. By the time I reached the age of twelve, whenever there was a blizzard that meant it was time for me to shovel what seemed like a long driveway leading to our suburban ranch-style home on the edge of the city's southern border among a small collection of fellow Afro-American families, most of whose fathers worked in factories. In the countryside around Fort Wayne the terrain was flat with corn and soybean fields stretching endlessly. And in the region where we lived the only time you saw large numbers of Afro-Americans was when you traveled to the major cities—163 miles northwest to Chicago, or 170 miles northeast to Detroit, or 227 miles east to Cleveland. By contrast, in Georgia, where my family was originally from, Afro-Americans were all over the state, except for the extreme northern reaches that were part of Appalachia. In Georgia the countryside was filled with fragrant pine trees, and, except in the coastal plain, the terrain was rolling. The soil in the dirt back roads was a beautiful deep orange and rust-red. In Georgia it was fun to travel to the south-central part of the state, visit my first cousin Jimmy, then go to our grandpa Pearson's 475-acre farm and throw watermelon rinds at the hogs and watch them fight each other in their efforts to devour them.

So while I grew up I never really understood why we had to live in Fort Wayne, Indiana. Magnavox was a big employer of Afro-Americans. So were International Harvester and General Electric. By contrast, my father was a physician. In that city of 175,000, about 25,000 of whom were Afro-American, we were among the Afro-American elite. Most Afro-Americans in Fort Wayne lived in the central city. Those of us in Southern Heights, as our neighborhood was called, consisting of about thirty families, were considered the bourgeoisie simply because we didn't. There were two other Afro-American "suburban" enclaves even smaller than ours, one of which had a physician. The other six Afro-American doctors lived in predominantly Caucasian neighborhoods.

The way we ended up in Fort Wayne was that in June 1955 my father graduated from Meharry Medical College in Nashville, Tennessee, one of only two predominantly Afro-American medical schools in the country at that time. Subsequently he completed an internship at St. Lawrence Hospital in Lansing, Michigan. After that he began the life of a nomad. Where, he tried to figure out, could a Negro general practitioner set up a practice with any chance for prosperity? For a little while he served as physician at a place called Muscatatuk School in Butlerville, Indiana. Then in the summer of 1957 he came to Fort Wayne to work as a replacement physician for the patients of Dr. Caesar Marshall, also Afro-American and a graduate of the other Negro medical school, at Howard University in Washington, D.C. By then, my mother and father, who had married right after he graduated from medical school, had a year-old daughter Carol and were expecting me in September, placing even more pressure on them to settle down somewhere. When Dr. Marshall returned in September he promised to help my father set up a permanent practice in Fort Wayne.

When I was a boy I didn't know that that was the way we had ended up there. To my young mind my father had been a virtual king among men. To my young mind he had a choice of several places to practice medicine because people everywhere had begged for his services. And for some strange reason he agreed to plunk us down in Fort Wayne, a twelve-hour drive from where all the "fun" was among our aunts, uncles, first cousins, and grandparents in the Deep South.

For me it was exhilarating to visit the South. In the middle of my childhood southern Afro-Americans threw off the shackles of Jim Crow. In 1963 Martin Luther King, Jr., made his famous "I Have a Dream" speech, the one that brought tears to everyone's eyes, the one where, to greatest effect, King opened a new vista on the Negro preacher's miraculous ability to use words, voice inflections, and all manner of sounds to bring other Negroes to a state of ecstasy. Prior to King, most Negro preachers had used that dazzling elocution and emotion to encourage their congregations to be patient and withstand the hell they faced on earth because there was a paradise

waiting for them in heaven. But in 1963 King made it seem that, after so many years of paradise eluding Negroes in the Deep South,
very shortly it was about to plop itself right down in the region.
And the following year it seemed as though it did—at least to me.
Nineteen sixty-four marked the passage of the Civil Rights Act,
bringing down the Jim Crow signs, which I don't remember, but I
must have seen, since from the time I was a baby, every summer we
made trips south to visit family. The following year came the Voting
Rights Act making it easier for Afro-Americans in the region to
vote. The year after that came calls for Black Power.

I was mesmerized. By the time I began the third grade I was intrigued by anything that smacked of large-scale social phenomena. I
read newspaper articles and books, and in the process learned what
life had been like for Afro-Americans under segregation: the vicious
lynchings; the separate drinking fountains; rides in the back of
buses; inferior schools; inferior jobs; the inability to eat in most establishments, stay in most hotels and motels, vote, or look Caucasians, especially Caucasian women, in the eye; the absence of
hearing yourself addressed by Caucasians as Miss, or Mrs., or Mister while you had better address them that way, or else!!! . . . I asked
my father what it had been like living under such a system. And always the answer came back the same way. "Oh, those crackers
never bothered us," his light-brown-skin, wavy-haired countenance
would insist. "They told each other, 'Don't bother those Pearsons,
they're crazy!'"

It was in this manner that my father imbued in me a sense of being exceptional. That is, a sense that while I was indeed a Negro,
since Negro was the preferred term among plenty of Afro-Americans at the time, I was first and foremost a human being with all the
possibilities ahead of me available to all other ambitious, hardworking human beings. Certainly to a degree it was a snobbism.
For part of the message was that it was other Negroes who were
forced to put up with racist insults, but not we Pearsons. Just like
my teachers would teach me in my predominantly Caucasian elementary, junior high, and high schools, America was the land of the
free, home of the brave, where anyone could aspire to be and do
anything as long as he or she put in the work to get there. And my
father tried to assure me that even in Georgia, despite the existence

of racism, the Pearsons had put in the hard work and gotten their just rewards.

Of course the truth was much more complex. Our family had been more prosperous than most other Afro-Americans in their area. But they, like all Afro-Americans back then, also paid the high price exacted to live in rural Jim Crow Georgia, causing the traits of caution and a warped sense of self to become second nature. They registered some instances of discreet victories over Jim Crow, such as the fact that in an era when most men wore hats as part of their daily attire, men in my father's family only wore them on their farms in the summer to shade them from the hot unrelenting sun, or in the winter to conserve warmth. But never when they went to town or attended any social gathering, because Afro-American men were expected to remove their hats in the presence of Caucasians, while Caucasians never reciprocated. And my grandmother and grandfather Pearson did fear for my father's safety because as he grew into adulthood he was the least likely of their nine children to say "Yes, sir" and "No, sir" to Caucasians, which was virtually required of Negroes. But ultimately to survive, my father, like the rest of his family, had to, in the main, surrender to Jim Crow.

When I reached college I discovered another aspect of the truth about the circumstances that preceded me. After finishing his internship in Lansing, Michigan, my father considered returning to Georgia—specifically to the town of Gainesville in the northern section of the state, where he would have had admitting privileges available to him on a segregated ward of the local hospital. But he knew what those wards tended to be like—second-class, in the rear of the main building or often in the basement with only a couple of beds. He probably wouldn't have been able to avail himself of the physician's lounge or the physician's parking lot. It's questionable if he would have been able to perform minor surgery, a privilege common to general practitioners in small towns and medium-size cities as recently as the 1970s and a privilege my father enjoyed in Fort Wayne throughout his practice. And places like Gainesville were usually as good as it got. In plenty of places in the South, Afro-American physicians had no local hospital privileges, and had to turn their patients over to Caucasian physicians when they needed hospitalization. The only other alternatives were the few hospitals in southern cities and towns built specifically for Afro-

4

Americans, either owned by the city and second-class, or those opened by Afro-American physicians themselves. Working in a decent, clean Afro-American–owned hospital in the Deep South was an alternative my father could have easily pursued, because in 1950 a member of our family opened the largest private hospital for Afro-Americans in the state of Georgia.

Uncle Joe was my maternal grandmother's oldest brother. The real world knew him as Joseph Howard Griffin, M.D., physician and surgeon. In 1950 at a cost of the then fabulous sum of $250,000 (if he were to build the hospital in 1999 the cost would be approximately $1.6 million), he built Griffin Hospital and Clinic in the town of Bainbridge, about thirty miles north of the Georgia-Florida border. He financed it all with his own money. The great Ralph McGill, editor of the *Atlanta Constitution*, came and spoke at the hospital dedication ceremony, then wrote a column about it calling the opening an example of the Negro's determination to make a valuable contribution to the South. One of the most influential Afro-American newspapers in the nation at that time, the *Pittsburgh Courier*, featured a large spread on the hospital.

By any estimate Uncle Joe was a wealthy man. When I was a boy my mother regaled me with stories about traveling from Jacksonville, Florida, where she grew up, and visiting his palatial home with its multi-car garage and big shiny Packards and Cadillacs when she was a child. In 1961 Uncle Joe allegedly loaned an Afro-American farmer $95,000 to purchase a valuable piece of property local Caucasians didn't want him to have. In 1970 I watched as he pledged $250,000 worth of stock in Coca-Cola to Meharry as a celebration of his fifty-fifth year since graduation. Two years later the pledge was turned into an irrevocable trust, consisting of stock in Coca-Cola and other "blue chip" companies that was worth $750,000 in 1972, the dividends of which would go to Meharry and two other institutions in perpetuity. But the donation wouldn't take place until after not only his demise and that of his wife and only child, but the demise of the last of his three grandchildren, who, while alive, could live off of the trust's dividend earnings. (But they couldn't touch the stock, per se. In other words, stock that was worth $750,000 in 1972 has ballooned in value by several million dollars, and will have ballooned even more by the time the last grandchild is gone. This was designed to ensure Meharry and the two other institutions a permanent yearly donation of a significant amount of money.)

After finishing his internship my father could have practiced with Uncle Joe. But he was advised against it. Rumor had it that Uncle Joe was too autocratic. There was one other reason he decided against it. But I wouldn't discover that until later.

In the meantime while I was growing up, my father, Uncle Joe, and Uncle Joe's youngest brother, my uncle David—an obstetrician-gynecologist who also practiced in south Georgia—provided me with images that were unusual for an Afro-American boy to grow up with. They were among a select few who sit at the top of the social order among all people: the physicians—kings on a hill whom most people look up to because they're alleged to know the secrets of curing life; kings who were placed on an even loftier pedestal among Afro-Americans who had precious few examples to be proud of.

At that time I had no understanding of what hatred based on this nation's racial obsession had done to their lives. That was something they and the rest of my family purposely kept from me in order to communicate to me that there was nothing beyond my reach. From my father's side of the family came the assurance that the racists "didn't bother us, they told each other those Pearsons are crazy," while from my mother's side came stories about the courage of my maternal grandfather, who was an independent small businessman, and a legendary tale about Uncle Joe.

The year was 1937. A Negro in Bainbridge named Willie Reid, accused of raping and murdering a Caucasian woman, was killed by prison guards allegedly because he was in the process of trying to escape. His body was turned over to a local Negro undertaker (Caucasians at that time would have nothing to do with burying a Negro). But the Caucasians of Bainbridge decided that his murder while "trying to escape" hadn't been enough. They spirited his body out of the funeral home, took it to a local high school football field, and burned it. Many in the mob, which included young women, proudly took pictures next to his charred corpse. Still that wasn't enough. They tied what remained of Reid's body to the end of a rope, hitched it to a car, and dragged it through the Negro section of town. And while doing so they threatened the welfare of all the "uppity nigras," including, of course, Uncle Joe. But Uncle Joe exhibited no fear. Allegedly he simply got his gun and sat on his porch. And as the Caucasian mob rode by he told them, "The first one of you who tries to harm me or my family will be shot dead, and you and me will both have to go to hell!"

A shot was fired into the driveway. But no one was hurt. And there was no more violence that day against Negroes.

Such stories of incidents where family members successfully stood up to racial violence are common lore in middle-class and well-to-do Afro-American families. Yet when I turned thirty-nine I learned that Uncle Joe's life had been far more complex than legend made it seem. His climb to wealth had been made along a dog-eat-dog path, as the climb to wealth made by self-made millionaires usually is. Remaining in the South had forced him to become a man who wore many masks. In the tug-of-war between a philosophy of accommodation to Jim Crow (a philosophy proclaimed by Booker T. Washington in the 1890s in Tuskegee, Alabama, while Uncle Joe was a little boy growing up in Stewart County, Georgia, only about fifty miles away) and the more daring philosophy of directly challenging Jim Crow through the courts (a philosophy espoused later by men such as W. E. B. Du Bois, resulting in the founding of the NAACP), Uncle Joe hewed far more closely to the philosophy of Booker T. Washington. And there was one other thing he did.

It is often said that behind every great fortune is a great crime. I knew for quite some time that Uncle Joe did a tremendous number of good things. But I later learned that he exhibited human weaknesses, human frailties. Yet he was shrewd. And because he lived in the worst time period for Afro-Americans in the Deep South, in order for him to accumulate so much wealth that old saying had to be true.

CHAPTER 1

An October evening in 1996, and I am tired of shouldering a lot of heavy negative racial baggage. But being tired of it is one thing, being free of it another. And I am well aware that by now America has the largest Afro-American middle class ever, that two-thirds of us live above the poverty level, that there are more Afro-American members of Congress than ever, yet to a tremendous extent there is an intractable, stubborn quality to the racism we still face. However, it is not these facts that concern me, for the moment. I am not thinking about the problem in terms of, "Is it useless government programs that are to blame for the problems that we still confront, or continued racism?" Neither am I thinking of it in terms of the unrealistic "Pull yourselves up *solely by your bootstraps*" solution advised by conservatives. Rather, I am thinking about it on a far more abstract level, contemplating how our place in the American self-image has contributed to creating a certain gravity to our predicament, the dimensions on which partisan political philosophers on all sides don't seem to focus. I am thinking about it at the level where one begins in her or his heart of hearts, developing every aspect of who you are to take you where you wish to go. It is on that level that not long ago I concluded there was a way out of much of the conundrum of being the victim, that there's always been a way out, if you only have the confidence to pursue it. And I became convinced that such a path had been perfected by Jews. In my opinion they had refined the formula for escaping their seeming impotence: rigorous pursuit of knowledge for its own sake, the development of independent enterprise to advance in the face of adversity (that is, independent enterprise that ultimately *caters to everyone*). And there was one more element integral to the formula, something that could undergird the collective self-confidence of a racial or ethnic group: worshiping one's own original interpretation of God. Such a recipe isn't the complete solution, I decided, but it is a large part of it, a part, the missing elements of which have nothing to do directly with supply-side ultraconservatism or radical leftism, or anything in between. Instead, it has to do with reorienting your notion of who you are, and, in the case of Afro-Americans, doing so to the extent that we reject society's simplistic definition of who we are (a designation we mistakenly embraced in the late '60s), labeling us by the otherwise negative word "black."

As far as I could tell, the only Afro-American group who approximated any workable formulation of my idea of the proper religious element involved in escaping the rut of the victim were the Black Muslims. My principal objection, however, was that Louis Farrakhan's religious sect does so with a heavy dose of hatred mixed in, calling Caucasians the invention of an evil scientist, singling out Jews in particular for their venom. Such an attitude, I was convinced, blocks intellectual access to what both groups have achieved, encouraging Afro-Americans to feel like inherent outsiders to Western culture (when, in fact, we are an integral part of it, indeed its unique invention, harboring black African, Caucasian, and, in almost half of us, Native American ancestry). And my theory of the proper route for escaping the rut of the victimized was that after worshiping a God who places you at the center of the universe, without directing you to demonize everyone else, you can then face any challenge with confidence, including questioning the very existence of a creator (as do the large number of secular, ethnic Jews). Which leaves Afro-Americans in a bind. We're part of Western culture, but made to feel like outsiders. Most of us have a faith that tells us we have a savior who in most representations looks Caucasian, looks like the very group who has historically left us out in the cold. Indeed, the brand of emotional Christianity practiced in most Afro-American denominations instructs us against questioning anything in the Bible's New Testament ("Your arms are too short to box with God!"). I was convinced that such a quality of worship had sustained us through countless trials and tribulations, yet simultaneously and inadvertently served as a roadblock to our full intellectual blossoming ("Your arms are too short to box with Isaac Newton!") and forced us into a perpetual game of catch-up with the rest of America (except in the realms of entertainment and athletics). With such mind-sets, I concluded, we'd never be intellectual, economic, or scientific innovators on a large scale (with all due respect to the roll call of Afro-American pioneers who have come from our ranks). We'd always be left trying to convince everyone else that we belong in the room. So, given this dilemma, I decided that the best alternative, religiously speaking, was for us to develop an independent secularity of some kind, or some form of agnosticism recognizing the possibility of God, but without belief in hard-and-fast perceived facts about his (or her, or its) existence.

Applying the correct formula for escaping the rut of the victim had been on my mind for a long time. My daily encounters forced me to grapple with the issue. As an editorial page writer for the *Wall Street Journal*, a self-professed independent thinker among conservatives, I felt victimized by my colleagues for not being a conservative, and due to the nature of the articles they wanted me to write, almost all of which dealt with "black pathology" in the ghetto. And then one April day I heard about a book written by Daniel Jonah Goldhagen called *Hitler's Willing Executioners*. Besides advancing the theory that there was a unique quality to the anti-Semitism in Germany that caused ordinary Germans to participate in the Holocaust not reluctantly, but with relish, the book touched on how Jews handled the most intense victimization imaginable, leading to the Holocaust. I decided to write a feature editorial comparing what they confronted in Nazi Germany just before being marched to the death camps with what Afro-Americans faced at the same time under Jim Crow in the American South. And then in August, just before leaving the *Journal,* I flew to the South to cover a story that reminded me of the Jim Crow past as it related to my own family, by virtue of the fact that it took me to Georgia.

Flying to the state to cover the funeral of Alice Hawthorne, the woman killed in the Atlanta Olympics bombing, brought me face-to-face with a heritage that hewed to one element involved in escaping the rut of the victim: finding a way to work for yourself, the path to economic independence. I had long been proud that the men in my family had taken that road. And the family member I was most proud of was Joseph Howard Griffin. Thoroughly steeped in this heritage while growing up, and leaving Indiana to visit family in the South every summer and savor it, had undergirded my self-esteem. Though all of the men in my family were Christian, most were, only to a remote degree, joining A.M.E. congregations that frowned on the carried-away spirituality that is the stereotype of Afro-American faith, and even then, most of them attended church only irregularly. While my father instilled in me the notion that our family had been granted special treatment under Jim Crow, insisting that Georgia racists used to say, "Don't bother those Pearsons, they're crazy," he also repeated a refrain that, over time, bored me, while it served its purpose. Whenever I approached him expecting praise for good grades or any other extraordinary display of intellectual accomplishment, he'd say, "You're supposed to do that, you're a Pearson." The only time during my upbringing when I veered from this self-image bordering on arrogance was in elementary school when, as a precocious third-, fourth-, then fifth-grader paying attention to the news, I briefly flirted with Black Power ideology (the revenge of the victim, a revenge directed against buying into predominantly Caucasian culture), trying to fit in with the mood of the day among young Afro-Americans.

Otherwise, given my upbringing, to a certain extent I felt like an honorary Jew. Of course, I wasn't treated that way. When I got to college (Brown University), I was treated, first and foremost, as a victimized "black." In later years, wherever I worked as a journalist, it was the same thing (though, by then, I also *felt victimized*, and often wrote about the predicament to preserve my sanity). The gap between how I viewed my inherent potential and how most non–Afro-Americans viewed it was often as wide as the distance between opposite banks of the Mississippi River. And by the fall of 1996, after leaving the *Journal*, I wanted to explore in a detailed manner how and why the men in my family were able to provide me such a strong inheritance of self-confidence and pride, since they accomplished what they did in the South during an era far more oppressive to Afro-Americans than the one we now live in.

With this in the forefront of my mind, on that night in October 1996, my interest had been piqued by a newspaper ad stating that another product of the Afro-American bourgeoisie, a former leader of the civil rights movement who had written his autobiography (*An Easy Burden*), was going to speak at New York City's premier Jewish cultural center and one of its principal havens for secular intellectual exchange—the 92nd Street Young Men's Hebrew Association (92nd Street Y). Andrew Young, born the son of a New Orleans dentist, had been an ordained Methodist minister (I decided not to hold that against him), key aide to Martin Luther

King, Jr., U.S. congressman, ambassador to the U.N., mayor of Atlanta, and co-chair of the Atlanta Olympics Committee. He was a real operator, in my estimation, a real achiever, someone who had been on the front line of dismantling Jim Crow, and then gone on to maneuver his way around the usual ruts of racial victimhood. I didn't like everything he stood for, particularly his recent consulting work for corporations that appeared to be exploiting Third World workers. But I was curious about him, and interested in hearing him speak to an audience of Jews, the ethnic group I admired, the ethnic group I envied. An additional reason I wanted to hear Young was that I had encountered him at Alice Hawthorne's funeral. He appeared, along with Billy Payne, the architect of the city's successful Olympics bid, and Zell Miller, the governor of Georgia, to pay his respects to an innocent games volunteer he hadn't known. The stoicism in his demeanor, and that of Payne and Miller, shocked me. We were at a funeral, the funeral of a woman who would still be living were it not for their successful bid to host the 1996 Olympics. The rest of the church was very emotional, while they sat stone-faced and declined an invitation from the pulpit to speak (later, at a second funeral service in Atlanta, they would have something to say).

Young's behavior in particular (in light of the fact that he started out an ordained minister) set my mind wondering if another key ingredient to prosperity, escaping the rut of the victim, involves turning on and off your moral conscience, facing the rest of the world with a certain pragmatism, weighing the pros and cons of who is and isn't expendable to advance your personal well-being, which must be brought about before you can do anything truly influential to advance the well-being of your ethnic or racial group. Was that the way Andrew Young was able to leapfrog from serving within Martin Luther King's inner circle, rending the conscience of the nation, to being the wheeler-dealer it is necessary to be as a member of Congress, ambassador to the U.N., mayor of Atlanta, and corporate consultant? Might he shed some light on the subject at the 92nd Street Y? I grabbed my coat and headed out of my Brooklyn apartment to hear the Columbia professor interview him, then field questions from the audience, including possibly my own.

On my way there by subway I thought of how in my *Wall Street Journal* essay comparing the Jewish and Afro-American experiences,

I theorized that America had been a godsend for Jews, that ours was a new nation founded by outcast Europeans—Protestants and Catholics escaping state-sponsored religious persecution, former convicts, maverick entrepreneurs—tired of old European cultures set in their ways, cultures divided by class, where almost everywhere Jews were treated as the ultimate niggers. And since the new Americans were escaping their own versions of persecution or economic stagnation, building a "new world" in need of all the enterprising assistance it could get, a welcome mat had been extended to Jews. In Europe they had had plenty of practice perfecting the skills this "new world" would need, actively writing the book on the escape hatch for the victimized, having been moneylenders (since moneylending was illegal for Christians in so many European nations), peddlers, merchants, major contributors to European culture due to their love of scholarship, etc. And they worshiped their own religion, from which Christianity was born. Jews introduced the world to monotheism. Still in Europe they couldn't escape victimization, periodic pogroms designed to get rid of them ("The evil Christ killers!"). By contrast, in America they certainly would face anti-Semitism (and still do), but it would never become woven into the fabric of the nation, requiring constitutional amendments to correct, as happened in the case of Afro-Americans, due to the institution of slavery.

In my opinion, these differences were the principal seeds that caused the growth of antagonism between Afro-Americans and Jews. In America it was inherently easier for them to escape niggerization. Besides having honed the attributes for escape, they often looked like their tormentors, whereas even when we did look like Caucasians, telltale physical signs of "blackness" were used to keep us out in the cold. Yet despite these differences in our lives, I dreamed of the day when applying greater thrift and enterprise, love of scholarship, and intellectual self-confidence would become as thoroughly instilled, collectively, among Afro-Americans as it seemed to be among Jews. And I concluded that the men in my family had applied much of this formula, especially Joseph Griffin. And that Andrew Young, to a great degree, had done much the same thing, but on a different frequency (the political wheeling and dealing of public office, lucrative consulting work . . .).

So that night at the Y, I looked forward to an interesting dialogue between Young and the professor from Columbia University, before an audience primarily of Jews, with whom, collectively, Afro-American relationships in the last thirty years or so had become strained. There had been the break after the civil rights movement, a movement that so many Jews had contributed to financially, and in a few cases with their own lives (Andrew Goodman, Mickey Schwerner . . .); there was the recent Leonard Jeffries controversy; and, of course, the issue of Afro-American fascination with Louis Farrakhan. During the audience question-and-answer period, I expected one or more of those subjects to be raised, after Young detailed a few choice anecdotes from his life, perhaps even tossed out a few pearls regarding how he managed to become the prosperous Afro-American now sitting before us.

The overwhelming majority of the audience appeared to be Jewish. During the interview, Young talked about the New South, among other things, calling it a land of racial cooperation, as if he were selling us on moving down there. However, he gave away no candid tips on his personal success. During the question-and-answer period I decided not to ask him anything about that. Instead, I accused him of engaging in overblown hype about how good things were racially in the region. He judiciously talked his way around my criticism. Then he fielded another question, one of the ones I had predicted. "What about Farrakhan, Mr. Young?" asked an elderly Jewish man. "Why is he so popular among blacks and what can be done about that?"

Young responded shrewdly to the question. Given my knowledge of Jewish history I understood the questioner's paranoia. Yet, despite my admiration for Jews, I also felt defensive, once more like a victim who understood the frustrations that allowed Farrakhan to captivate so many Afro-Americans. I realized that part of that feeling derives from the fact that Jews, who once felt impotent and collectively victimized, had now left those of us who still feel that way to fend for ourselves. In recent years, so many Jews had grown indifferent to Afro-American life. Like others who see themselves as white, so many of them had grown tired of us, so many no longer empathized with what we go through. Jewish indifference toward us and rapid assimilation in contemporary life, I told the questioner after the event was over, was every bit as much to blame for Farrakhan's popularity among Afro-Americans as anything else. But he would have none of it. He began shouting at me, insisting that what I said wasn't true. I insisted that it was. Then what he said next really enraged me. "We were responsible for your freedom!"

Part of me understood that he wasn't referring to the personal me, but rather, the collective one. Still the bigger part felt like he was referring to me personally, as though his comment was a cavalier, patronizing slap in my face and the faces of my entire family. He didn't know a thing about me, about us. Referring to either the personal or collective Afro-American as owing our entire debt for freedom to Jews was an insult that overlooked and disrespected the long history of suffering, of courage, of strength and audacity that I felt all Afro-Americans could claim, despite my frustration with what we hadn't yet achieved. But, more pointedly, it was the personal side that felt offended, enraged that he disregarded my great-grandparents, grandparents, parents, aunts, and uncles. The male in me was especially offended about his disregard for the men, especially his disregard for Joseph Howard Griffin.

So I yelled right back at him, filling him in on the accomplishments of my great-grandfathers, grandfathers, father, and uncles. I filled him in about Uncle Joe. It was me, one man against a group of middle-aged and elderly Jews, whose counterattacks began to drown out everything I had to say. By then Andrew Young had disappeared into a crowd of admirers who had moved into the adjacent room. The handful of other Afro-Americans in attendance had gone, too. I was making no headway, convincing no one of the rightness of what I had to say. I decided to give up, to simply back down, retreat, head for the elevator and out the door of the 92nd Street Y, back into the streets of Manhattan.

Again, I pondered the legacy the men in my family had left me. Once more, I wondered how they accomplished anything to be proud of in the Jim Crow South, given the documented history of oppression that immediately comes to mind when thinking of Afro-Americans in the land of cotton, kudzu, magnolias, Spanish moss, Scarlett O'Hara, and the Ku Klux Klan. Once more I recalled how during my most recent visit to Georgia to cover Alice Hawthorne's funeral, I had come across Young, an encounter that led me to his speaking engagement at New York City's premier Jewish cultural center. And when I arrived in the city of Albany, Georgia, where Ms. Hawthorne had resided, I got up on the morning of the first funeral service held for her, and was surprised by the presence of a Jewish-owned restaurant downtown, a large eat-in affair specializing in bagels, a place where I was grateful to have breakfast, saving me from the vast expanse of fast-food emporiums in the area. Though I knew that a handful of Jewish merchants settled even the small-town South, I hadn't expected any to open up a large bagel restaurant deep in southwest Georgia, 190 miles from far more urbane Atlanta. Whenever I thought of bagel restaurants, I thought of the presence of large numbers of Jews, and I knew there weren't a large number in Albany, or anywhere else in Georgia outside of Atlanta. Then after my breakfast, upon making my way over to the church and viewing Ms. Hawthorne's body hours before the service, I was reminded of the enterprising success of one of the branches of my family, a level of success that also reminded me of what I admired about the Jewish community, what I admired about the possibilities of escaping the worst manifestations of victimhood. One night several years earlier in the town of Dublin, where all three of my father's brothers lived, my cousin Alfred called me and another of my first cousins down to the family funeral home to help him and one of his assistants lift a very overweight woman into her casket (it wasn't Ms. Hawthorne's size that reminded me of this, since she had been slender, just the fact that I was viewing her body). The Alfred O. Pearson family had inherited the Dudley Funeral Home, one of several businesses owned by my aunt Thomaseanor's very resourceful father, Herb Dudley, who had been known as Mr. Black Dublin.

During segregation Dudley had built one of the most impressive Afro-American business empires in the South. His friends had included my uncle Joe, as well as 1936 Olympic gold medalist Jesse Owens, Martin Luther King, Jr. (who often stayed at the Dudley Motel when traveling from Atlanta to Savannah, since Dublin is midway between the two cities), and an entire roll call of famous Afro-American entertainers who traveled the "chitlin circuit" of southern towns during Jim Crow and who were relieved to stay at the Dudley Motel because there was nowhere else of quality to sleep for miles. However, after segregation crumbled, most of the enterprises he owned (including, in addition to a motel and funeral parlor, a twenty-four-hour gas station, a restaurant, beauty parlor, real estate company, and, at one point, an ice skating rink, lumber and sawmill, and a casket factory) were closed, leaving just the beauty parlor, funeral home, and modest real estate holdings, all owned by the Alfred O. Pearson family since Dudley's daughter, my aunt Thomaseanor, had been his only child.

How could it be, I wondered once more, that anyone like the man at the 92nd Street Y had the arrogance, the audacity to imply that no such enterprising Afro-American had played a role in facilitating our freedom? Granted, it would have been nice if there had been more Herb Dudleys and even nicer if after segregation, the Dudley Motel had grown into a national Afro-American–owned motel chain serving the entire general public, a chain to rival Holiday Inns or Comfort Inns or any others. But there were a number of reasons this hadn't occurred, reasons I wasn't completely privy to, as well as the satisfaction, the thrill Afro-Americans felt in 1964 to finally be able to stay in motels the law had previously prevented us from doing anything in except cooking and cleaning. In addition, there had been the reality that Caucasians had never been used to patronizing Afro-American businesses the way they had the businesses of each other or those of Jews. And they hardly had any intentions of doing so after Jim Crow, all factors contributing to the depressing legacy wherein burgeoning enterprise still wasn't second nature to enough Afro-Americans. The effects of this truth were graphically presented to me once more after viewing Ms. Hawthorne's body, when I decided to drive around the neighborhood surrounding the church since there were still a couple of hours left before her funeral. Where there weren't the same old crumbling boarded-up houses or dilapidated structures housing people to be found in such poor Afro-American communities, the commercial activity was the usual—liquor outlets primarily owned by non–Afro-Americans, fast-food chains like Churches or Popeye's. And there were the poor Afro-American men standing around waiting for nothing just like the men I've seen in countless ghettos.

Attending a funeral was sad and depressing enough without pondering this other reality. The very emotional, moving service provided me one more taste of Afro-American Christianity. Now I was in the mood for something else. I was in the mood for recalling what my family had done to escape the worst manifestations of victimhood. I realized that I was only sixty miles from the town where my uncle Joe had built his hospital. So after the funeral I decided to drive to Bainbridge to ponder my great-uncle's legacy, to gaze once more at the building that had housed Griffin Hospital and Clinic, and visit his daughter, my cousin Mary Louise, who still lives in his old home.

I hadn't been back to Bainbridge since the summer of 1977, when I was in college. Uncle Joe was quite old and frail by then, eighty-nine years of age. His strong resemblance to my maternal grandmother was evident (or my grandmother at that point resembled him). She was his youngest sister in a family of sixteen children. Having been born in 1888, he was the oldest of the twelve children my great-grandfather Griffin had by his second wife. When I last saw him he was having lunch in a room in the front part of his home, being fed by Mary Louise, a widow, who even in her adult life lived in that large house with her parents, husband, and children—two boys and one girl. He was happy to see me and asked if my father was still practicing medicine in Fort Wayne. We engaged in more of the polite niceties that extended family engage in on such occasions. Then I said my farewells, got in my car, and headed forty miles south to visit my aunt and his niece, Barbara Richardson Cotton, who taught history at Florida A&M University in Tallahassee. That was the last time I saw him. He died two and a half years later, the last week of December 1980, just a little more than one month before he would have turned ninety-three.

Fresh from Alice Hawthorne's funeral, as I headed down state highway 253 I savored the deep orange and rust-red clay-based soil evident in the back roads coming off the two-lane highway, the tall skinny pine trees, and oak and other broadleaf trees with Spanish moss defining the south Georgia countryside. I had to admit there was something vaguely entrancing about the Deep South, a sentiment that survived my childhood. Yet from the vantage point of the age of thirty-eight I was just as struck by the rampant lack of worldliness demonstrated by its people. Over the past year I had concluded that most southern Afro-Americans and Caucasians alike rebel against intellectual growth. Like Afro-Americans, the Caucasians as a whole tend to be extremely Christian (less pronounced in their Christianity yet still wedded to what they swear are the direct words of God) and unlearned, a fact that becomes just as obvious as the uniqueness of the region's countryside. Once you leave Washington, D.C.'s Virginia suburbs heading south, you begin to notice plenty of billboards, bumper stickers, and large signs in front of a plethora of churches instructing that Jesus is the light and the way. Plenty of radio and cable TV programs profess the same thing. Now I was in south Georgia's version of this phenomenon.

As I crossed the Flint River that abuts Bainbridge just as it does Albany, it became clear that the town was even sleepier than Albany (Georgia's sixth largest city), since it has only approximately 11,000 citizens. Instinctively I made a right onto Broad Street and staring me in my face on the left was my great-uncle's old hospital, a sizable plain two-story brick structure looking just like it did when he built it. The difference was that instead of the original sign reading "Griffin Hospital and Clinic," on its façade is a sign reading "PX Printing." The structure is just two blocks from the center of town, calling the lie to the notion that in every town and city in the South all Afro-American enterprises were shunted off "across the tracks" from everything important. Griffin Hospital and Clinic seemed as if it had been an integral part of this town that had always been run by Caucasians (though about half of its population throughout its history has been Afro-American), specifically another family named Griffin, whose patriarch went on to become the last staunchly segregationist governor of Georgia until the election of Lester Maddox.

In the town square next to a lovely gazebo is a plaque commemorating the life of that man, Marvin Griffin, who also earned dubious distinction as perhaps the most corrupt governor in the state's history. In 1958 while in office, he openly, indeed quite publicly, advised the governor of Arkansas, Orval Faubus, to defy the Supreme Court's school desegregation order. In the process he received accolades from racists all over the nation. His family ran Bainbridge for many, many years and still owns the town's only newspaper. My great-uncle interacted with them, not because he agreed with what they stood for but because, as one power dealing with another, he had to.

The town seems pleasant, Old South pleasant, as if, unlike Atlanta, it embraces rather than flees the region's stereotyped image. I drove south past the town square and entered a neighborhood of lovely Victorian homes and Greek revival mansions with abundant Spanish moss hanging from the broadleaf trees surrounding them. It was all Caucasian and looks like the perfect setting for a film like *Fried Green Tomatoes,* or *Forrest Gump.* Then I swung back north to the center of town, up two blocks, and parked my car across the street from my uncle's old hospital. I got out and walked around.

At one corner across from the town square is a drugstore where I bought some film to take pictures. I asked the young Caucasian woman who sold me the film and appeared to be in her late teens if she had ever heard of Dr. Joseph Griffin, who was once a prominent physician in town. She replied no. She then asked the fifty-something Caucasian pharmacist behind the prescription counter. "Of course I've heard of him," he replied. "When I was a boy I used to run errands at his hospital. It was right down the street. But now it's owned by a company called PX Printing."

"I know," I replied. "I'm Dr. Griffin's great-nephew."

"Is that right? He was an interesting man. If you go walk into the printing company they probably wouldn't mind giving you a tour of the building."

"I might just do that."

I decided, though, to save the tour for later. In the meantime, after taking pictures of the hospital I got back in my rental car, turned right onto Calhoun Street, and on the left Uncle Joe's lovely old brick home came into view. It was the only impressive residence of its kind in this particular section, which was predominantly Afro-American. I pulled into the driveway, got out, and knocked on the door. In a little while Mary Louise's small, caramel-colored, elegant personage complete with a short gray-and-black Afro answered the door. "Why, what do you know," she said in her cultivated southern lilt, a large smile spreading across her face as she prepared to embrace me. "It's the author of the family."

CHAPTER 2

The old-fashioned Afro-American southernness at the core of Mary Louise's greeting warmed me. After we hugged she ushered me inside. I told her what had brought me to the area.

"Yes, wasn't it a shame!" she remarked. "Just pitiful!"

"And after her funeral I decided since I was so close to Bainbridge, I'd drive on down."

"Albany's not *that* close. It was so nice of you to make the detour!"

Glancing again at her petite frame, keeping in mind that she is all of seventy-three years of age, I reminded myself that her appearance fuels that adage Afro-American men sometimes state among themselves when debating the wisdom of marrying outside of the "race": "Well, you know, when women get old, black don't crack!"

She no longer uses most of the house. Yet it is still adorned with her parents' elegant furniture. In the expansive living room hangs a large painting of Uncle Joe. To the right of the living room is a spacious room that includes a television set and bookcase, the place I last saw Uncle Joe. In the opposite direction past the living room, opening out to the left, is the study, which looked largely as it did on my previous visit. There are family photos on a piano, including a picture of Uncle Joe when he was about sixty. Heading to the back you see the staircase on the left leading to the second floor, which contains large bedrooms that have been mostly closed off. Then behind the staircase, the formal dining room. Behind it to the left is another room that Mary Louise has converted into her bedroom, and to the right, the kitchen. And just off the side entrance to the house, where I parked my rental car in the driveway, is what is now her main sitting area, where there are family photos, too, one with Uncle Joe and three of my other great-uncles, his younger brothers. And there are two photographs I'm familiar with from childhood visits to my maternal grandparents' home—one of Great-grandfather Robert Griffin taken, it appeared, when he was about in his mid-forties, the other of Great-grandmother Mary Griffin when she was an old woman.

Ever since her mother and father died, which was within five days of each other, Mary Louise, whose husband died several years before her parents, has lived in this house alone—most of the time. For the past year or so her son Joe, who is in his early fifties and suffered a heart ailment while living in California, has temporarily moved back in. At that moment he wasn't home. We chatted politely in the main sitting area filling each other in about family, then went on to discuss the current state of the world about which we were in almost total agreement. I told myself that not only is Mary Louise elegant, she is a sharp woman.

Besides coming to see my uncle's old hospital, visit his old home, ponder his legacy, and talk to Mary Louise, there was one other task to complete in Bainbridge—visiting another cousin in town. Her mother was another sister of Uncle Joe's, one of my grandmother's older sisters, Agnes Griffin Ford. Aunt Agnes's daughter Mary Agnes is also an attractive woman. Much taller than Mary Louise, she has chocolate skin, wears her hair straightened, is also a widow, has two grown daughters, and is in her late sixties— the same age my mother would be if she were still alive. In fact, it was because Alice Hawthorne's brown-skinned beauty reminded me of my mother that I was drawn to writing about the tragedy of her death. That, and the fact that she died at the age of forty-four, the same age my mother died after her eight-and-a-half-year battle with systemic lupus. So to complete the circle of my trip south, to obtain closure with regard to the reasons for the story idea and thus the odyssey, I wanted to see Mary Agnes because she and my mother were running buddies while growing up. On another trip she'll regale me with stories about their college days when my mother attended nursing school in Augusta, while she attended college in Savannah.

"Edith would come down to Savannah and we would go to parties. She was so shy. Now your mama, she was a shy one! We'd go to parties with our cousin Robie, and if anyone bothered us we'd sic Robie on them! Edith and Howard were my favorite first cousins. When your mother died and Howard died shortly after, I thought the world had ended."

ing the last decade of the nineteenth century in rural Georgia at a time when lynchings in the state occurred almost every week? (At the turn of the century, Georgia led the nation in that category.) Where did the audacity originate that caused him to decide not only that he would become a physician, even though there was not one Afro-American physician in his county, but later on, that he was going to build an eighteen-bed hospital, then later still a fifty-bed facility with the most modern, up-to-date equipment available in the 1950s, an almost unheard-of accomplishment at that time for a private hospital owned by an Afro-American? I was beginning to suspect that given the absolutely nightmarish conditions that existed in rural and small-town Georgia for Afro-Americans in his heyday, his drive must have exceeded the drive in all but the wealthiest Caucasian men—that it had to rival that of men like John D. Rockefeller, Andrew Carnegie, and Joseph Kennedy; that with such drive, had another avenue of success been available to him, my great-uncle would have become immensely wealthy rather than just wealthy; that had he been born Caucasian he would have been mentioned in the same breath as such men. And while on my trip to Georgia for the Alice Hawthorne story, after leaving Bainbridge, I continued on to Tallahassee, since it was just forty miles farther south. And as I continued driving I continued to dwell on these thoughts of how my enterprising great-uncle escaped the worst manifestations of victimhood. The more I thought about it the more I began to suspect there was something else to his identity that was totally missing from my aunt's book. I could feel it. And I was sure that she knew plenty of what that something else was, that the reason she didn't expose it to the light of day was directly due to something I once heard her sister, my aunt Elaine say: "Barbara wrote that book for Uncle Joe. If someone wrote the *real* story of his life it would be a very different and very interesting book."

Aunt Barbara had written *Non Verba Opera: Not Words but Works* under a number of constraints. The price of full cooperation from Uncle Joe, the price of sitting down with him and recording hours of taped oral history, the price of continuing to receive Mary Louise's pleasantness, the price of shoring up, providing a few more bricks to the façade we Afro-Americans construct to maintain our dignity rather than tell the world or even ourselves everything about who we are, was agreeing to write that slim volume that would have easily passed muster with John Johnson, publisher of *Ebony*, were he to decide that he might want to excerpt it on the pages of his magazine as one more storybook, Dale Carnegie–in–brown–face tale to motivate Afro-Americans.

Yet on that day, that visit, I decided not to tell my aunt of my intention to further investigate Uncle Joe's life. I feared I might offend her professionally. So the following morning, after a pleasant get-together, I solidified my plans, my resolve to return to the area later for the investigation. For the moment I would depart and head for the section of the state where my father is from to contemplate the legacy of his side of my family. So the following morning I rose and drove to southeast Georgia, choosing first to visit Savannah, since, despite countless trips to Georgia during and after my childhood, no one in the family had taken me or my two sisters there, even though Savannah was a mere hour and a half from my grandfather Pearson's farm. The reason *he* never took us, my father had told me one day the previous summer, was because while he was growing up, Savannah was, of all the major cities in Georgia, the worst hands down for Afro-Americans. He said it was wise to stay away because it was so easy for an Afro-American with any pride about himself to get in trouble there. And he carried over his aversion for the town into this post–Jim Crow era.

But visions of and allusions to Savannah from recent films and the book *Midnight in the Garden of Good and Evil* aroused my curiosity anew. So the following morning after my three-and-a-half-hour drive due east northeast from Tallahassee I saw why the city is considered such a gem. Among all of Georgia's municipalities Savannah is by far the loveliest. Its stately townhouses and twenty-one squares are a stark contrast to everything else in the state, rendering it the only city that gives off a sense of cultured urbanity anything like the cities of the U.S. Northeast. I had read and been told that it is a quirky locale, but it is also a showcase of the Old South along with New Orleans; Charleston; Richmond, Virginia; Natchez, Mississippi; and Wilmington, North Carolina. Still, it was hard to believe that Savannah is even part of Georgia, which I'm sure is a sentiment many residents of the town feel from the opposite direction. To them it must be difficult to believe that the rest of Georgia, given its Bible Belt, molasses-slow, redneck aura (which is rapidly being devoured by a relatively fast-paced Atlanta-orchestrated, generic, service-based economic virus of some kind), is part of the Georgia founded in the eighteenth century. I toured many of the town squares, at the center of which are statues or fountains, noticing one that contained the image of John Wesley, founder of the Methodist church. From 1735 to 1738 he preached Methodism in Savannah before returning to Europe to actually launch the denomination. I thought about how I had been raised attending a church that was derivative of the denomination—the African *Methodist* Episcopal church. In an old cemetery were other prominent progenitors of aspects of my heritage that I had taken for granted—men such as James Oglethorpe, who had gotten the colony of Georgia off the ground.

An hour and a half west of town is a sector of the state that could hardly be more of a contrast. Known as the wiregrass region, it was very sparsely settled during the antebellum era, primarily because its soil was considered too poor for large-scale cultivation. After the Civil War the land became prime frontier property ripe for the purchase by any aspiring farmer willing to try to make a go of raising crops in its less-than-ideal loam. Great-grandfather Law Pearson came from Coffee County, Georgia, about seventy miles to the south, where he had been a slave before buying his freedom, and eventually accumulated eight hundred acres of land just outside of the town of Dublin. And upon reaching adulthood his son Nathan, the father of my father, traveled about thirty miles southeast and purchased 475 acres.

I headed to Interstate 16 for the drive back to Atlanta so that I could make my return flight to New York City and file my Alice Hawthorne story. An hour and a half into the drive I took the Vidalia exit, then the turnoff for the nearby town of Glenwood, then the rough black asphalt road that led to my grandfather Pearson's farm. The house my grandparents lived in while I was a child was still standing, but empty. It looked weather-beaten but not dilapidated. Across the road from it still exists the clearing where my grandfather built his original house, a large wooden structure with a long porch across the front. By 1956 that house was badly in need of repair. So my grandparents moved to the smaller house I was familiar with across the road. While I was growing up, however, my grandfather still used an equipment shed and smokehouse that he built adjacent to the original house. In that original clearing the only things still standing are the dark gray, withered, wooden skeletal parts of the shed and smokehouse that have yet to collapse—the sort of dilapidated structures that are common sights in the rural South.

By now it was night. I drove down the deep orange dirt lane leading to the family graves that comes off the main road facing the farmhouse. Upon arriving at the graveyard I didn't get out because I didn't have a flashlight. I just sat in the car and tried to squeeze all the sentimentality bubbling to the surface out of my system. When I parked in front of the house my grandparents lived in while I was a child, visions came to me of my grandfather sitting on the porch in his felt hat and overalls with his dog Bullet by his side. And of how, when the entire family got together, at dusk he would have all of us younger grandchildren pile into the back of his pickup truck. Then he'd climb into the cab to drive us through those red clay backroads of the farm, as if to make up for the fact that he wasn't effusive in demonstrating his affection. He was an extremely quiet, small, dignified man, who bore a striking resemblance to the late Ethiopian emperor Haile Selassie, a look that implied that the word "esteem" was invented specifically to describe him, an esteem that signaled to everyone that this man was too regal to be treated as if he was a nigger. Which was why I wanted to believe the standard reply my father gave to my questions about what it was like to grow up in that racially repressive environment: "Those crackers said, '- Don't bother those Pearsons, they're crazy!'" To my young mind, it seemed that if anyone was stupid enough not to realize you should treat a man of such deportment with homage, then certainly he and the rest of the family would have forced you to.

Of course my history studies told me that this couldn't have been totally true. And my later investigations of family lore would expose plenty of the husks within the family legends my father told me, proving that despite my grandfather's regal bearing, he had made plenty of compromises. His daughter Mamie, who married a man named Louis Jordan, who has a nephew named Vernon Jordan—known to the rest of the world as President Bill Clinton's best friend—would be most revealing in this. "Pop knew he could only go so far with those crackers," she reminisced when I pressed her. "He knew that if you wanted to survive you had to be smart enough to know the right situation where it was okay to preserve your dignity. He used to say, 'You gotta be smarter than the white man, know when to tuck under and when not to.' He believed that sometimes you could be a man, other times you couldn't."

Aunt Mamie recalled one particular time when he chose not to be a man and she had been with him—a good example of the type of incident my father would never have told me about and perhaps wouldn't even remember because it would be in the best interest of his self-image not to. They stopped at a gas station in Glenwood owned by a Mr. Sears. "Now Mr. Sears thought Pop was great," she recounted. "Pop pulled up to his gas station. I must have been in the sixth or seventh grade. When Mr. Sears saw him he went to his ice bucket and retrieved a bottle of Coke for Pop. And as he gave it to him he said, 'Look at this Nathan. He's one of the finest coloreds in Wheeler County.' That made me real mad, the condescension of his statement. You see, he could call Pop Nathan, *but Pop had to call him Mr. Sears*. And Pop was just beaming away. You see, they liked Pop because he abided by their rules, was quite hardworking, and he paid his bills on time."

Nathan Pearson: Born in October 1882, he stood about 5′9″ in height and never weighed more than 150 pounds, had light brown skin, blue-gray eyes, curlyish hair (among Afro-Americans, often called "good hair," meaning far less kinky than the typical Afro-American's) as a result of the family racial mixture (his father was the son of his slave master, while his mother, Mary, daughter of her slave master, was also one-quarter Native American), and wasn't educated past the third grade because after that he was required to work on his father's farm, which he did until he was twenty-one. Then he set out on his own with all his possessions in a knapsack (an alleged detail that for me sounds just a bit too romantic). He had accepted no compensation from his father, so from that time worked farm labor jobs for pay, saving up his money until he had enough to begin purchasing the land for his own farm. He believed that idleness was a sin stating, "I'll never be accused of raising a lazy young'un!" And he never was. When it was time to pick the cotton crop in the fall, upon reaching the age of four each child he and my grandmother Bessie McClendon Pearson had—five girls and four boys—would receive a small cotton sack that was draped over her or his shoulder for the purpose of toddling along after the adults and older children and plucking the stray bolls of cotton they had missed. Recalled Aunt Mamie: "He did it in such a way that you sort of felt it a privilege to join in the activity." Everyone's chores fit their age levels: care for a pet animal, clean up the yard, milk the cows, feed the pigs, sweep the porches . . .

Though he was a Christian, Grandpa wasn't hyperreligious in the sanctified carried-away tradition that is the stereotype of Afro-American Christianity. In fact, he rarely attended St. Paul A.M.E. Church with the rest of the family. And not only did he frown on singing, shouting, and dancing in the aisles at church, he didn't believe in dancing period, not even at parties (he didn't believe in parties at all, frowned on card playing, and forget craps!). He worked six days a week, twelve to fourteen hours a day during the summer, even worked in the light rain, and while doing so in the fall and winter wore a leather cap and jacket and high-top boots. He ate three meals a day, took a half-hour rest at noon, and at the end of the workday napped in his chair through the rest of the evening before retiring to bed, only to sleep soundly until dawn. Grandma Pearson kept the books. And Grandpa allowed others to sharecrop some of his land, sometimes including poor Georgia crackers (who, according to my father, when about to work our land, would tell another of their peers, "I'm gonna go work for one of them rich niggers.").

Reportedly he had such a good reputation in the area that it wasn't difficult at all for him to obtain bank loans until his tobacco, cotton, and corn crops came in. But discretion based on the area's racial reality was never far from the surface of his persona. One day he had to go to a bank in nearby Mount Vernon to conduct business with a banker named Duncan McCrae. But that particular week was a bad one because local crackers had severely beaten a Negro man in nearby Ailey for having had the audacity to try to organize Negroes in the area to vote (he would die later of his injuries). So Mr. McCrae advised Grandpa to wait a week, then return, because the crackers were so riled up that they were going after any Negroes they considered to be uppity. And any Caucasians who helped them. "They don't like me any more than they like you," Mr. McCrae told him, referring to the fact that middle-class Caucasians were also disliked by the poor crackers who predominated in the area. Grandpa tucked in his dignity and discreetly worked on his farm for a week before returning to do business with Duncan McCrae.

He said he could never work for "whites." It was beneath his dignity, which was also why when the great migrations of Negroes from the South took place, he felt it was foolish to move North since the jobs they were migrating to required working for Caucasians in factories. But by owning your own farm, he felt, you could get around all of that. He wouldn't allow his wife to work for them either or his children, as long as they lived under his roof—especially the girls. Just such an opportunity presented itself when the oldest three, all girls, were teenagers (all the children were born a year or two apart). The local Caucasian mailman had a Negro maid. One day she became ill. So he knocked on the door of the Nathan Pearson home to ask if one of the Pearson teenage daughters could replace her for the duration of her illness. But Nathan Pearson knew what tended to happen in such situations: Afro-American maids often ended up being coerced by their Caucasian bosses into having sex, a practice that dated back to slavery, which was why he looked the way he looked. And he knew that if any of his daughters were placed in that predicament he'd have no legal recourse. There would be only one face-saving, pride-preserving alternative, and that would lead to his being lynched. So he told his daughters the answer was no, "Because I don't want to have to go kill myself a white man."

Despite all his hard work, independence, and pride, tucked just beneath the surface of who he was would remain that ever-present race-based fear. After constructing a home for his family he didn't paint it. No Afro-Americans in the community had painted houses. The reason? That was considered too uppity. If it was painted he told his family, "The crackers might come and burn the place down with us in it." Then there were the times when the local Ku Klux Klan would parade through their rural Negro community in search of a Negro girl who kept having children out of wedlock, with the intention of beating such ways out of her. Rather than having the audacity to try to prevent it, Grandpa, like all the other Negro men in the area, decided it was best to ignore it all, largely because she wasn't someone they wanted to shine any light on anyway, highlighting a negative racial stereotype, even though it had to have eaten away at their sense of male pride that they were unable to protect her. Instead, Grandpa insisted on protecting what was definitely his. "Every time the Klan paraded down the road to get her, he'd take his gun and hide in the bushes on our property line to ensure they didn't do any damage to our property," recalled Aunt Mamie. "For that day and time it was a brave act."

But there were other times when he seemed not so brave, and counseled his children as to why such gestures really amounted to a certain necessary cunning in order to survive. After leaving the farm, his daughter Lavester, the second-oldest child, to whom I am so close that she is a virtual surrogate mother to me now, graduated from Talladega College in Alabama in 1938. She was valedictorian of her class (my grandparents would send all nine of their children to college, which was unusual in that day and age for rural southerners, period, to do). However, Grandpa couldn't afford to send her to graduate school to earn a master's degree in French the way she wanted. So she had to teach high school. All Afro-American high school teachers in the public school systems of Georgia at that time had to be selected by Caucasians. She got Grandpa to drive her to her first interview. Prior to attending Talladega Aunt Lavester had attended Ballard High School in Macon. Ballard was a private school for Afro-Americans that had been established by New England missionaries. Only a fortunate few Afro-Americans were able to attend a school of that caliber. At the school the Caucasian teachers from the North taught the students the same way they would have taught them if they were New Englanders. That is, the youths weren't instructed to be deferential to Caucasians in the manner it was customary back then to teach Afro-American children to be. The same was true at Talladega.

So when Aunt Lavester sat for her interview she answered the questions put to her by the Caucasian woman with "Yes" or "No." This was a potentially fatal mistake since Afro-Americans were always supposed to answer Caucasians with "Yes, ma'am" or "Yes, sir," etc. According to Aunt Mamie, who was also there, Grandpa was sitting with Aunt Lavester while she answered the questions. Upon hearing that she wasn't attaching "ma'am" to her answers, he started fidgeting. Aunt Lavester also answered questions with "I did" or "I did not," which was another trick that proud Afro-Americans used to avoid being deferential in the way expected. Grandpa continued to fidget. "After the interview when we got back to the car, Pop let her have it. He told her, 'You cannot do that! I have to live here with these crackers, but you can go away!' He was terribly upset."

And he feared most of all for my father. "Pop was always scared for your daddy," Aunt Mamie recalled, "because he just wouldn't buckle under [to Caucasians] the way he was supposed to."

A hint that this had been true even while he was growing up was graphically demonstrated to me when I was thirteen, and my father and I traveled to Georgia because my grandfather was on his deathbed. (He would die weeks later, after which we and the rest of our immediate family would return for his funeral.) It was the spring of 1971, seven years after the end of Jim Crow. Though public facilities were no longer segregated, other old habits were dying a slow death, and in the hospital where my eighty-eight-year-old grandfather lay half-asleep, an elderly Caucasian woman stuck her head in the door of his room. Upon seeing my grandfather on the bed she said, "Oh, uncle. I'm so sorry you're sick. I'll be prayin' for you." "Uncle" was the traditional appellation Caucasians attached to Negro men (particularly older Negro men) during Jim Crow, part of the etiquette of "respect" for them, while Negro women were referred to as "auntie" (the rationale behind creating the marketing names and faces of Aunt Jemima and Uncle Ben). And apparently the tradition was still alive at that time in east south-central Georgia. Not missing a beat, my father, sitting in the chair next to the bed, looked up at the woman and replied, "Now if he's your uncle, that must make us first cousins. And I don't remember my father introducing you as a member of our family." The woman was taken aback. Calmly, but firmly, my father walked up to her and continued, "Things like that aren't said anymore. When you're talking to my father, refer to him as *Mr.* Pearson." Sheepishly the woman apologized, and closed the door. But I got the sense that normally local Afro-Americans would have still accepted what she had done.

My father was the middle child in his family, the shortest of the four boys, the most bookish, a fastidious dresser. The only one of Nathan and Bessie Pearson's children who would attain the level of prestige that went with becoming a physician—in fact, the first person period in Wheeler County, Georgia, to earn an M.D. degree—he absolutely detested working on a farm. He and his sister Lavester were more interested in books than any of the other children were. In fact, my father had such a burning desire to learn from books that one day when he was about eleven, in the middle of the Depression when money was scarce, he browsed through the Sears catalogue that came to the house periodically in the mail. There was the Bible and that catalogue. That was it, as far as books in the house went. So Lavester read and reread and reread the Bible. And my father scoured and scoured and scoured the Sears catalogues. One day while scouring one of them he came upon an ad for a set of encyclopedias. All you had to do was fill out the order form. So he did. And to his surprise the encyclopedias arrived in the mail C.O.D. He wasn't the only one who was surprised. So were my grandparents. They were surprised and angry because at that particular moment they couldn't afford to pay for the encyclopedias and, feeling a sense of shame, had to send them back.

My father was a determined little fella. And according to Aunt Mamie he had a Napoleon complex, an agitation, an irritation, an exactness about him that annoyed the rest of his family (and me, too, throughout my own childhood). Recalled Aunt Mamie: "One of my chores used to be ironing. I'd iron all the boys' shirts and sometimes the iron would have a slight carbon stain on its face because in those days you heated up the face of the iron in the fire. If that happened, it was okay with all the boys except your daddy. One little stain, or one wrong crease and he'd have Mama make me iron his shirt all over again. I'd be ready to kill him." No one knew where such an attitude came from since his father had also been the shortest boy in his family, and he was no taller than his father.

All of this my aunt would tell me later. For now as I rode through the farm it came to me that all the belief in honest hard work exhibited by my grandfather Pearson and passed on to my father had gone into making me who I am (for I had long heard stories about that aspect of his persona). I also recalled the reply my father always gave to my question about what it was like growing up on that farm under all that racial oppression (a reply I never really believed but was still proud to hear), as well as his calm, detached declarations that whatever excellence I demonstrated was supposed to come naturally to members of our family. The declarations amounted to an improvised family ethnicity. They were tantamount to migrating to a "new world" (the North), and starting from scratch, as though he, as though *we* had no connection to the messy past grappled with by southern historians. Wasn't this the American way? Tear down the old, start from scratch, lie to yourself about what the past was like if you have to (*certainly lie to your children*), but work hard, forge ahead, keep moving, don't *really* look back because, as Satchel Paige once said, something may be gaining on you. How very American. And if you're Afro-American and successful at it, you might just produce a son who is confident, defiant, and, plenty of people might one day say, often angry and arrogant (arrogance is the *first* refuge of intelligent, ambitious Afro-American males forced to live with an enduring social oppression).

Upon returning to New York City, confidence, defiance, and anger caused me to write a subversive editorial feature about the death and funeral of Alice Hawthorne. I described the memorial service held for her in Albany, but I also accused the city of Atlanta of greed, insensitivity, and hyperbole in its handling of the Olympics and wrote that the games should have been halted for one day in respect for her memory, rather than immediately resuming the competitions and holding a memorial to her at the closing ceremonies. I wrote that such a day could have also been used to assess what the games really ought to be about since they weren't being conducted by amateur athletes anyway, but instead by professionals masquerading as amateurs. How *un-American* of me.

I had spent virtually all the patience of Bob Bartley, conservative editorial page editor of the *Journal.* We simply had different ideological philosophies, a difference I had made clear from the beginning of my employment, but a difference he thought he could change, only to discover otherwise. The end came during the last week of August, and it resulted from what I did after learning that the editorial page wouldn't print the next story I wrote. Upon returning from a trip to California during the Republican National Convention, I penned an editorial feature castigating Jack Kemp for switching his stand opposing California's Proposition 209, banning affirmative action on the part of the state government, and his stand opposing Proposition 187, which sought to deny state aid to illegal aliens and U.S. citizenship to the children of illegal aliens born in the U.S. Kemp reversed his positions on those issues after he was chosen by Bob Dole as his running mate on the 1996 Republican ticket (though on Proposition 187 Kemp continued to denounce its stance on U.S. citizenship). And since I wrote for a staunchly Republican editorial page, they weren't about to print the piece. Instead it was reedited and printed in the Sunday View-points section of *Newsday,* a move that violated the policy stating that no full-time editorial staffer could publish an op-ed in another newspaper. I could think of no better or more altruistic end to my tenure on the page. Yet as I should have surmised, I would soon discover that altruism didn't always motivate the relative whose life I admired most.

CHAPTER 3

"My name is Bertram Ehrlich," the man said on my voice mail at my office in Brooklyn. "I saw your ad in the *Bainbridge Post-Searchlight* looking for people to talk to about Dr. Griffin. I knew Dr. Griffin very well. I had a drugstore across the street from his hospital and could tell you a lot of things about him, some things you'll want to hear, some things you probably won't. I can be reached at ——— here in Atlanta, where I just moved. I'm looking forward to hearing from you."

Mr. Ehrlich's message was the first evidence I came across, other than the hints of my aunt Elaine, that my uncle Joe wasn't as benevolent as my aunt Barbara's book had made him seem. And he had me wrong. The things he thought I wouldn't want to hear about my great-uncle were the things I was most eager to hear, because such things would finally enable me to come as close as possible to getting a complete picture of him. The name "Ehrlich" caused me to suspect this man was Jewish. His accent was clearly southern. Was I about to meet an example of the type of person who had piqued my curiosity when I stopped in that bagel restaurant in Albany—a southern Jew?

By now it had been eight months since my confrontation with the elderly Jewish man at the 92nd Street Y. Two weeks after speaking with Mr. Ehrlich I made the thirteen-hour trip by car to interview him in person. He instructed me on how to find his new residence, which is in a senior citizen apartment complex just off I-285 on the north side of the Atlanta metropolitan region. I am very familiar with the Atlanta area since my younger sister Jennifer lives here (as did my older sister Carol, before attending medical school in Minnesota), as does my aunt Lavester and several first cousins. I can't count the number of times I've visited, or passed through on the way to visit relatives farther south (by now, what Afro-American doesn't have a relative in the Atlanta area, since it is America's premier "black mecca"?). It is also the fastest growing of all our large metropolitan areas (a mecca for all Americans), giving the impression that the only things welcome on its expanding freeways, next to its shopping centers, near its high rises, and in its burgeoning housing subdivisions are automobiles. Every time I return, something monstrously new has been constructed (or is in the process of being constructed), particularly in this section of the metropolitan area. So I'm having trouble finding Mr. Ehrlich's apartment complex, since my bearings in the area have been thrown off by a wider expressway and new commercial establishments.

As I search I think about how successful Henry Grady, editor of the *Atlanta Constitution* in the 1880s, and his compatriots were in igniting the spark at the previous turn of the century that ultimately led to all this sprawl. And how so much of that success was kicked off on the occasion of another major event that, like the 1996 Olympics, brought the rest of the nation and the world to Atlanta, an event during which, at the behest of a twenty-three-year-old lawyer and minister named I. Garland Penn, Negro physicians, predecessors of my uncles and father, formally organized themselves into the National Medical Association. They had just listened to a keynote speech by Booker T. Washington where he conceded to southern Caucasians just what they wanted from people of black African descent. That concession speech, in turn, set the tone for the behavior of most of the men in my family for most of their lives.

The Cotton States and International Exposition was held in Atlanta in the fall of 1895, when my uncle Joe was seven years old growing up 110 miles to the southwest on a farm along the banks of the Chattahoochee River that partially separates Georgia and Alabama, while my grandfather Pearson, a twelve-year-old, was growing up on his father's farm 120 miles to the southeast. By that year things had grown pretty awful for Negroes. In one of my *Wall Street Journal* feature editorials I explained why, collectively, we've invested so much faith in the federal government. These days, the facts bear repeating since in their restless rage to forget the past, to move on to the new (as in asking, "Why are we still talking about black hardship?" "Why do blacks always look to the federal government to do things for them?") Americans tend to forget pertinent facts from the past that have bearing on the present (a tendency I sometimes have to check in myself, as when I ponder why more Afro-Americans haven't, on our own, moved farther away from the impotence of victimhood). Facts such as, at one point after the Civil War and freedom from slavery, all the promise of full citizenship rights for Negroes was being fulfilled in the South at the behest of the occupying Union Army, along with the Thirteenth, Fourteenth, and Fifteenth Amendments to the Constitution. Yet it didn't take long for a sentiment to grow among citizens in the North that was amazingly similar to the implications of the racial and socioeconomic views of today's conservatives.

A popular Democratic poster during Pennsylvania's 1866 congressional and gubernatorial campaign portrayed the federal Freedmen's Bureau, which had been formed to help the newly freed slaves, as "an agency to keep the Negro in idleness at the expense of the white man . . ." It depicted a dark-skinned, kinky-haired man with bug eyes and thick lips lounging in a field, the Capitol building emblazoned with the words "Freedom and no work," while in the upper-left-hand corner was a drawing of a Caucasian man tilling a field, with his home in the background and a wife and child. In the lower left was a depiction of another Caucasian male splitting logs with the saying that the Caucasian male "must work to keep his children and pay his taxes." In other words, the federal government was "wasting" its money on one specific branch of the poor—"the lazy, freed Negroes." But it was at the behest of the Republican Party that this federal money was being "wasted," since at that time it was the Republicans who believed in federal intervention to ensure racial equality, while the Democrats believed in a limited federal government that shouldn't involve itself in matters best left to the states—matters such as race. In their view, such intervention trampled on the personal liberties of those who wanted nothing to do with the newly freed slaves, the same way many conservatives today insist that federal social programs and affirmative action oppress middle-class Caucasians, highlighting a problem that hasn't yet seemed to go away. When you psychologically cripple a group of people, how do you cure them? Should it be through libertarian benign neglect ("tough love" or "tough hate," depending on your perspective), or through massive social intervention that often removes their incentive to act on their own?

The rationale for benign neglect—the racial stereotypes of Negroes depicted in the Pennsylvania poster—amounted to insisting that the former slaves would always be crippled, no matter what was done. Was there a grain of truth to the stereotypes? There were, in fact, several grains of truth (most stereotypes tend to have at least a few grains of truth to them, or else they would never become stereotypes). But that was no rationale for concluding that they applied to all Negroes. And plenty of evidence supports the conclusion that government intervention in the form of the Freedmen's Bureau wasn't useless at all.

As for the racial stereotypes, there were numerous reasons for the grains of truth, reasons having to do with the way the newly freed men and women had been encouraged to behave by the institution of slavery. The man who designed New York City's Central Park, Frederick Law Olmsted, took upon himself the task of traveling through the South in the years 1853 to 1861. He ventured from Maryland all the way to Texas and back. These were the years in which there was a heated debate taking place in the North over the institution of slavery, ultimately leading to the political tug-of-war that caused the Civil War. Olmsted discovered a world where, contrary to contemporary notions about the antebellum South, most people, period, including Caucasians, were poor; a world where most slave owners owned not the numerous slaves housed in a slave quarters behind a Greek revival mansion, on the front porch of which sat the slave master sipping his mint julep, his wife dressed in a Scarlett O'Hara hooped dress with Mammy at her beck and call, the children playing in the yard with the little "pickaninnies" not yet trained to treat them as masters and mistresses, but a world where most masters lived in simple wooden cabins, owned three or four slaves, and their entire families, dressed in coarse homespun clothing, had to work alongside their slaves in the fields. Even Caucasian families like these—meaning living at that relatively high standard of living—were in the minority, since most Caucasians in the region were too poor to afford any slaves.

The region became full of so many Negroes because where there were large-scale slave owners who invariably lived on the most fertile land, those owners indeed owned many slaves, and were often absentee masters who left their large plantations to their overseers while they and their families lived in relatively cultured towns such as Charleston; Savannah; Richmond; Memphis; New Orleans; Natchez, Mississippi; and Wilmington, North Carolina. And Olmsted wrote that in most of his encounters, the slaves were indeed lazy, having to be forced to till a field, forced to properly set a table and serve their master and his family or overseer, forced to repair farm equipment.

Maybe we should be suspicious of Olmsted's conclusions. Maybe we should assume that, given the era he lived in—one where it was almost impossible not to be extremely racially biased in some way, since even Northern abolitionists who found slavery morally wrong tended to support its abolition with the added stipulation that the former slaves be returned to Africa because they were innately unabsorbable into American culture—Olmsted, too, was biased. That for any Caucasian *not to be biased* against people with black African blood in some way was an extraordinary feat bordering on an ability to walk through walls. But, then again, maybe we shouldn't be suspicious of what Olmsted wrote. For it only makes sense that the slaves would have behaved as he described. In most cases they had virtually no incentive to work hard. Where was the payoff? In most cases a fifteen-year-old slave boy forced to till a field could only look forward to becoming a fifty-year-old slave "boy" forced to till a field. Indeed, what alternative did he have in protesting his condition other than performing his tasks as shoddily as possible, when he did perform them? There was no use even in looking forward to taking pleasure in the diversion of an attractive slave girl (since the desire for sex is behind so much of what *all* people do), because, as Olmsted discovered, any and every female slave with any looks to her automatically became the concubine of the master, his son (or sons, if he had any), or if he had one, his overseer. (One planter told Olmsted, "There is not a likely looking black girl in this state that is not the concubine of a white man.")

Writing from jail, a Mrs. Douglass of Virginia—who was tried, convicted, and punished during the antebellum era for the crime of teaching a number of slaves to read—laid bare a truth about her culture that receives short shrift from most historians and sociologists of that period:

> This subject demands attention. . . . It is one great evil hanging over the Southern Slave States, destroying domestic happiness and the peace of thousands. It is summed up in a single word—amalgamation. This, and this only, causes the vast extent of ignorance, degradation, and crime that lies like a black cloud over the whole South. And

the practice is even more general than even the Southerners are willing to allow.

Neither is it to be found only on the lower order of the white population. It pervades the entire society. Its followers are to be found among all ranks, occupations, professions. The white mothers and daughters of the South have suffered under it for years—have seen their dearest affections trampled upon—their hopes of domestic happiness destroyed, and their future lives embittered, even to agony, by those who should be all in all to them, as husbands, sons, brothers. I cannot use too strong language in reference to this subject, for I know that it will meet with a heartfelt response from every Southern woman.

It would have probably met with a heartfelt response from every male slave, and plenty of female slaves, as well. Imagine night after night being sequestered in your hovel while a slave girl you have taken a liking to is being "humped" by your master or his son or one of their acquaintances. Or imagine that the slave girl is your sister or your daughter. Or imagine she is the woman who passes in slave society for your wife. And you can hear her moans, their moans. Among many such slave women there was a dread of these encounters. However, among many of them, too, there was the desire to pull the "white" man down off his "high perch" or get pregnant with children whose lighter skin would move them a notch higher in caste rank. Among many as well there developed an anger at, resentment toward, and ridicule of Negro men who could not protect them, or provide for their survival needs like Caucasian men could (either before or after the end of slavery), or protect them from Caucasian men when their sexual advances *weren't* wanted.

It must have been a major blow to the ego of the male slave and his male descendants. If he expected fidelity from the slave woman he was with, she had to be a woman who wasn't physically attractive (quite often when an attractive slave woman was chosen by the master, she then became as much off-limits to the male slave as a Caucasian woman), while over in the "big house" the master wouldn't abide any Caucasian woman having sexual relations with a slave, and would indeed have the slave severely physically punished if he so much as found out such a thing. (Though such liaisons, in rare instances, did occur, when they were discovered physical punishment was the more likely penalty because slaves were too valuable to the master's net worth to kill, whereas after slavery the more common physical punishment for such a "transgression" was a torture death for the Negro male.) No such humiliation for the master. Maybe the master was his own father or his half-brother—since in this world there was no birth control being used. And it was in the master's best interest to increase the ranks of his most valuable property, the slave, by having his slave women breed. And in the interest of having such women breed he mated the male slaves with whatever slave women he didn't want, though in plenty of instances, with such women, the male slaves had families. And when that male slave got up in the morning he had to go to work toiling in a field for the master, with nothing more to look forward to but spending the remainder of his life toiling in a field for him (unless he had free relatives who could save enough money to buy his freedom for whatever price was being demanded, or he was the master's son or lived in a major city like New Orleans, Charleston, Savannah, or Baltimore, in which case he might get the opportunity to buy his freedom and become one out of ten people of black African descent in the antebellum South who composed the "free people of color").

And, as was the case with so many slave women, the only thing keeping him from going totally insane over his predicament was the hope that after he died there would be a heaven that would grant him his just reward for enduring so much hell on earth, which is why in church he danced, got happy, enraptured himself in Christianity, the only religion his master allowed him to have. And in case after case he passed on to his descendants a reluctance to engage in labor, a reluctance they took with them into freedom after the Civil War. In case after case he passed on to his male descendants a disrespect for slave women since he considered so many of them to be licentious—and in case after case, after slavery, such men disrespected the descendants of such women. In case after case he passed on to his male descendants the feeling of powerlessness he had over the welfare of his children, so they didn't take responsibility for their children either. He passed on to his descendants, too, his extremely emotional religious faith, his enrapture with "the Lord."

Without question there were plenty of male slaves and former male slaves for whom all of the aforementioned description didn't apply. But there were enough for whom it did apply, meaning that there were several grains of truth in the caricature of the Negro male lounging in a field on that 1866 poster in Pennsylvania, a caricature that included a drawing of the U.S. Capitol with pillars depicting the alleged characteristics of such a former slave. His supposed likes? Pies, stews, fish balls, idleness, white sugar, apathy, white women, indolence, sugar plums, candy. It was only natural, only human, given the background of slavery, that in numerous cases, what the poster depicted was true. For it not to be true would have required a superhuman collective strength and determination that, so far, no group of people on earth has demonstrated, because no group of people on earth were born from a set of circumstances approximating those that went into the creation and designation of the American Negro. Numerous Negroes did find the strength and incentive to dream big and work hard after slavery, *but the fact that any of them found any reason to muster that strength is truly remarkable,* given the circumstances they came out of, and the circumstances they would be relegated to after the federal government pulled out of the South, signaling the end of Reconstruction (which, again, is something I often have to remind myself, given how often I become exasperated with what we haven't yet achieved).

By the 1870s the fallout from the buildup and ultimate popularity of negative stereotypes like the ones in the Pennsylvania poster would be dire indeed. During Reconstruction, southern aristocrats, the former pillars of the Confederacy, weren't allowed to vote. But by the 1870s throughout the region they had been reenfranchised, and local governments were turned back over to them. They drove Reconstruction Republicans out of office and appealed to the racial allegiance of their "white brethren" to disenfranchise and further subjugate people with black African ancestry, bringing about an approximation of the slavery they had just been freed from. Since more than one-fifth of adult Caucasian males had lost their lives in the Civil War, one of their chief concerns was the sexual future of Caucasian women in a region where large sections of the countryside were populated by more newly freed men than Caucasian men. Would such men do to Caucasian women what Caucasian men had done to slave women and would do to numerous freed women for the foreseeable future? Thus began an obsession with the preservation and protection of "white womanhood." So nothing became higher on their list of taboos than any kind of cordial equal relationship between Caucasian women and newly freed men, or any kind of alleged violation of Caucasian women by males with any noticeable black African ancestry—hence the excuse for so many lynchings and murders such as the one that took place in Bainbridge in the 1930s, leading to the dragging of Willie Reid's charred corpse past the home of my uncle Joe as a threat to all the "uppity nigras" (my uncle's "uppitiness" being his prosperity, and thus possible attractiveness to a wide range of women).

At no time was such gruesomeness as common as in the 1880s and '90s. Once a rape accusation was widely accepted as true, lynching notices were printed in newspapers and thousands of Caucasian spectators arrived from miles around, including schoolchildren, to watch the victim get castrated, or skinned, and finally hanged or shot or burned to death, after which often the perpetrators and spectators took turns taking photos next to his limp mangled remains and "souvenirs" from him—maybe one of his testicles, or his penis, or a finger, or toe, or a piece of his liver, heart, lung, or his ear. Most of the time such hideous deaths were recorded by local coroners as having occurred at the hands of "unknown perpetrators." And along with this reign of vigilante terror came a sharecropping system that kept most Negro farmers in virtual peonage, and by the 1880s the formal Jim Crowing of public accommodations, standard references to Negro men as boys and "uncle," while Negro women became "auntie" and girl and gal, and the casting in stone of the southern practice of spending barely any money on the education of Negro youth.

The most dignified, ambitious Negroes were psychologically devastated. In 1886 on his way back to his native Jacksonville from his first year at Atlanta University prep school (financed by northern philanthropists) on a first-class train ticket was the young mixed-race James Weldon Johnson, who would later become the first Negro to pass the bar exam to become a lawyer in the state of Florida, the first to publish a daily newspaper in the state, the founder of the first high school for Negroes in the state (the high school attended by my mother), part of the first successful Negro Broadway composing team in the nation (Johnson would also compose the lyrics to "Lift Every Voice and Sing," considered by many to be the Negro national anthem, while his brother would compose the music), a diplomat in Latin America, executive secretary of the NAACP (during which he would unsuccessfully lobby for the country's first antilynching legislation), and one of the nation's first successful Negro authors. Steeped in dignity during the tail end of the Reconstruction era by a landowning father who had become headwaiter at a Florida resort, and a talented mother who became the first Negro high school teacher in the state, raised to believe that there was nothing he couldn't accomplish, and traveling with two fellow students from similarly dignified backgrounds, Johnson presented the conductor their tickets. The conductor told them to move to the inferior-quality Jim Crow car, and he offered no refund of their first-class tickets. Johnson and his companions refused to move. Caucasian passengers stared with indignation. Nearby a Negro Pullman porter paced nervously. The other first-class passengers became more indignant. Someone shouted "Baxley!!!" The Pullman porter pulled Johnson to the side and told him that "Baxley" meant Baxley, Georgia, a small town only sixty miles from where my grandfather Pearson, then three years old, was growing up; a town the train would pass through, and where earlier a group of Negro preachers had been pulled off the train for refusing to abide by the new Jim Crow laws. According to the porter, the townsmen forced the preachers to dance by shooting guns at their feet; the preachers were made to dance for hours until they dropped from exhaustion. The porter told Johnson that the conductor would wire the Baxley residents so that when the train arrived they'd probably be waiting to do the same thing to James and his companions. So it would be best for them to accept the humiliation of getting up and sitting in the inferior Jim Crow car. Weighing the situation, Johnson relented. The seeds of cautious acquiescence (and camouflaged ambition, and patience *that justice could one day be brought about, but not now*) were successfully planted.

The response from the retreated North to such threats and conduct of violence unless Negroes surrendered to Jim Crow was nothing but silence (and in 1896, from the U.S. Supreme Court, official sanction via *Plessy* v. *Ferguson*), along with widespread agreement that it was okay to treat Negroes that way. Things were better for Negroes in the North because they were a relatively minor presence there until the first large waves of Negro migrants summoned by industry during the First World War. But things weren't so good that Negroes didn't suffer from much prejudice and restrictions on their freedom (and, on occasion, violence), since most Caucasians in the North believed in the same insulting stereotypes of Negroes popular among their southern counterparts.

By 1895 most of even the proudest and hardest-working Negroes concluded that the only way to survive was to *slowly and patiently* prove their worth as citizens, a philosophy promoted by Booker T. Washington, the principal of a new trade school, the Tuskegee Institute. Washington's precise theory was: "Harmony will come in proportion as the black man gets something that the white man wants, whether it be of brains or material." But in practice it boiled down to an acquiescence that was often humiliating, a modus operandi he had perfected in Alabama among local Caucasian residents of Tuskegee, a once prosperous antebellum town where he promised that his trade school would teach most Negroes to become valuable tradesmen in a Caucasian-dominated economy, that Caucasians could trust him, and where he demonstrated his sleight of hand in carefully dealing with them by convincing them that he had not provided aid to a local Negro lawyer forced to flee a lynch mob because in his home he hosted a Caucasian preacher as though he was equal to Caucasians.

Washington made the promoters of the proposed exposition in Atlanta comfortable because it sounded like he promoted the perfect solution to the South's "Negro problem," a matter that northern industrialists were concerned about as they considered investing their capital in the South, an investment that "forward thinking" southern leaders like Henry Grady were desperate to bring to a devastated land still trying to recover from the Civil War.

In order to host the Cotton States and International Exposition designed to boost northern and international investment in Atlanta and the rest of the South, just as the Olympics would aim to do in 1996, the promoters needed $200,000 from the federal government. So they traveled to Washington, D.C., to testify at a hearing scheduled to decide if they would get that money (a decision similar to one the International Olympic Committee would make almost one hundred years later on whether or not Atlanta would get the go-ahead to host the Olympics). And for good persuasive measure the industrial leaders brought along Booker T. Washington, the son of a

Virginia slave woman who had been the concubine of her Caucasian master, their relationship resulting in his birth, just as nearly one hundred years later, Billy Payne would bring along Andrew Young, a man whose light brown skin and other physical features carry the evidence that his great-grandmothers or his great-great-grandmothers were also the concubines of their Caucasian masters.

When Washington spoke, which was near the very end, he did what was expected of him. He disarmed the congressmen to whom he shared a racial connection through his master-father, put the self-important politicians at ease that he wasn't "uppity" by stating that for fifteen years he had done his best to avoid politics or political gatherings and told other Negroes to do the same. Instead he had preached the gospel that it was best to leave politics to "the white man." It was best for Negroes to learn how to be good bricklayers, carpenters, cooks, tillers of soil. . . . But it was best, too, for them to strive to acquire property, keep out of debt; that the route to full citizenship was a gradual acquisition of respect through thrift, patience, and abiding by the laws laid down by their former slave masters, the best of whom had their best interests at heart.

Washington perfected a tightrope walk that Garland Penn became good at as well. He suggested that Penn, who was also of mixed heritage, serve in his stead as the superintendent of the separate Negro pavilion that was to go up at the Atlanta exposition. It was to be a pavilion featuring a large medallion with a handkerchief-headed "Auntie" on the exterior, a condition that apparently Washington and Penn were willing to accept, indicating the extent to which compromising their dignity had become a way of life.

While perfecting the same modus operandi as Washington, Penn decided to push for the altogether radical idea of having a Negro actually speak at the opening ceremonies. The plan of the organizers had been to use Washington to help secure funds for the fair, and construct the separate pavilion with the handkerchief-headed logo designed to show the progress patient and obedient Negroes were making in the New South, but certainly not to have a Negro included among the procession of speakers at the opening ceremonies, even one speaking last of all. But Penn had the idea that further progress could be made if a Negro spoke, even if he spoke last. And what better Negro, what safer Negro to do the honors than Washington himself? So he prevailed upon the exposition organizers to allow it. And across the country his victory in doing so was hailed as a major achievement.

It was a revolutionary idea even in the North to have a Negro speak at such an event, even last for only five minutes. There was much curiosity across the country, and after the initial ecstatic reaction among them to the news, much nervousness among Negroes, much hand-wringing, much fear that Washington, this "chosen representative of the race," would make a mistake. A mistake could be anything. It could be a mere cough at the wrong moment, excused if done by a Caucasian male, but perhaps laughed at if done by a Negro. A mistake could be momentarily losing one's place in the prepared text, an embarrassment for anyone, but a potentially grave mistake for "the chosen representative" of a people believed to be so ignorant that Caucasians came from miles around to the first commencement exercise at Tuskegee handing out diplomas to Negroes who had adequately learned to become good housekeepers, good bricklayers, and good carpenters because they couldn't believe that a Negro could learn anything in a classroom.

And the fear, the ambivalence was great within Washington himself, who was convinced that one wrong word, one utterance that was deemed too radical, too militant, too uppity, too suggestive that Negroes deserved immediate rights, could ruin the entire exposition, could ruin the future of his school, dependent as it was on the goodwill of the Caucasians in next-door Alabama. One wrong utterance could even endanger his life.

The September day of the opening ceremonies to the exposition that would draw 800,000 visitors over one hundred days was a hot one. As would be the case 101 years later when it hosted the Olympics, Atlanta was packed with people from across the country and many from around the world. The previous night Booker Washington did not sleep in the Negro hotel where he was housed. Over and over and over again he reviewed the text of his speech. He knelt down and prayed. On the morning of September 18, 1895, when it was time to proceed to the fairgrounds at Piedmont Park on the northeastern side of the city, the cream of Atlanta's Negro citizenry as well as other prominent Negroes of the day from across the nation called on him as if to massage the psyche of a great fighter, a great hope about to enter the ring and do battle for the entire "race." They gathered up Washington, then joined a long procession of carriages headed from downtown to the fairgrounds, a long procession where they were relegated to the very rear as though an afterthought.

Despite having plenty of allies, Washington's position on the question of the proper course Negroes should follow in light of the tremendous opposition of Caucasian southerners to the concept of racial equality, hadn't, as of yet, totally prevailed among the region's Negroes. There were still those who insisted on following the course prescribed by the promise of Reconstruction: pursuit of immediate equality in a region where, collectively, Caucasians were never able to boast of a high degree of economic and intellectual sophistication on their part, either. Atlanta was somewhat of a Deep South Athens for Negroes. And apparently, just before the official opening ceremony for the exposition, a principal spokesman for the opposite viewpoint from Washington's, who was promoting immediate equal educational rights for Negroes leading to equality in all social and political arenas as soon as possible, had delivered his speech to thunderous applause from many other Negroes attending the exposition. What Dr. J. W. E. Bowen, a theologian from Gammon Theological Seminary in Atlanta, said has been forgotten by most historians because of the manner in which Washington's philosophy ultimately prevailed. But the pressure on Washington to make a speech that would convince virtually all Negroes that his was the best course to follow became all the greater due to Bowen's eloquent address:

> The Negro's place will be what he makes for himself. . . . One class contends that he must earn it by staying in the three "R's" and they make special efforts in ridiculing the higher education of the Negroes, even for leaders in church and state. Yes, he must learn the three "R's"; he must master the king's English and then he must plume his pinions of thought for a flight with Copernicus, Kepler and Herchel; he must sharpen his logic for a walk with Plato, Immanuel Kant and Herbert Spencer; he must clarify his vision for investigations with Virchow, Huxley and Gray, he must be able to deal in abstruse questions of law as do Gladstone, Judge Story and Judge Speer; he must fortify himself to divine rightly the Word as do Cannon Farrer Foster, Bishop Haygood, Dr. John Hall and Dr. H. L. Wayland. In short the education of the Negro must be on par with the education of the white

man. It must begin in kindergarten as that of the white child and end in the university as that of the white man.

Bowen probably spoke those words in the Negro Pavilion. (It is not clear where he made this speech, only that, indeed, he did deliver it.) In any case, he wasn't part of the official entourage for the opening ceremonies.

Washington and his supporters brought up the rear of that long procession. When they finally reached the fairgrounds they entered a packed auditorium. In a segregated section sat a kaleidoscope of Negroes from across the country called together by Penn: lawyers, physicians, pharmacists, dentists, entrepreneurs, maids, cooks, skilled and unskilled laborers, all gathered to possibly chart a new course following the road map forced upon them by Caucasian southerners, a road map where they were to be shunted off to the side, separated, forced to develop as a people, slowly, and primarily as unskilled and low-skilled laborers. At the sight of Washington and Penn alighting the stage, there arose a great cheer from the segregated Negro section.

The program was an hour behind schedule. The crowd had been restless. Those in the Caucasian section had been whipping it up the way restless crowds whip things up. When the speakers finally walked across the stage they too began to cheer. But when it was seen that at the end of the procession of dignitaries two of those alighting the dais were Negro, whereupon the Negro lawyers and physicians and pharmacists and dentists and entrepreneurs and tradesmen and farmers and unskilled laborers increased their applause, the Caucasians abruptly ceased clapping at all. Some indignantly called for "the niggers to leave the stage," wondering why the proceedings were being "ruined" with their presence. But soon enough their catcalls died down and the speeches began. After a while the band played the "Star Spangled Banner." The crowd cheered. Then the band played "Dixie." The Caucasians in the crowd went wild, not only out of conjured southern pride, but also as if to intimidate Washington and Penn. Former Georgia governor Rufus Bullock, who had been the Republican governor of the state during Reconstruction and a relative moderate on the question of race, and was now deposed yet not without some honor in a city that prided itself on its relative racial moderation compared to other southern cities, told the crowd that it would now be favored with an address by a great southern educator. The audience applauded. But when the Caucasians saw that this "great educator" was Washington their applause abruptly ceased. Former governor Bullock addressed them again: "We have with us today a representative of Negro enterprise and civilization." The cheers resumed. The "moment" was at hand.

As Washington began to speak, Caucasians in the audience found themselves interested in what he had to say despite themselves. Cognizant of the fact that the first thing a person perceived unworthy always does is thank his benefactors for being beneficent, Washington showered them with excessive thanks for allowing him to speak, a trait that survived from slavery, a trait that became woven into the collective Negro psyche when in the presence of Caucasians, a trait our forefathers would teach their children, and their children would teach us, and so on. Next he urged Negroes to remain in the South, something our forefathers were beginning not to do in hope of living somewhere where they could enjoy their full rights as U.S. citizens, though Caucasian southerners at that time certainly didn't want them to leave because they needed their cheap manual labor in an era before technology rendered their presence unnecessary. Next, as though he were speaking to a group of masters about their good and faithful dogs, he reminded the Caucasians of the Negro's patience and loyalty. They liked that. They listened even more intently. He tried to recover some pride, speaking of Negro desires for self-improvement and opportunities in the southern economy. That was all we asked for, he said. And if given that, the Caucasians would be assured of the continued presence of "the most patient, faithful, law-abiding, and unresentful people the world has ever seen."

But he ingratiated himself, too, with what he knew would be for them humorous anecdotes confirming their notions about Negroes. Don't expect too much too soon from us, he said. "Starting thirty years ago with ownership here and there in a few quilts and pumpkins and chickens gathered from miscellaneous sources [read *stolen*], remember that the path that has led from these to the inventions and productions in the Negro building has not been trodden without contact with thorns and thistles." With those words he had won them over. So he went for the knockout punch. He assured them that just as they desired, "In all things purely social we can be as separate as the fingers, yet one as the hand in all things essential to mutual progress."

They went wild with cheers, with applause. Caucasian southern maidens dropped flowers at his feet. Caucasian males roared and as he left the stage reached out their hands for him to shake and patted him vigorously on his back. From the Negro section there were cheers, too, but also expressions of ambivalence. Some shed tears of gratitude, tears of pride because "the chosen representative" had dazzled a large gathering of Caucasians, had confirmed that "one of our own" could be impressive at a skill Caucasians had reserved only for themselves. Such pride for the moment overwhelmed notice of the insulting humorous characterizations of Negroes woven into his speech. Such pride for the moment overwhelmed notice of the tone of the speech assuring Caucasians that we would be obedient. The enthusiastic reaction to Washington's speech from southern Caucasians meant that he would become the clear leader of Negroes, and the position represented by Bowen would be soundly defeated. (In later years, it would be inherited and promoted in the North by W. E. B. Du Bois, a founder of the NAACP, although at the time Washington made his Cotton States Exposition speech, Du Bois actually praised what he had to say.) Washington set the tone for making a deal Negroes would continue to make in exchange for whatever peace they could find in the Caucasian world, a deal we would make in exchange for whatever enticing carrot would be offered as the route to our individual prosperity, a deal each generation would teach the next to make even as another part of each generation dreamed of the day when it wouldn't be necessary.

Several days later, Dr. Robert F. Boyd of Nashville gathered together the Negro physicians, dentists, and pharmacists attending the exposition. They met at the First Congregational Church in Atlanta and asked Garland Penn to preside as they formed what would be called "The National Association of Colored Physicians, Dentists and Pharmacists." The organization's charter stated that the purpose of the new organization was the "banding together for mutual cooperation and helpfulness the men and women of African descent who are legally and honorably engaged in the practice of the cognate professions of medicine, surgery, pharmacy and dentistry, and to promote their literary and scientific development." (Eight years later the name would be changed to the National Medical Association, and several years after that, the organization's membership would be limited to physicians.)

Washington's concession speech generated hope among such attendees that the overt oppression they had endured would come to an end, alternating with fear that it really wouldn't. "As fast as merit shows up, prejudice will break down," they were told by Caucasians of alleged goodwill. "Keep out of politics, make any concession consistent with manhood. Let white men know you are glad to be a Negro. Don't push, but be proud of your Negro blood." Though every now and then even from these mouths came the rationale for Negro trepidation. Upon letting his guard down from being a salesman for his vision of the New South, Henry Grady, in a moment of candor, had once put the case bluntly: "The white race must dominate forever in the South, because it is the white race!"

During the 1896 Tuskegee commencement exercise, in a moment of agitated candor, while Booker T. Washington, still basking in glory from his triumphant Atlanta speech the previous fall, sat and watched, William C. Oates, governor of Alabama, fearing that the crowd had grown too hopeful and too uppity because of their enthusiastic claps for a Negro who spoke just before him, rose to the podium and angrily stated: "I want to give you niggers a few words of plain talk and advice. No such address as you have just listened to is going to do you any good; it's going to spoil you. . . . You might as well understand that this is a white man's country, as far as the South is concerned, and we are going to make you keep your place. Understand that! I have nothing more to say to you!"

The blunt professions of Oates notwithstanding, Negroes living in Atlanta grew increasingly confident in the years following the Cotton States Exposition. Their physicians and lawyers, professors at the five Negro colleges, teachers, ministers of prominent churches, leading business persons, all sought an alliance with their Caucasian counterparts in an effort to uplift the respective poor of their perceived races who were flooding into the city from the countryside in search of new opportunities. Caucasian Atlanta demanded that the Negro elite control the poor Negro masses whom they hadn't really expected to arrive in such numbers. As a response the Caucasians of the city started expanding Jim Crow through city ordinances, employment discrimination, and violence. In 1902 Garland Penn, ever the organizer and now a theology professor at Gammon Theological Seminary, organized the Negro Young People's Christian Education Congress, designed to promote the attributes of "the best" Negroes so that Caucasians would agree that there were two factions: the educated ones who strove to improve themselves, and those at the bottom, too many of whom did not. Two hundred speakers at the conference sought to unite the six thousand in attendance across denominational lines, to tackle the ignorance of those at the bottom and demonstrate through diligence and hard work, rather than protest and radicalism, that educated Negroes deserved the same rights as everyone else. Because this was the era when the façade of Victorian purity was pursued with a vengeance by the upper and middle classes of America, causing dancing, card playing, craps, gambling, and recreational sex, particularly the premarital variety, to be viewed as sins, issues such as motherhood, "social purity," and child marriage as a social crime were raised at the conference. Widespread was the belief, growing out of the recreational ends to which slave women had been put, and the crude frivolity allowed the slaves as relief from the harshness of their existence, that recently freed people were the gravest threat to the furtherance of those values. Hence the conviction that Victorian mores had to be stressed among them at every turn.

Caucasians of the city applauded this "right thinking" designed to address "the difficult upward march of [Negro] development." They were relieved to hear that "right thinking" Negroes tacitly agreed that interracial social equality and economic inclusion would not be on the agenda. Instead "right thinkers" taught that as a group Negroes had to earn their way to securing social and political rights. They applauded the efforts of Penn and his allies and in exchange promised to support Negro schools and churches. Educated Negroes got to work helping to promote "the Atlanta Spirit," encouraging upwardly mobile Negroes to move to the city for its five Negro colleges, skyscrapers, and climate. They encouraged the upwardly mobile to save their money and strive to buy their own homes, and most of all, to avoid ever being accused of rape—especially the rape of a Caucasian woman.

By the summer of 1906 such accusations were not uncommon.

The Negro population of the city had continued to swell as did the Caucasian population, particularly unskilled poor migrants from the countryside, many of whom liked to spend their weekends in dance halls where not only did they dance, they gambled, drank, bought and sold sexual favors, shot craps—just the kind of behavior that "right thinkers" were doing their best to eradicate, since upon detecting such activity among any Negroes, Caucasians tended to paint all Negroes as licentious menaces. Brawls and knifings took place among them, too. In the main, such behavior was limited to their ranks. But the fear continued that it wouldn't take long before Caucasians in the city raised the specter of that most dreaded accusation: widespread assault of Caucasian women. In the countryside, they reasoned, such Negroes could be controlled since most lived on Caucasian-owned plantations and worked as sharecroppers. In the city they thought this was impossible. Increasingly, Caucasians in Atlanta viewed the swelling ranks of such unrefined migrants as a threat to further "positive" growth.

The increasing Negro presence caused so much concern that in the summer of 1906 the city welcomed Booker T. Washington—who was back this time for a national conference of his recently formed Negro Business League—with more than a bit of trepidation. The conference went without a hitch, and Washington assured Negro and Caucasian Atlanta that the course he promoted of patient, obedient thrift and development among Negroes was the right course. But tensions were increasing, had indeed been exacerbated by the recently victorious Georgia Democratic gubernatorial candidate Hoke Smith, who campaigned for governor on the platform that further control of the "Negro menace" was in order.

That summer the Atlanta press began reporting incidents between Caucasian women and Negro men that they classified as rapes, incidents that included a case in which an English woman allegedly had one of her eyes put out, nose destroyed, and legs broken so that she was maimed for life. The papers encouraged Caucasian women to arm themselves, Caucasian men to protect "white womanhood," and called for the formation of volunteer patrols to supplement the city police. Tensions increased accordingly, and on September 22, 1906, violence began and rained down for three days upon all the Negroes of Atlanta. Negro barbershops, which had established a monopoly on such business in the city (including in

Caucasian areas where they only cut Caucasian hair), were indiscriminately attacked. Caucasian mobs pulled Negroes off streetcars, out of their jobs in hotels, and entered their neighborhoods and assaulted them on their own property and burned down many of their homes. Negroes armed ourselves, their men with guns across their knees prepared to die defending their families. Eventually respected Caucasians came to the defense of Negroes they considered upstanding. And peace was restored. But not before Negro men, even in respected middle-class communities, were arrested at gunpoint because of the death of a Caucasian police officer in the melee, as against the death of as many as twenty Negroes. For the death of the officer Negro leaders formally apologized, while no Caucasians formally apologized for the deaths among Negroes.

This had more of an adverse effect on Negro self-esteem. Despite strong evidence that most of the accusations of widespread rape of and attacks on Caucasian women had been fabricated, Penn and other leaders sought détente on Caucasian terms. Pleaded his brother, William Fletcher Penn, a physician whose stepson, Louis T. Wright, would go on to become the most esteemed Negro physician of his era, "If sober industrious, upright life, accumulating property and educating his children as best he knows how is not the standard by which a colored man can live and be protected . . . what is to become of him? . . . Tell us what your standards are for colored men. What are the requirements under which we may live? . . . What shall we do?"

What they did was inadvertently set the stage for severely crippling Negro advancement. In exchange for peace with Caucasian Atlanta, in exchange for the assurance that Negroes would not be massacred, Negro leaders encouraged docility from the masses. They admonished the masses of Negroes in Atlanta to obtain jobs as low-skilled laborers and domestics, to be prompt and obedient, work hard for low wages, and never quit their jobs suddenly; all this would ensure their protection by Caucasians. And they worked with the Caucasian establishment to apprehend those accused of crimes.

The leaders were thrust between a rock and a hard place. In other words, segregation forced a certain level of cooperation between educated Negroes and the masses. Yet after such watershed events as the Atlanta Riot of 1906 (duplicated elsewhere with similar riots in many cities and towns across the country), the educated could do nothing that ultimately interfered with Caucasian desires for a cheap, pliable, and basically ignorant Negro labor force. However, the elite would conclude that this route to advancement, this straddling of two motives (advancement as well as complacency) could eventually lead to economic and social freedom. "I was in the Atlanta Riot," Garland Penn told the Negro physicians, dentists, and pharmacists attending the National Medical Association convention in Washington four years later. "I got out of it, too. I said to myself as I walked up and down in my room that night, 'Penn, what have you done for this mob to come after you?' I got the answer. By race identity. In spite of myself I am linked with my brother down on Decatur Street [an Atlanta street known for tawdry activities and dance halls] and the lesson comes to me that I am no safer than he will let me be, and that with all of our struggles upward, we have got to touch the man in the gutter and lift him up. You may want to get away from it," he told the physicians, dentists, and pharmacists. "For it is always the tendency of the intellectual man to want to get away from it. It would be a good thing if this organization and the [Negro] Business League and other organizations would get together and compile their issues in one, namely: collect information concerning the progress of the Negro race and have that progress printed for distribution throughout this country so that we may put our case in its proper place."

Negro physicians were mobilized to serve as role models, economic pillars, and healers all rolled into one. Just as with physicians everywhere, they were the beneficiaries of the most occupational prestige and respect. But given the desperate collective situation, Negro physicians took on an even greater relative importance in the Negro community than Caucasian physicians held in theirs (even though at the turn of the century the Negro masses were still struggling to trust their medical acumen). As a result, they had their work cut out for them, another reason being that along with the commonly held belief in Negro licentiousness and brutality went the widely held belief that Negroes were a menace to the rest of society because they carried disease. "Morality among [Negroes] is almost a joke, and only assumed as a matter of convenience, or when there is a lack of desire or opportunity for indulgence, and venereal diseases are well-nigh universal," claimed Thomas Murrell, a Caucasian physician. "As an illustration of this, in clinic and private practice, I have never seen a Negro virgin over eighteen years of age. Consultations with older men of the profession have yielded only two undoubted cases. Of course, there are many more, but it is terrible to hear a man in active practice for fifty years, practicing both in country and city, proclaim his experience to be the same as my own."

"I have a considerable gynecological practice, both institutional and public," countered John A. Kenney, Sr., school physician for Tuskegee Institute and general secretary of the NMA. "Hundreds of girls and young women from thirty-five states and territories of the Union, Cuba, Puerto Rico, Central and South America have been under my care for gynecological troubles. I have been deeply impressed with the very large and overpowering percentage which show no sign of defloration. . . . Will our readers [of the *Journal of the National Medical Association*] inform the writer through these pages of that class of Negro virgins as pure and chaste as those of any other race. . . . What is most unfair is his attempt to condemn even our refined classes along with the slum product among whom he undoubtedly has had large experience. . . . I am appealing to the Negro physicians to send in statistical evidence to rebut these easily refuted assertions."

The first fully recognized Negro physician was a freed slave who practiced medicine in eighteenth-century New Orleans. Dr. James Derham was born in Philadelphia in 1757. His master, Dr. John Kersey, taught him how to compound medicines and assist with patients, since at that time apprenticeship was the usual and accepted method of becoming a physician. Upon Kersey's death Derham was purchased by Dr. George West and then by Dr. Robert Dove, who took him to New Orleans where he freed him in recognition of his medical ability. By 1783 the twenty-six-year-old Derham had built a medical practice in New Orleans estimated to bring in the then fabulous sum of $3,000 per year. He was considered one of Louisiana's most capable physicians. "I have conversed with him upon most of the acute and epidemic diseases of the country where he lives and was pleased to find him perfectly acquainted with the modern practice on these diseases," testified Benjamin Rush, one of the era's most prominent physicians. "I expected to have suggested some new medicines to him, but he suggested many more to me."

However, Derham was an exception to the rule that Negroes

generally weren't accepted either for apprenticeships in medicine or training in medical schools. During the early nineteenth century the way to get around that was to pledge that after receiving your medical training you intended to move to the new colony of Liberia, established in West Africa for newly freed Negro slaves. After attending medical lectures sponsored by the American Colonization Society, on June 21, 1834, a Virginian named Charles Webb made the move, only to succumb to a tropical disease four months after arriving.

Others studied medicine under the same promise: a Philadelphian named Washington Davis, a Washingtonian named John H. Fleet. James McCune Smith, on the other hand, made no such promise, so had to sail to Scotland and earn his M.D. at the University of Glasgow, which he did in 1837, only to return to New York City to combat similar attitudes to those John Kenney urged Negro physicians to combat seventy-three years later. Smith wrote an essay, "Comparative Anatomy of the Races," challenging the popular belief that there were intrinsic differences between Negro organ systems and the organ systems of those classified as Caucasian. Another essay by Smith, "The Influence of Climate on Longevity, with Special Reference to Insurance," belied the notion that Negroes were inherently of weaker stock. He collaborated with Frederick Douglass on speeches and writings, opposed the resettlement of newly freed slaves in Africa, and engaged in public debate with the likes of South Carolina senator John C. Calhoun (a former vice president and secretary of war who staunchly defended slavery and states' rights). The subject, of course, was the biological capacities of the Negro, a debate Smith is said to have won.

By promising to immigrate to Liberia upon graduating, John V. de Grasse and Thomas J. White earned admission to medical school at Maine's Bowdoin College, graduating in 1849. However, neither kept his promise. White never really practiced medicine. De Grasse did, hanging his shingle in Boston, even gaining admission to the Boston Medical Society. But like the handful of other Negro physicians during that time, he still had to brave extreme doubts about his competence, even from other Negroes.

By 1850 there were nine Negro physicians in New York City, four in New Orleans, two more elsewhere in Louisiana. By 1890 there were 909 across the country; by 1900, 1,734; by 1910, 3,409 for a Negro population of 12 million—one Negro physician per 3,520 Negroes, compared to one Caucasian physician per 624 Caucasians, though such a statistic is misleading since by 1910 plenty of Negroes still lacked faith in the competence of Negro physicians. This caused the *Washington Post*, subsequent to an address by Booker T. Washington calling for four thousand more, to respond:

> Now, nobody disputes the right of a Negro to practice medicine. . . . However there is room for doubt that 4,000 more Negro doctors would find the demand for their labors considerable enough to pay the expenses to keep themselves alive. An indefinable something resides in the breed that disinclines the Negro to give countenance and patronage to members of his own race who open a store or an office. Whether this peculiar form of the boycott is a survival of the full dependence of the Negro upon the dominant race in slavery days or some more deeply seated cause is for the 'ologists to tell us, our province going no further than to point to the effect.

Nevertheless Negro physicians didn't starve. Many even became financially well off, despite also having to overcome additional obstacles to practicing the profession, including the availability of no more than thirty-five hospitals where they could admit patients, primarily makeshift facilities with a handful of beds, opened by a handful of physicians among their ranks. Most were educated at struggling medical schools opened to train them because most other schools still refused to admit Negroes: Howard University, Meharry, Leonard, Lincoln, Flint, Knoxville, West Tennessee, Chattanooga, and Louisville Medical Colleges, all but two of which—Howard and Meharry—would be forced to close by 1915, along with numerous other medical schools for Caucasians that wouldn't make the grade in the estimation of Abraham Flexner. Flexner was designated by the Association of American Medical Colleges to evaluate medical school quality because the country had expanded so rapidly and, given the nation's penchant for allowing capitalism to flourish untrammeled wherever greedy men saw a good opportunity, medical schools had started sprouting like toadstools. From the initial founding of respectable ones at the University of Pennsylvania (1765), Columbia (1768), Harvard (1783), Dartmouth (1798), and Yale (1810), there grew to be over four hundred claiming the ability to teach students to become physicians. The admission requirement of most, including the respectable ones, was only that the prospective student be able to pay the fee. Often all it took was for a handful of physicians to organize and declare themselves a school. They didn't even need a laboratory or infirmary, and were aided by the fact that the scientific basis of disease wasn't yet well established.

In 1909 and 1910 Flexner toured the country, visiting each medical school for a day, and noted in his resultant report that it was tremendously important to produce Negro physicians since Negroes were such "a potential source of infection and contagion."

Nevertheless, Caucasians who trained Negro medical students became objects of contempt for plenty of other Caucasians. Howard University School of Medicine opened on November 9, 1868, with an initial enrollment of eight students and five teachers, one teacher being considered Negro. The university proper had been opened nearly two years earlier and was named for General Oliver O. Howard, an officer in the Union Army who had fought in twenty-five battles during the Civil War, lost an arm, and survived several bouts of cholera. After the war he had been named head of the Freedmen's Bureau, which was so heavily criticized by Democrats of that era as an agency designed to keep the Negro in idleness at the expense of "the white man." The bureau aided in the launching of Howard as well as Atlanta and Fisk universities, the latter two schools ultimately being taken over by northern churches and philanthropists. The bureau also established 4,000 elementary and high schools in which 9,000 teachers taught 250,000 Negro pupils, which was hardly concrete evidence that the bureau kept Negroes in idleness at the expense of "the white man." And Negroes donated from their own pockets and homes one-sixth of the initial proceeds and equipment needed to keep the schools functioning. The Negroes who were pouring into Washington were primarily from across the Potomac in Virginia. In that thoroughly planned city, rather than integrate them with Caucasians, the solution for the time being, it was decided, was to squeeze most into alley dwellings that inevitably became eyesores. They would not be condemned and flattened until the era of Franklin Roosevelt's New Deal, after photographs of alleyway shanties in newspapers and magazines with the Capitol dome in the background finally proved to be too much for the citizens of a nation that claimed a belief in democracy and equal opportunity.

Naming Negro schools after people like General Howard would become a tradition, the object of which was to honor Caucasians of that era for the charity work of dedicating their lives to uplifting the debased, a group General Howard may have felt a kinship with due to having lost one of his arms. The stated aim of the new medical school was "to assist [the] agencies already at work in the relief of the ignorance and personal suffering in the District of Columbia and the country at large." However, neither its faculty or student body was ever limited to Negroes. Indeed, most of both initially were predominantly Caucasian, but over time the medical school became predominantly Negro, its teaching infirmary—appropriately named Freedmen's Hospital—launched in a former army barracks, since at that time Negroes weren't accepted for treatment in regular medical facilities.

Six years later, in Nashville, Tennessee, five Irish brothers expressed a desire to contribute to the reconstruction of their area of the South with the then princely sum of $15,000 for the "training of Negro youth in medicine." This act of charity was precipitated by the fact that one of the brothers, the Reverend Samuel Meharry, had once been a needy farmer and was befriended by the same type of loyal, patient, faithful Negro that Booker T. Washington later praised in his speech at the Cotton States and International Exposition. The Negro man even shared his home briefly with Meharry until the young man could get back on his feet. A little more than a decade before the brothers made their intentions clear, when the Civil War was in its last days, a young Caucasian named George W. Hubbard arrived in Nashville to enlist in the Union Army, which had occupied the town during most of the conflict. He rode in on the day the Confederacy surrendered, but chose to stay and teach the newly freed slaves pouring in, primarily from the farms and plantations of western Tennessee. While doing so he earned his medical degree at Vanderbilt University, and upon graduating learned of the charitable intentions of the Meharry brothers. They made their bequest to Central Tennessee College, established by the Methodist church as a school for Negroes; it was planning a medical department because "the difficulty of securing proper medical attention for the colored people was very great and the mortality alarming." The college hired

Hubbard to serve as initial dean and faculty member of its new division, Meharry Medical College, which became Meharry Medical College of Walden University when in 1900 Walden became the new name of Central Tennessee College. Eventually Walden closed, but Meharry continued as an independent medical school, saved by the report of Abraham Flexner. By 1910 and in the years to come, Meharry would expand its physical plant, faculty, and student body, primarily through the aid of enrollment fees and philanthropic foundations, while Howard's medical school would survive through enrollment fees as well as annual federal subsidies (and some foundation support). Together, the two schools, up until the mid-1970s, produced 80 percent of the Negro physicians who diagnosed diseases, treated them, performed surgery, and served as role models in Negro communities. Yet within that same span of time, lack of endowment, coupled with plenty of discreet racial antagonism and opposition to its well-being from Vanderbilt would force Meharry to the brink of extinction, while Howard's medical school would fare only a little better.

CHAPTER 4

Thus the medical alma mater of my great-uncles, father, and, for a brief time, myself began as an expression of the benevolence of five Irish-American men. And within our families there is Irish blood infused in the usual manner it was introduced into the veins of Afro-Americans—discreetly within slave shacks by men who went "slumming" between the thighs of slave women, inadvertently siring children they considered "polluted" because they weren't purely European but contained the blood of black Africa. And after those slaves were freed, some Irish-American men donated money to launch a separate medical school for "our polluted kind." And eventually Uncle Joe—evincing an indomitable will for an outcast— did well enough as a physician to return to that alma mater as its largest alumni benefactor.

According to Mr. Ehrlich—newly settled in the metropolitan area where the political and social rights of people of my heritage were abdicated in 1895 during Washington's famous speech; site of the further compromising of our collective dignity subsequent to a brutal municipal riot against us in 1906; birthplace in the year 1929 of the man who'd do more than any single individual to bring about the restoration of our civil rights thirty-five years later—there were both good and bad things to know about Meharry's most generous alumni benefactor, my great-uncle Joseph Howard Griffin. But first I had to find where Mr. Ehrlich lived.

As I continued searching for the address, my mind also continued ruminating. Once again, I pondered the extent to which we either sugarcoat or ignore our heritage in order to generate self-esteem and lead productive lives. Once more I thought of how my father had been an expert teacher of how to put the unpleasant behind you. The summer of my mother's death, 1975, just before he dropped me off in Providence, Rhode Island, to begin my freshman year at Brown, we four immediate survivors of Edith Pearson sat together one evening in the family room of our home at 1008 Wilson Drive in Fort Wayne, watching TV. Suddenly a program about death and dying came on. "You kids shouldn't be watching this," my father told us. It was a more telling demonstration of how the only way he knew to get on with the rest of life was to bury unpleasant experiences. He never discussed with us the reality of racial acquiescence he saw all around him and engaged in while growing up in Jim Crow Georgia. Not once did he or my mother discuss with us children the slow process of her dying. It was only in the last three months of her fading life, spent in a bed at Parkview Hospital, that they even admitted it was reaching its end. And after she died, not once did we discuss how we felt about witnessing it. Sometimes I concluded that my father was like that because he was a physician and there was no greater enemy, no more potent reminder of defeat to a physician, than death. Other times I attributed his reticence to the emotional reticence that also appeared to grip his siblings and parents. They were so stoic in demeanor that if you closed your eyes at a Nathan Pearson family get-together you might think you were attending a gathering of WASPs.

By contrast, on my mother's side of the family you could hear the Griffins and Richardsons laughing and talking a mile away. The liquor flowed freely and, among the men, so did the philandering. But the legend of my great-uncle's medical accomplishments remained intact, unquestioned, or digressively but respectfully hinted at in all its real dimensions, with a knowing wink, by my aunt Elaine. I had no problem imagining Uncle Joe in the company of the most respected pioneers in the Negro medical universe. Now as I searched for Mr. Ehrlich's residence I wondered, Did he really belong among the most respected pioneers in the Negro medical universe? I discovered that in the years leading up to his enrollment in medical school in 1911, such men paved their own paths in surgery—the specialty he practiced and loved—because they were left with no other alternative.

By the end of the nineteenth century, Howard and Meharry were turning into the principal sources of Negro physicians. Yet most people, especially Negroes, went to the doctor only after home remedies proved unsuccessful. If you were admitted to a hospital that usually meant you were having surgery. The prospect of being operated on frightened most people. When they were told the man wielding the scalpel would be a Negro surgeon, their fright often turned into hysteria. Weathering such adversity, by 1892 when nothing else could be done, surgeons at Howard's Freedmen's Hospital amputated thighs, legs, toes, and feet; repaired hernias, lacerations, and dislocated shoulders; removed hemorrhoids; set fractured bones. But other than to repair a hernia, they were too nervous to penetrate a patient's abdomen. They sprayed the area of the patient's body to be operated on with a weak solution of carbolic acid and, when amputating, left the ligatures hanging out of the end of the wound long enough to rot off. There was much talk among them of "laudable pus." In 1893 Hoke Smith was the Secretary of the Interior. His administrative jurisdiction included Freedmen's. Thirteen years before returning to Georgia and calling Negroes a menace, then being elected governor, Smith decided to install a new surgeon-in-chief at Freedmen's. He chose a man named Daniel Hale Williams, a man whose name eventually became a standard refrain during the Negro History Weeks of my youth, and is still a standard refrain today during Black History Month.

With the arrival of Williams came a new, more progressive era in the training of Negro surgeons. There would be no more talk at Freedmen's of "laudable pus" because he rendered pus "unlaudable" by sterilizing surgical instruments in a wash boiler containing a metal strip full of one inch holes sitting on iron blocks to keep the instruments above water. Later, he installed a steam sterilizer. At two o'clock on Sunday afternoons in an amphitheater he successfully penetrated his patients' abdomens for operations other than hernia repairs. And any curious layman could watch. His assistants were all fellow Negroes. Critics called his public displays an invasion of the patient's privacy, an act of unethical self-promotion. Defenders called it the most direct means of reassuring the public of a Negro surgeon's competence.

While operating Williams let his hands do most of the talking. Outside of the operating room he was viewed as preoccupied, boorish, and withdrawn. His hair was straight. He wore a bushy mustache. He carried himself with dignity. And even though he was light brown in complexion with so much Caucasian ancestry diluting his black African blood that he might have passed for a swarthy

Sicilian, or Latino, he proudly identified himself with all others harboring any detectable black African ancestry. Eight years after graduating from medical school at Northwestern he founded Chicago's Provident Hospital, one of the first Negro-run hospitals in the country, and a nursing school along with it. Two years later he was credited with being the first surgeon anywhere to successfully operate on the pericardial sac surrounding the human heart (thus he is recorded in history and remembered every Black History Month as the first surgeon to successfully operate on the human heart). At Freedmen's he replaced red bandanna nurses (who effectively served as maids) with nurses trained in a nursing school he founded. He appointed the hospital's first interns. He required that they wear dark blue uniforms with white armbands bearing a red cross. He launched a horse-drawn ambulance service. Still he had problems getting Freedmen's personnel to accept proper discipline and decorum. His efforts got him into hot water with other physicians there. In 1897 he was removed, and turned so bitter about his days at Freedmen's that later when a fellow physician asked if he should accept an appointment there, Williams replied, "I'd rather have my son sell newspapers on a street corner!"

But Williams had no son. He had no children at all. He did have a wife. Often it was said that she was the only person who delighted him. He began asking parents to name their sons after him. He wanted to be remembered. He wanted to be vital. Yet no one made less effort than he did to make friends. It was said that once he moved on to new surroundings he forgot about his former associates. During the height of his professional success he was expelled from a fraternal organization. He returned to Provident Hospital. But the man who had replaced him as surgeon-in-chief had an ego that wouldn't budge, was Booker T. Washington's personal physician, a leader in the Urban League, and a clever diplomat. Unlike Williams he made friends easily and fought enemies ruthlessly. Dan Williams had no stomach for a battle. He decided to ply his trade at Cook County Hospital and elsewhere.

In 1899 George Hubbard invited him to begin holding annual one-week surgical clinics at Meharry. He accepted, and assumed the title Visiting Clinical Professor of Surgery. Negro physicians from all areas of the South brought their most perplexing cases to Nashville for Williams to operate on. His surgical demonstrations became the great event of the school year. In 1903, at the convention of the National Medical Association, he met Dr. John Kenney, seven years before Kenney would admonish Negro physicians to defend the chastity of middle-class Negro girls and young women. Kenney read a paper on the treatment of shock that impressed Williams so much he invited Kenney to serve as his anesthetist at his annual Meharry clinics. They began an exciting collaboration that further motivated Meharry's students and practicing Negro physicians in the South. Williams had found his new mission. He made numerous pilgrimages to the annual meetings of Negro medical societies in Virginia, North Carolina, South Carolina, Georgia, Alabama, Mississippi, Louisiana, and Texas. When the American College of Surgeons was formed in 1913 to certify a surgeon's competence for the skeptical public, he was the only Negro invited to join. As a result of his acknowledged skill and determination he influenced the training of every promising Negro surgeon of the first two decades of the twentieth century, including the man who would mentor my uncle Joe at Meharry, John H. Hale.

As a first-year student, Hale watched Williams's first surgical clinic at Meharry, saw his clean efficiency, witnessed his calm under pressure, and decided that nothing could be more fascinating than being a surgeon. He never missed a Williams clinic. Upon graduating from Meharry in 1905 and finishing his internship at Mercy, its affiliated hospital, a year later, he hung his shingle out in Nashville. Because the scientific basis of medicine was still in the process of being established, mandatory formal training in distinct specialties was still a thing of the future. At that time an aspiring surgeon needed only an M.D., courage, boldness, and someone willing to apprentice him in the operating room. The American College of Surgeons was still seven years away. A surgeon would be weeded out if he gained a reputation for a high mortality rate among patients. Hale found a mentor in a fellow physician named John T. Wilson, an earlier Meharry graduate who had opened his own hospital. Wilson was considered a genius, who, upon witnessing someone perform an operation only once, could then successfully perform the same procedure himself. His mortality rate was low. Patients didn't become hysterical upon learning that he was to operate on them. He was large, attractive, and, unlike Williams, made friends easily. He captivated his protégés, and John Hale proved to be his most talented one. Hale was a handsome man of light brown complexion who wore his kinky hair closely cropped. In portrait his face appeared serious, on the edge of becoming sad. To increase his skill in the operating room he learned not only from Wilson but made repeated visits to the Mayo Clinic and the Crile Clinic to observe what surgeons at those institutions were doing. By the time Joseph Howard Griffin arrived at Meharry in September 1911 to begin his medical studies, Hale's star in the Meharry constellation was swiftly rising.

The summer of 1911 my great-grandmother Griffin couldn't understand why her oldest son would want to give up a lucrative job (for that day and age) paying him $50 per month working as a brick mason in the southwest Georgia town of Blakely, approximately fifty miles south of the family's 495-acre farm, to attend medical school, where for at least four years he'd make no money at all. It was more money than he had ever earned in his life, at a trade he had learned while he was a student at Georgia State Industrial College in Savannah. He had graduated that May, valedictorian of his class. Georgia State Industrial (later renamed Savannah State) wasn't even recognized as a true liberal arts college by national standards because it merely taught the rudiments of traditional liberal arts courses while heavily emphasizing the teaching of trades to its students. This situation was largely a result of the compromise Booker T. Washington had made with the Caucasian South at the Cotton States and International Exposition, as well as the message wealthy northern Caucasian philanthropists were certain they had heard in that speech and others he later made.

The result was a profound handicapping of the liberal arts education available to Negro students so that resources could be concentrated on teaching them the tools for "useful living." To Washington this amounted to pragmatism. Yet it became hopelessly entangled with the desires of Caucasian racists who were eager to see Negroes remain their subordinates. Like Tuskegee, Georgia State Industrial taught brick masonry, carpentry, plastering, painting, blacksmithing, wheelwrighting, tailoring, shoemaking, laundering, auto mechanics, agriculture, dairying, poultry raising. But it also taught algebra, geometry, trigonometry, physics, English, rhetoric and composition, argumentation, penmanship, introduction to economics, history, biology, botany, zoology, applied sociology, public health, Latin, French, and Spanish, and a course in "good morals and good manners." All students were required to spend as much time "in the pursuit of industrial training, or on the farm as agricultural students" as they spent studying traditional college courses. In 1905 the school's library housed a mere six hundred volumes.

Yet there was at least one professor there who insisted on preparing his brightest students to pursue careers other than in agriculture or the trades. D. C. Suggs had earned his bachelor's degree at Atlanta University and his M.D. at Leonard Medical School, one of the medical schools that would be forced to close by 1915. But he couldn't pass his medical boards. So he taught science courses at Georgia State Industrial. At Atlanta University he had been exposed to an educational philosophy at odds with that prevailing at Georgia State Industrial. Atlanta had been founded by Ivy League New Englanders eager to train the brightest Negro prep school and college students of the region in their own image. Faculty members expected them to scale the greatest intellectual heights rather than learn a trade (later the prep school and undergraduate divisions closed and Atlanta became strictly a graduate institution). As Washington's educational philosophy stressing vocational training for Negroes became more popular among northern philanthropists, increasingly they disfavored the philosophy of Atlanta University. Faculty member W. E. B. Du Bois, who had begun a protracted study of Negro life, became such a liability to the institution that by 1910 he agreed to leave and work for the NAACP so that the school could survive. Yet it wasn't unusual for the Negro industrial and agricultural colleges to hire Atlanta University graduates, as well as graduates of Fisk and Howard, which were also bastions of liberal arts education. They needed such graduates to teach their liberal arts courses, and welcomed them as long as they agreed to behave—as in, not rock the boat by giving their students workloads that subtracted from their "industrial" and agricultural apprenticeships.

For the most part, at Georgia State Industrial Suggs "behaved." But he motivated his brightest students to become scientists or physicians, rather than brick masons, carpenters, mechanics, haberdashers, shoemakers, or farmers. He provided them as thorough a grounding as he could in biology, botany, physics, and chemistry so that upon arriving at Meharry in September 1911, after saving $180 to pay his tuition, Joe Griffin felt prepared to tackle the medical school curriculum.

Though John Hale was there pioneering in surgery, along with his mentor J. T. Wilson, and Dan Williams was electrifying each second semester with displays of his virtuosity with a scalpel, Meharry was still a struggling institution: there were handicaps in the preparation of its students that had to be overcome; ever-changing standards in the medical profession to be met; and the permanent difficulty of expanding its facilities and faculty in a moderate-size Tennessee city where Vanderbilt would always cast a shadow like a large elephant.

The school term preceding Joe Griffin's freshman year saw the completion of the first wing of the medical school's very own teaching hospital. It was opened in December 1910 and was named for George Hubbard, who was sixty-nine and still dean. Prior to the opening of that first forty-five-bed wing, privately owned thirty-bed Mercy Hospital and J. T. Wilson's twenty-five-bed infirmary were the only clinical facilities available. Each January for one week, in the cramped confines of Mercy's operating room, over one hundred students and physicians took turns trying to observe Daniel Williams at his best, craning their necks for a good view. With the opening of Hubbard they were relieved of the strain. Its surgical amphitheater seated up to one hundred students and physicians in a semicircle for skylighted views of the latest operating techniques performed on a spanking new white-enameled steel table.

The city's Negro population and its twenty-three Negro physicians proudly pointed out that they raised one-fifth of the $15,000 it cost to construct the first wing, and supplied all of its furnishings. They boasted of how its redbrick structure, painted walls, and polished wooden floors were a stark contrast to the pitiful hovels of the city's Black Bottom where most Negroes lived. In almost every city in the nation the Negro death and disease rate was much higher than that for Caucasians. There was so much of it in ghettos like the Black Bottom that an image of licentiousness leading to a high rate of syphilis wasn't the only stereotype hounding Negroes. They were also dogged by the belief that they were the principal hosts of the tuberculosis bacilli and carriers of pellagra.

TB, also called "the Great White Plague" and consumption, was to the early twentieth century (with regard to the general public's fears) what AIDS became to the 1980s and '90s (though its victims recovered if the disease was detected early enough). Often, stricken carriers took on the appearance of walking cadavers. Healthy people treated them like lepers, were mortified of coming into accidental contact with their coughed-up sputum on floors, horse buggies, cars, and sidewalks. Across the nation TB sanitariums mushroomed. Cities passed antispitting laws. The myth grew that half of all Negroes meeting their maker were dying of the disease. Negro barbers, waiters, cooks, and domestics lost their jobs.

The incidence of TB per 100,000 people was four times higher among Negroes as among Caucasians. But half of all Negroes dying weren't succumbing to TB. Negro physicians tried to explode the myth while treating TB symptoms with oral administrations of iodine, and swabbing the chests of sufferers with the same substance. Mindful that those they were treating and advising were less than fifty years removed from legal bondage, and still largely wedded to the prescriptions of voodoo and hoodoo doctors, herb vendors and "patent medicine men," the physicians forced cod liver oil down plenty of throats, as well as lime-and-soda syrups. They instructed sufferers to abstain from sex, advised them to exercise outdoors, and told them to avoid crowds. Negro fraternal and professional groups formed antituberculosis leagues and fanned out to churches to teach their poverty-stricken brethren the proper way to prepare and serve food, bathe, ventilate their abodes, wash their hair, clean their teeth.

Scientific developments and educational innovations came about ever faster. Meharry faculty and students struggled to keep pace. Flexner's report on medical school quality would soon lead to the stipulation in every state that no graduate of an unaccredited medical school could take a state board exam and face questions like: Beneath what point on the anterior chest surface are the cardiac valves? What arteries supply the heart and where do they originate? Give the nerve supply of the anterior abdominal wall. What structures are severed in a tracheotomy?

Though Meharry was of higher quality than most of the other medical schools across the country that would soon be forced to close, it still faced a daunting mission. The notion that sick people expecting to live through their illness should be admitted to a hospital wasn't yet fully accepted in society. The belief that those learning the medical profession should be required to do so in hospitals was also an idea still fighting for uniform acceptance. For a medical school to train its students in a sizable clinical facility was a sign of its progressiveness, and the major determinant in whether it would receive accreditation. By 1911 Howard, Meharry, and Leonard were the only Negro schools successfully meeting that standard (though Leonard wasn't doing well enough to gain accreditation, which ultimately led to its demise). Of the three, Howard was the most advanced. By 1911—the earlier difficulty of Daniel Hale Williams in establishing proper discipline and decorum notwithstanding—Freedmen's Hospital provided 278 patient beds for Howard's students compared to a total of 100 patient beds spread among three hospitals for those receiving their medical education at Meharry. And both Freedmen's and Howard received annual federal subsidies, while Meharry and its affiliated hospitals were completely private.

More to the point, Washington, D.C.'s, Negro community was twice as large as Nashville's. At that time it was the largest urban Negro community in the nation with the most Negro physicians. The city was the capital of the Negro bourgeoisie. No other Negro community set as high a standard of education. By contrast, in the former Confederacy—where the lion's share of Negroes still lived—standards in general weren't as high. Less exacting standards meant that from the beginning of the twentieth century until 1925, despite having fewer clinical resources, Meharry graduated far more M.D.s than Howard—in some years seven times as many (the Howard class of 1917 had only thirteen graduates while Meharry had ninety-seven). Another reason for its much higher enrollment was economic: Meharry needed as many students as possible to pay its faculty.

The class of 1915 included Joe Griffin and eighty-four others. The school year lasted from September to April. During the first two years students spent all their time in the classroom learning chemistry, embryology, histology, pathology, anatomy, physiology and something called electrotherapeutics. The faculty were an integrated lot. And one of them, a Negro physician, had what he considered to be the better fortune of receiving his medical training at

Harvard. In class he never let an opportunity go by to remind Joe and his classmates, "When I trained at Harvard, this is what we used to do . . ."

While my great-uncle studied he hardly had any spending money. Often he was hungry. He worked part-time as a bellboy in the Hermitage Hotel and sometimes gathered pieces of bread and scraps of meat left over from the hotel's restaurant after it fed its Caucasian patrons to make his meals. By the time he began his clinical years all of Hubbard Hospital had been completed. It could comfortably accommodate seventy-five patients, one hundred in an emergency. Over half of the 336 patients it treated during the eight-month school year were admitted for surgery (195). Thirteen appendectomies were performed, seven salpingo-oophorectomies, and a host of other -ectomies. During his weeklong surgical clinic, Daniel Hale Williams completed eighteen operations. During the rest of the academic year John Hale completed thirty. Among the 141 medical admissions were patients suffering from typhoid fever, malaria, pneumonia, intestinal catarrh, pleurisy, diabetes, nephritis, hysteria, and rheumatism. Yet only 2.7 percent of the hospital's patients died.

Across the nation the number of Negro hospitals continued to grow. By the end of 1913 there were no less than seventy. But there'd never be enough to serve the total need of Negroes for good medical care. Negro physicians continued to make a few inroads into the developing specialties, primarily at Freedmen's, but also at Hubbard. John Kenney and his skeletal staff gratefully accepted the keys to a brand-new hospital, built to further the work they were doing in that area of the South. It was the gift of Elizabeth Andrew Mason, granddaughter of John A. Andrew, governor of Massachusetts during the Civil War, who recruited and launched the 54th Regiment of Massachusetts—the famously brave and heroic Negro Civil War battalion. For that accomplishment and Mason's generosity, the hospital was named for him. She shelled out the $55,000 it cost to construct and equip an imposing two-story redbrick facility featuring wide porches, Greco-Roman cement columns, and enough beds to treat fifty-three patients being cared for by the scarce supply of Negro medical doctors in Alabama and western Georgia.

Most of those physicians remained general practitioners partly because so few hospitals where the specialties were developing accepted them for any training, and partly because after passing the state board exam where they intended to practice, plenty of Negro physicians were content to hang out their shingle, then never again pick up a medical text or journal. Of course they weren't alone. Such habits were hardly peculiar to physicians considered Negro. But the movers and shakers, the prodders, the leaders among Negroes in medicine were especially sensitive, especially embarrassed, especially concerned. "Too few are willing to pay the price—to delve deep down amidst the intricacies and mysticisms of science, to, day after day, year after year, doggedly and determinedly follow the labyrinthine meanderings of the scientific way," complained Kenney. "We must add something to the stock of medical knowledge, we must discover something not already known."

There were a host of Caucasians making their presence felt, stamping their names on parts of the human anatomy, along with medical equipment and procedures to cure diseases. They engraved their sobriquets on Hunter's canal, the canal of Knuck, Hesselbach's triangle, Malpighian bodies, Metchnikoff's theory, Roentgen rays, Wright's opsonins. But only one pioneering mark had been left by a physician with the blood of sub-Saharan Africa. Though mainstream medical journals and the lay press hailed Daniel Hale Williams's sewing up of the pericardial sac as the first successful operation on the human heart, no part of the human anatomy or any surgical procedure was named for him. Still, Williams continued to visit Meharry each winter and, scalpel in hand, perform what seemed like surgical magic.

Despite experiencing occasional pangs of hunger and struggling to make ends meet, Joe Griffin was able to observe him, too. And when my grandmother's oldest brother reached Hubbard's wards he demonstrated such a degree of diagnostic excellence and skill at assisting John Hale in the operating room that when the medical degrees were awarded in April 1915 he graduated valedictorian of his class. His classmates had elected him class president. Said the yearbook: "Joseph Howard Griffin, from rural Georgia—If he makes the doctor he has made the student, his success will be certain."

After once more reading Mr. Ehrlich's directions and retracing my route a third time, I came upon a modern-looking apartment

CHAPTER 5

Indeed, Bertram Ehrlich hailed from a family of southern Jews. They had settled in Bainbridge because Thomasville, forty miles away, though larger, was hostile to the sons and daughters of Israel. It had something to do with the Civil War. Jewish peddlers in Thomasville were suspected of spying for the Yankees. So from that point on Jews weren't welcome. They found Bainbridge, just northeast of the confluence of the Flint and Chattahoochee rivers, more hospitable. It was a locale that, if it played its cards the right way, could become the major trading center of southwest Georgia, since the Flint and Chattahoochee rivers combine where the damming of the Flint River forms Lake Seminole, defining the southwest corner of the state. Then out of it comes the Apalachicola River which begins at the Florida border, and heads farther south to pour into the Gulf of Mexico, from which ports around the world can be reached.

Obviously, Bainbridge didn't play its cards the right way, and Albany, farther up the Flint River, became the major urban center of southwest Georgia. But that wasn't because Mr. Ehrlich's grandfathers hadn't done what they could to move the town forward commercially.

After I rang the doorbell, a short, slightly stout man eighty-three years of age answered. We exchanged greetings and Mr. Ehrlich ushered me into a modest-sized, nicely furnished one-bedroom residence in that spacious, atriumed suburban Atlanta complex that features a range of social events and health care services for residents sixty-five and older. He told me that he was a widower with three grown children, one of whom was a daughter living in Atlanta who had convinced him to move to this retirement community to be near her and his grandchildren. At my encouragement he detailed the beginnings of the Ehrlichs, as well as the Kwileckis on his mother's side—the two most prominent Jewish families in turn-of-the-century Bainbridge. I encouraged the digression because it was important to me to know as much as I could about the first person to volunteer what he promised would be a candid assessment of my great-uncle. I was curious, too, about the saga of two Jewish families in a small southern town. And in the back of my mind was my encounter at the 92nd Street Y. It figures, I decided, that someone Jewish would play such an integral role in aiding my mission, proving once more that through thick or thin, among those who see themselves as white, Jews have figured prominently and most compassionately in Afro-American life. It appeared that this was about to hold true right down to the task at hand, though I was sure that it still wouldn't prove that Jews were responsible for my freedom.

Mr. Ehrlich elaborated on the Jewish experience in that pocket of the state. Later, I learned that his grandfather, Henry Ehrlich, was born in Germany in 1849. While still a teenager, Henry followed his two brothers to the U.S., landing in Savannah not long after the Civil War ended. By that time his brother Abraham had migrated farther west to Bainbridge, where he opened a store. Abraham died in 1872, and Henry arrived from Savannah to take over the business. His brother had turned it into one of the most impressive in town, offering customers such delights as barrels of fresh lobster and cases of fresh strawberries.

As is true of the origins of so many American municipalities, the location that is now Bainbridge initially had been settled by Native Americans. They called it Pucknawhitla. When an English trader established a trading post on the site in 1765 it became known as Burgess Town. Later a militia installation was built on the site and it became Fort Hughes. In 1823 the state legislature stipulated that that section of the state, which was the southern half of Early County, would henceforth become Decatur County. The following year it decreed that Fort Hughes would become the county seat and would henceforth be known as Bainbridge, in honor of Commodore William Bainbridge, commander of the U.S.S. *Constitution* during the War of 1812.

In its early years the town's advantageous location turned it into the fastest-growing settlement in southwest Georgia. Numerous barges plied the Flint, Chattahoochee, and Apalachicola rivers, stopping in Bainbridge to trade the wares and crops from the plantations, farms, and timber operations. These had sprouted up in the region after the Creek, along with the Chickasaw and Cherokee

Native Americans, had ceded the region to the U.S. and made the seven-hundred-mile journey west along what became known as the Trail of Tears. Their destination was the federally designated Indian Territory, land the U.S. government promised would be theirs forever. Forever, though, lasted only until oil was discovered, at which point Indian Territory, too, was overrun by non–Native Americans, who in 1907 carved out of it the state of Oklahoma.

Meanwhile, back in southwest Georgia, in the last decades of the nineteenth century, as the state recovered from the Civil War, as many as two hundred boats known as Fannies, along with barges and a nascent railroad line, stopped in Bainbridge. The town became home to five opera houses, two theaters, a horse racing track, twelve saloons, and numerous hotels. When eventually railroads outpaced barges as the preferred mode of transportation, lack of a railroad bridge across the Flint River slowed the town's growth, enabling Albany, Valdosta, and Thomasville to overtake it. But Henry Ehrlich decided he was there to stay.

After taking over his brother's store, he met his future wife in Albany, married her in 1877, and brought her back to Bainbridge. They would have eight children. In addition to his store, in conjunction with a partner, Henry launched a lumbering enterprise. It featured its own small railroad to transport lumber to customers in the outlying county. Later still, along with a handful of other movers and shakers, he founded Citizen's Bank and Trust and rose to the position of bank president. His merchandise emporium grew even more and he opened a large cotton warehouse, adding cotton purchasing to his line of businesses. Later still, near the county's northern border he purchased large tracts of land and turned them into what became known as the Ehrlich Plantation, where sharecroppers raised cotton and other crops.

Mr. Ehrlich's maternal grandfather, Isadore Kwilecki, was also born in Germany, the same year as his paternal grandfather. He, too, arrived in Bainbridge as a teenager. He came with other relatives after starting out in Tampa, Florida. By the close of the 1870s he opened a general merchandising store, then gradually turned to offering hardware and building supplies. From there he expanded into purchasing real estate and constructed his own building downtown, the ground floor of which became the first of the town's five opera houses, where traveling shows, light opera, and local entertainment groups—all Caucasian, of course—decamped and entertained Caucasian audiences. In conjunction with his four sons, Isadore opened other merchandise emporiums—one in the nearby town of Moultrie, another in nearby Quincy, Florida, another in nearby Chattahoochee, Florida. He became one of the organizers of Temple Beth El and was named its first president. In subsequent years he made several visits to Germany to bring more members of his family to Georgia. After he died in 1934 his descendants used the money from his estate to bring even more relatives out of that country, since by then Hitler had risen to power.

From all this I concluded that, in essence, the Ehrlichs and Kwileckis got a head start on becoming prosperous by pioneering the availability of much needed products and services to the residents of southwest Georgia while my family was just emerging from slavery. As tended to be the case for most German Jews—the first Jews to settle the U.S.—the small number who settled in southwest Georgia did their best to assimilate as rapidly as they could among others eventually deemed Caucasian. They moved to Albany and Valdosta as well as to Bainbridge, where they were so eager to assimilate that they held their temple services on Sundays, rather than Saturdays, the traditional Jewish sabbath. Except for a Star of David, the architecture of the synagogues in the area was virtually indistinguishable from many of the surrounding Protestant churches.

The option of being accepted to a similar degree didn't come about for my family or any other Negroes. So rabid was the determination to keep at arm's length during daylight hours anyone even thought to harbor black African ancestry that even the lightest-skinned Negroes, barely distinguishable from those considered pure Caucasian, were forced to live in a netherworld where they held themselves above their darker brethren but also acknowledged kinship. (Some experts believe that a significant percentage of southerners who are considered Caucasian have in fact at least one black African ancestor—a female slave whose offspring from her role as a concubine eventually became so light in skin color that they "passed" as Caucasian.)

Both the light-skinned and dark-skinned commingled in my family, primarily on my mother's side. And they did so to some extent in a reversal of the stereotype that up-and-coming Negro men marry women lighter-skinned than them (both of my grandfathers were light brown in complexion while my maternal grandmother was dark-skinned and paternal grandmother brown-skinned; my mother's skin, too, was much darker than my father's). From somewhere deep inside of both families developed the determination to make the most of any economic opportunity that became available to a Negro in their area, a determination that appeared to outpace that of most of the other Negroes around them.

Great-grandfather Robert Griffin and his brother Shorter were brought to Stewart County, Georgia—ninety miles north of Bainbridge and thirty-five miles south of the cotton mill city of Columbus—by their father, William, when they were toddlers. William Griffin migrated to the county from Troy, Alabama, located in the southeastern part of the state. That was where he had been a slave. Robert's mother was the offspring of her Caucasian master and a slave woman who was half Creek Native American. Robert never really knew his mother because she was sold during slavery. After freedom his father brought him to a Georgia county, which, like all the other counties in the southwestern section of the state, was predominantly Negro. Stewart County abuts the fall line where the Piedmont Plateau becomes the Atlantic coastal plain, making it very hilly. Lumpkin, the county seat, straddles the summit of the county's highest hill. By 1850, twenty-five years after the Creeks ceded the area to English, Scottish, and Irish settlers, including those who brought slaves, a person could stand on the courthouse steps in town and observe groups of slaves in all directions as far as the eye could see, cultivating or harvesting so much cotton that only one county in the state produced a greater volume.

During the Reconstruction era William Griffin became a local sharecropper. At first, upon reaching adulthood, so did his sons Robert and Shorter. Robert's first wife died not long after giving birth to their fourth child, a girl just like the others. He took as his second wife my great-grandmother, a dark-skinned fifteen-year-old girl from the county named Mary Watson. On February 1, 1888, Joseph Howard Griffin was the first child born to them. They would have eleven more. My grandmother, who was given the same name as her mother, was the tenth. The family labored on sharecropped land until 1899, when Robert saved enough money to purchase a 395-acre tract along the banks of the Chattahoochee River from a

Caucasian named John Elliott (since my grandmother wasn't born until 1909, she only knew her father as a landowner). In later years he purchased an additional hundred acres in adjoining Randolph County. He bought it from a local judge. Unlike most of the rest of the region, most of the land sits on flat terrain. For the land that sits along the river, the hills don't begin until about a mile from the riverbank, and only a couple of miles down the road is a site where early nineteenth-century Caucasian settlers skirmished with the Creek Native Americans who eventually surrendered the land.

Robert Griffin was the first Negro to purchase land in the county (only 8 percent of the Negro farmers in Stewart County were able to purchase their farms). He never had a formal education but did learn to read and was the principal leader among Negroes, serving as their adviser, confidant, and informal ambassador to Caucasians. A sign of the times he lived in was his acceptance of what Caucasians in the area considered a respectable means of addressing him: They called him "Uncle Bob." Whenever something had to be discussed between Caucasians and Negroes in the river area they sought out "Uncle Bob." (Former President Jimmy Carter, who grew up in Sumter County, about thirty miles away, also had relatives in Stewart County; many years later, upon meeting my uncle Joe at a reception, Carter recalled that Stewart County relatives spoke highly of "Uncle Bob.") Great-grandfather was also superintendent of the local A.M.E. church Sunday school and held offices in Negro fraternal organizations such as the Knights of Pythias. At church he told his children to always sit up front, not in the back engaging in foolishness as so many youths were fond of doing.

In imitation of the Caucasians who owned large tracts of land, he liked to refer to his farm as "my plan-ta-tion." But because he couldn't afford large-scale equipment and sophisticated fertilizers, the crop yields from it were meager. Still the other Negroes in the area considered the family to be rich, not only because they owned a large farm but because they lived in a relatively large house and rode in a nice horse and buggy. Great-grandfather was a strict disciplinarian, and Uncle Joe was whipped frequently because he was always doing something mischievous. One day he decided to experiment by trying to "cure" one of the farm's turkeys with a solution of medicine that smelled like turpentine, a concoction he had seen his father administer to a cow suffering from what was known as "hollow tail." Then he decided to ride him, after which the turkey began fluttering around, then dropped dead. For that he received a whipping. But he also informed his father that he wanted to be a doctor. Allegedly Great-grandfather's taciturn response was, "If you want to be a doctor, go on. Be one!"

Yet first Uncle Joe had to overcome the severe educational limitations on Negroes in the county. Caucasians decided that very little was to be spent on the separate schools housed in Negro churches that they forced Negro youths to attend. Per-capita expenditures were as low as $1.68 per Negro child compared to $19.23 per Caucasian youth. As was common throughout the South, the school year for Negro youths started only after harvesting season was over and lasted only until the following spring cultivating season began (which meant that in such a mild southern climate it lasted for just four to five months). By contrast, Caucasian youths were in school almost twice as long. Salaries for Negro teachers were less than half those for Caucasian teachers. Caucasian administrators chose Negro teachers and didn't require them to meet very strict standards. In those days they preferred the relatively poorly trained industrial school graduates to those educated in genuine liberal arts colleges, not only because of their poor training but because they believed they could trust them to safely teach the Negro youths "their proper place."

The Negro teachers were paid so poorly that most in Stewart County couldn't afford a place to live. So they rotated living with Negro families in the area. Each day they'd gather their charges in one of the small clapboard Negro churches—each age and grade mixed together—and teach them from outdated books handed down from the Caucasian schoolchildren after they received new ones. None of the books went beyond the sixth grade. After that, Negro youths were expected to work the fields. If they were lucky and their families had the money, they might get the opportunity to attend one of the few private high schools in the region for Negroes. But there were none in Stewart County. So for that they'd need to leave home.

Uncle Joe liked school so much that Great-grandfather allowed him to keep going back after finishing his sixth-grade readers. But eventually he got bored going through the same books over and over again. His teacher, "Professor" Eddie Lee, approached Great-grandfather about possibly sending him to Payne High School in Cuthbert, Georgia, about thirty-five miles away. ("Professor" was a term Caucasians back then used to describe any Negro school-teacher, in lieu of just John or whatever his first name was, which was the normal way they addressed Negro men, doing all they could to avoid attaching "Mister" in front of their names.) He would have to board with a woman named Fannie Clark. Great-grandfather came up with the tuition, plus room and board, and sent Uncle Joe off to Payne.

Though it was called a high school, its curriculum was really no more sophisticated than that of a respectable elementary school. The principal, "Professor" John Lewis, had originally taught at Atlanta's Morris Brown College. Payne was part of the A.M.E church school system that included Morris Brown. And though Lewis's background and resources were limited, he did the best he could to provide Payne's students a decent education. But it wasn't enough. Uncle Joe breezed through Payne. After receiving his certificate he wrote several colleges and discovered that he could attend Georgia State Industrial for forty dollars per year. He found odd jobs and saved up eighteen dollars. Impressed with his diligence, Great-grandfather decided to give him the additional twenty-two dollars to enroll in a college that essentially was no better than a decent high school. At that time many medical schools didn't require a liberal arts education. It wasn't until two years after he enrolled that Meharry changed its admissions criteria so that new entrants would need a liberal arts degree and a set number of premedical requirements.

Despite lacking the best preparation for medical school, Uncle Joe appeared to have a good aptitude for learning. After graduating valedictorian of his class at Georgia State Industrial in 1911, then valedictorian at Meharry in 1915, he completed his internship at Hubbard Hospital, then spent a few months observing surgery at Chicago's cavernous Cook County Hospital (at that time the largest hospital in the country) and another few months observing in the Department of Surgery at the University of Pennsylvania School of Medicine. (At that time there were no surgical residencies anywhere for Negroes, and only a few places such as Hubbard and Freedmen's where they could do their internships.) The year was 1917 and the U.S. had just entered World War I. So he enlisted in the Army Medical Corps, was given the rank of first lieutenant and sent to Fort Leonard Wood in Missouri, where he examined incoming recruits. He was released after a few months at which point he returned to Georgia, passed the state medical board, and headed back to Stewart County to set up a small office in Lumpkin, in the back of a store owned by a Negro man. But Caucasians made things difficult. They didn't want a Negro doctor in the county. That was considered too uppity. In three months he was gone. Next he tried Columbus for one week. But conditions there weren't to his liking either. Then he spent a week in Albany, which he didn't like. It was the fall of 1917.

Back in Bainbridge, Henry Ehrlich's son Julian, Bertram's father, who was four years older than Joe Griffin, was forced to leave school after the third grade because in early childhood he suffered from seizures. (As he became older they stopped.) When he reached his teen years he began working for his father. In 1909, in conjunction with a partner, he opened a drugstore. By 1917 he was in his sixth year as sole owner of what became Ehrlich Drug Company. He never attended pharmacy school, choosing instead to employ registered pharmacists. In 1912 he received one of the first Rexall franchises in the country. According to Bertram, because his father's pharmacy constantly filled physician's prescriptions, he knew a lot about local medical conditions. He became increasingly concerned about the Negro population of Bainbridge and the surrounding county, who composed most of its residents and were its principal supply of unskilled labor. Caucasian physicians, like those elsewhere in the South, administered only a rudimentary level of treatment to them. Many had never seen a physician at all. Negroes weren't eligible for admission to the town's two hospitals. There was only one elderly Negro physician in Bainbridge, and he was near retirement. Julian Ehrlich felt another Negro physician was needed to take care of the needs of Negroes in Bainbridge and the surrounding counties. He had recruited one who proved to be no good, so Julian encouraged him to leave town, which he did. Then he heard about the young Negro physician who had left Lumpkin and was moving about looking for somewhere else to practice. He urged Joe Griffin to set up practice in Bainbridge.

The town, though, was hardly a racial Shangri-la. Paranoia about the "Negro menace" was still white-hot throughout the South and across the nation. The country was still enthralled with the notions expressed in Thomas Dixon's 1905 novel, *The Clansman*. Within a few months of publication it had sold over a million copies to people eager to read a take on the Reconstruction era portraying barbaric Negroes ("mulattoes" in particular) lusting after "fair white maidens," corrupting city halls and state legislatures, and further intimidating "good white citizens" with their "dominance" of the region until the Ku Klux Klan came to the rescue of "white civilization." The novel became so popular that Dixon turned it into a traveling play. In 1915 it became the notorious landmark film *Birth of a Nation*. One night in Bainbridge after watching the play, excited audience members left the theater, headed straight for the town jail, and lynched a Negro prisoner.

But Joe Griffin knew that if he held every racial incident that occurred in the history of every town in the nation against it, he'd never set up practice anywhere. At that time any place that allowed a Negro physician to practice without giving him trouble was considered progressive. Part of the impetus for bringing him to Bainbridge was fear of further Negro flight from the area. Many were leaving due to damage of cotton crops by the boll weevil (damage that would reach devastating levels by the 1920s). Upon U.S. entry into World War I, Negro out-migration accelerated. Labor agents from the North traveled south to recruit them to work in factories. Caucasians in Bainbridge feared greater losses to places like East St. Louis, Chicago, Detroit, and Cleveland. Something had to be done to convince Negroes to stay. One ploy the town newspaper used was to print stories of desperation suffered by Negro workers who migrated north. Another enticement, the thinking went, could be the arrival of a good young Negro doctor to take care of their medical needs. But desperation soon got the upper hand. It didn't take long before many towns and cities in Georgia, Bainbridge included, passed "work or fight" laws requiring every able-bodied Negro either to serve in the army, work outside of their homes, or face arrest and fines as a vagrant. That meant that any Negro waiting in a railroad station to board a train heading north was subject to arrest. Under the ordinances Negro women were required to work as domestics. Respected Negro citizens of Bainbridge became outraged. They called a mass meeting. They informed the mayor and the town's lawyer that they would resist the new ordinance "to the last drop of blood in their bodies." The city rescinded the requirement in the case of Negro families with a visible means of support.

Still Negroes in town felt humiliated. As soon as the U.S. entered the war, they resolved like most others across the country to support ceaselessly the struggle against Kaiser Wilhelm. They were relieved that the nation had found a new demon. Each week the Bainbridge newspaper featured a full-page ad for Liberty Bonds. It contained the helmeted, shadowy figure of a German soldier, sword in one hand, large club in the other, the word "Kaiserism" displayed across his image, as he sneaked up on an apparently unsuspecting America, with only the lighted sun of Liberty Bonds exposing him for proper destruction. Beneath him in large type were the words DRIVE THIS SHADOW FROM OUR LAND, and in smaller type "Show the military masters of Germany that Americans are not close-fisted. Convince them that we will make any sacrifice for the cause of freedom and democracy."

Negroes in Bainbridge and the rest of the county purchased Liberty Bonds and sent their young men off to war, most of them to dig trenches and otherwise serve Caucasian infantrymen. "The Decatur County Negro is above the average," the town newspaper assured its readers. "They are law-abiding, very few of them ever being disorderly, and they are loyal to their friends and they will be to their country."

When the town bid farewell to its first detachment of Negro soldiers, a celebration was held in the courthouse square. On the dais was the new Negro physician Joe Griffin, master of ceremonies. He introduced Harrison McIver, a postman, a well-respected and relatively well-off Negro citizen, as well as T. H. Bynes, also Negro, and chairman of the Committee on Arrangements, who told the gathering:

We are willing to join hands with the powers that be and force this great war to consummation. If an injustice has been done to us in the past, we have no time to discuss that. . . . The time has come that we have an opportunity to show to this great republic our loyalty to the stars and stripes. . . . We believe that this war is God's war and that it is the medium through which he is going to teach all men everywhere that they must fully recognize the fatherhood of God and the brotherhood of man. . . . Our boys are going willingly, feeling that the greatest good that shall come out of this war is for us, after we have again proven our worthiness to attain the blessings of this nation. We shall not cease working and fighting until the leader of this great nation shall say to us, you have done enough, come up higher.

Though for such occasions the town's Negro leadership eagerly accepted him among its ranks, Joe Griffin had to engage in an extra effort to gain the trust of the Negro population in his abilities as a physician. The notion that a Negro man of medicine didn't know as much as his Caucasian counterparts was still quite common—even among Negroes. It took a national disaster for him to earn their trust. By the fall of 1918 the nation was struck by an influenza epidemic that had its origins in Europe. Approximately thirty million people around the world would die from it, a little over half a million in the U.S. Residents of Bainbridge reeled from it. People venturing out in public were advised to wear face masks. Among the epidemic's victims was the town's leading physician. Joe Griffin was the only doctor in the area who knew of an effective treatment for the disease. He had learned to administer it while serving in the Army Medical Corps at Fort Leonard Wood. It consisted of a yellow powder of pharmaceuticals mixed with distilled water. He administered it to Negroes and Caucasians alike, working in Bainbridge during the day, driving to nearby Quincy, Florida, at night, and to plenty of rural locales in between. Caucasians prohibited him from driving up to their residences in his Ford Model T. They considered that too uppity for a Negro. So they picked him up from his office on Ward Street, drove him to their homes, then brought him back. He became known as "the Flu Doctor" and received a wide variety of remuneration for his services. Some could afford to pay his fee. From others he received livestock: in one case a full-grown Jersey cow, in another, a hog, in many other instances hams, pickles, chickens, turkeys. Receiving no money for his services angered him. But allegedly Great-grandfather set him on the right track, telling him, "Whenever a man brings you all he has, you accept it. You didn't go to medical school to learn how to fight, you went to learn how to practice medicine." The influenza epidemic established his reputation as a good doctor. At that point his practice began to flourish among Negroes, while after the epidemic most Caucasians went back to being treated by Caucasian physicians.

It was at about that time that he met the daughter of the leading

Negro citizen in town, Dr. J. W. F. Johnson, a prosperous dentist. Elaine Johnson had just graduated from Fisk University. Her mother, Lula Cooper Johnson, was a teacher. Lula's mother was the daughter of a Jewish man and his Negro concubine. Her father became the first Negro engineer on the Atlantic Coastline Railroad that ran from Waycross to Dothan, Alabama. He acquired property in Bainbridge and Waycross, which Lula inherited. In October 1919 Joe Griffin and Elaine Johnson would wed.

In the meantime, in the early morning hours of November 11, 1918, a shrill fire whistle began to blow, mingled with all the other bells and whistles in town. At first some thought there was a massive fire. Others guessed the real news and soon everyone was screaming with joy. A parade spontaneously formed. It included the town band, followed by the town fire truck, followed by hundreds of cars decorated with American flags. Children gathered in the town square and shot fireworks. An elderly Negro woman marched up and down Broad Street, the main thoroughfare, waving the American flag. For one day, at least, segregation took a backseat as other Negro citizens joined the march around the courthouse square and the celebration inside it, waving more flags and shooting fireworks with fellow Caucasian citizens.

But if any Negroes thought that their loyalty and aid in winning the war would finally lead to true democracy and equality, they soon discovered they were wrong. Caucasians throughout Georgia, as elsewhere in the South, made it clear to returning Negro veterans that seeing them in uniform or hearing that they were determined to no longer suffer the injustices of Jim Crow was an offense to their sensibilities. Roughly sixty miles northeast of Bainbridge, in the town of Sylvester, Daniel Mack, a Negro veteran, was sentenced to thirty days in jail for announcing that now that he had been to France and fought for democracy, he would no longer accept mistreatment from Caucasians. As severe as it was, even that punishment wasn't enough in the eyes of some local citizens. Before he could finish his sentence a mob broke into the town jail, dragged him out, and beat him to death. Closer still to Bainbridge, in Blakely, forty-three miles to the north (where Joseph Griffin had been a well-paid bricklayer), as soon as Negro citizen Wilbur Little alighted from the train after returning from the war, he was forced by a group of local Caucasians to take off his uniform and walk home in his underwear. Despite such intimidation he was resolute in his determination to wear it around town anyway. As a result, he eventually paid with his life.

Apparently no such incidents occurred in Bainbridge. Yet neither were Negro citizens to assume that anything was about to change as far as their rights were concerned, even though the town fathers did acknowledge the contribution returning Negro veterans made to winning the war. As happened elsewhere, they recognized the veterans within the traditional strictures of segregation by sponsoring, the following April, a separate Negro veterans' appreciation day in the town square. The speaker for the occasion was Henry Lincoln Johnson, a Negro lawyer from Atlanta, respected by Georgia's leading Caucasians because he was an accommodator who preached patience to the Negro masses. Indeed, as the main Negro Republican patronage dispenser in Georgia, he was such a powerful political operative that Booker T. Washington, who had died almost four years earlier, once feared Johnson would replace him as the principal Negro power broker in the nation. Now that the war was over, Johnson's assignment was to travel around the state and quell Negro hopes for immediate democracy and equal rights. He rose to the podium in Bainbridge as elsewhere and did just that.

No published record survives of exactly what he said. But the speeches given by other Negroes considered acceptable to Caucasians in that area of the South, and treated as proud and respectable by fellow Negroes, give us a good idea. A little over a year after the war ended, upon gaining reelection as Grand Chancellor of Great-grandfather's Grand Lodge of the Knights of Pythias, G. R. Hutto, the namesake of Bainbridge's Negro high school, declared to the assembled:

> Any man who would stir up race [hatred] is a dangerous man. I care not to what race he may belong, or what his position may be, and while others may preach the doctrine of hate, let us teach ours to love. Let every Pythian be a law-abiding citizen, and in addition to this, let everyone strive to own his home. The man who is a property owner becomes at once a contributing factor in his community, for he helps to support the government and provide for the education of his

children and this should be the aim not only of Pythians, but every Negro in the country.

With the doctrine of gradualism reinforced, in neighboring Alabama plans moved forward to build a hospital for returning injured Negro veterans. The location was to be Booker T. Washington's adopted hometown. In a way, this seemed like an odd choice since Howard or Meharry could have used the hospital to bolster the clinical resources available to their faculty and students. Indeed, Tuskegee was in the second tier of southern locales under consideration, and received the hospital only after city fathers in places like Atlanta, Durham, Memphis, Nashville, New Orleans, Birmingham, and Mobile exercised the option given them by the Veterans Administration to turn it down. The town and school of Tuskegee were only too happy to have the hospital (though ultimately it would house primarily mentally ill Negro veterans). The town was still run by Caucasians who did their best to tolerate the college, while the college did its best not to incite the wrath of Caucasian residents. This issue, though, would eventually incite their wrath. Caucasian men flocked to town to help build the hospital. Construction moved forward, increasing the demand for housing, precipitating the construction of a new hotel, pouring money into the coffers of Tuskegee merchants.

John Kenney was proud that he helped convince the government to put it in Tuskegee, buttressing John A. Andrew Hospital, adding a major piece to the Negro medical center he wanted to expand in the region so that one day a Negro physician might contribute something not already known to medical science. But once the facility neared completion Caucasians in the town decided that they couldn't stand for Negroes to enjoy the principal benefits of this new addition to the local economy. They sent a committee to Washington, D.C., to demand that the new hospital be staffed with Caucasians.

The committee was reminded that the main reason Tuskegee was chosen was so that the hospital could be staffed by Negroes. Members were reminded of their own state law preventing Caucasian nurses from caring for Negro patients. The committee informed the Veterans Administration that it had figured out a way around the law. Their plan called for each Caucasian nurse to have a "colored maid" who would take orders from her and serve Negro patients. VA administrators found the idea preposterous. They stuck to the original plan. But that didn't stop Caucasian Tuskegeeans. They enlisted the aid of others in the state, persuading them that "white supremacy" was at stake if the new hospital was run by Negroes. A committee marched into the office of Robert Moton, the man who had replaced Booker T. Washington as president of the college, and demanded that he go along with their plan. The message was clear. Moton was to either heed the directive or risk hanging by his neck as "strange fruit" in a noose secured to the limb of an oak tree draped with Spanish moss.

At that point neither his life nor John Kenney's was safe. Both fled campus. The Klan moved in. From across Alabama, in their trademark hoods and robes, they descended on the town at night, burned their cross, and paraded down the highway running through the college campus, their hooded profiles captured by the glow of their torchlights. Students and faculty remained disciplined, nonviolent, and kept their doors shut. But the Caucasian locals had overplayed their hand. Southerners outside of Alabama became embarrassed by the spectacle. Oscar Underwood, one of the state's U.S. senators, was running for President. His backers pressured Caucasian Tuskegeeans and their Klan allies to cease and desist lest he be further shamed in an election year. They did as they were told. John Kenney and Robert Moton won their fight and returned to campus. Yet the incident was indicative of the uneasy truce influential Negroes in the region were forced to work out with Caucasians—a trick requiring them to guess when they were crossing that invisible divide between the self-reliance and industriousness disingenuous Caucasians urged, and when such efforts would raise Klan paranoia, more than a few of the hooded Klan anonymities being those same respected Caucasians.

With the war over, Joe Griffin, newly anointed "the flu doctor," set out to prosper 140 miles to the south, as much as he could in Bainbridge and the Georgia-Florida-Alabama tristate area. When his patients needed hospitalization he drove them forty-one miles south to the only hospital in the area for Negroes—the recently constructed fifty-bed Florida A&M College Hospital in Tallahassee, that state's capital city. The school was the state's agricultural and mechanical college designed primarily to teach Negroes a trade. In the first years of his practice he'd drive his patients along the dusty road to Tallahassee for serious operations only. If the operation was not so serious he'd perform it at the patient's home.

The first unsupervised procedure he undertook was on a field-hand who worked on a plantation owned by multimillionaire William Bradley, of Columbus. The patient was a fifty-two-year-old Negro man. A Caucasian physician had been called in, examined him, and concluded there was nothing he could do for him. The overseer of the plantation heard about the young Negro doctor in Bainbridge. He called Joe Griffin, who drove up, examined the man, and diagnosed him as having a hernia that needed repair immediately. He began sterilizing towels and sheets, placed the instruments he would need in a pillow case, and boiled them in water he had instructed other tenants on the farm to prepare. The kitchen table of the overseer's house was scrubbed. The patient was placed on it and administered ether. The operation began. . . . It was a success.

For the next ten years he examined patients in his office, wrote prescriptions, performed house calls, minor home surgery, and surgery at Florida A&M, all within a social milieu typical of the small-town and rural South. Plenty of his patients were other share-croppers. One was a woman whose baby he was called upon to deliver into the world by a Caucasian plantation owner. The nervous man greeted him at the plantation gate: "Doc, I got a nigger sow down here trying to birth a young'un and the granny lady's there, but she can't handle it. I thought I better call you. You go down there and see what you can do with her, 'cause I want her back in the fields as quickly as possible, 'cause these crops, the grass is eating me up." Under the philosophy of gradualism Booker T. Washington had worked out, reinforced by Henry Lincoln Johnson, faithfully adhered to by Joe Griffin who was a loyal member of the local Negro Business League, there was nothing to say to that—only the delivery of a newborn to be carried out for an agreed-upon fee.

Other patients were the Negro men performing menial tasks in the turpentine distilleries, and cotton and tobacco and peanut warehouses, the Negro washwomen in the area's towns who picked up the laundry from the homes of families like the Ehrlichs and Kwileckis and the rest of the gentry, brought it back to where they lived, washed it, dried it, ironed it, then returned it for whatever low wages they could manage. Many were wet nurses for the children of such families, or their baby-sitters or their nannies, or the men who drove such families around, or the maids who cleaned up after them and prepared their meals, some becoming the secret lovers of husbands. A few were the lovely café-au-lait women in the elaborate bordellos who only serviced well-to-do Caucasians. Others were the Negro teachers and preachers and postmen and undertakers. Some were the town derelicts, the alcoholic asthmatics who would line up outside of the home that had been built for his family to receive injections from his youngest brother, David—when David came to live with him to attend Hutto High School for Negroes—paying in return twenty-five or fifty cents.

Every now and then mob violence pierced the façade of civility. It had become a tradition. From 1889 to 1918 Georgians led the nation, putting to death primarily without trial 386 victims, followed by Mississippi with 373, Texas with 336, Louisiana with 313, Alabama with 276, Arkansas with 214, Tennessee with 196, with Florida and Kentucky next, respectively, completing a solid southern block. And the following year Georgia again topped the list with twenty-one prey, almost twice as many as second-place Arkansas and Mississippi with twelve each (in the years to come Mississippi would eventually overtake Georgia). Of course, the overwhelming majority of victims of mob violence were Negro. And until 1950, Georgia had more Negroes than any other state in the country. But, interestingly, most Negro victims weren't accused of that most heinous violation sure to incite a lynching—the rape or assault of a Caucasian female.

This was true, too, in subsequent years. In November 1920, in Coffee County, where Great-grandfather Pearson had been born a slave and months before my own father was born about fifty miles away, a Caucasian farmer named Pearly Harper walked into a store in the Negro section of Douglas, the county seat, to sell some syrup. Two Negroes, Will Perry and Will Ivory, allegedly approached him. Harper and Ivory began to argue. There is no record of what they argued about. Given the times it could have been about Mrs. Ivory, who was outside waiting for the argument to end. Perhaps Harper was pressuring her to have sex with him. Perhaps Will Ivory had done some work for Harper and not been paid fairly, or his wife had done some work for him and hadn't received a fair wage. In any case, Perry allegedly went outside and told Mrs. Ivory to bring in her gun. Mr. Ivory then fired it at Harper, hitting him in the head, killing him instantly.

The sheriff arrived and arrested Perry and Ivory, while Mrs. Ivory escaped. Later she was apprehended and thrown in jail, too. As word of Harper's murder spread, Caucasian farmers poured into Douglas from a radius of ten miles. They made plans to rush the jail and capture the prisoners. In an effort to quell any possible disturbance the sheriff secured an agreement from the local Superior Court judge to call a special session rushing the case to calendar the next day, thinking that swift justice might defuse the situation. A relative of Pearly Harper begged the mob to allow justice to take its course. Many returned to their homes. Meanwhile, a group of them headed to a highway leading out of town under the theory that the sheriff might attempt to spirit the three prisoners to another county for safekeeping. At about one o'clock that morning the prisoners were taken from the jail, placed in an automobile, and driven down the Dixie Highway toward nearby Ocilla. Seven miles outside of town their vehicle was intercepted by the vigilantes. The sheriff surrendered Mr. Perry and Mr. and Mrs. Ivory, who stood in the middle of the road, shocked and silent, as shooters waited for the order to fire. Bullets from more than fifty guns then crashed into their bodies, transforming them into three bloody heaps of flesh, bone, and fiber lying in the middle of the road, not to be discovered until later that morning by travelers along the highway. The following day a grand jury was convened only to conclude that "the Negroes came to their death at the hands of unknown parties."

Weeks later, closer to Bainbridge, in neighboring Grady County, Jim Roland, a proud, respected, forty-year-old Negro who owned a two-hundred-acre farm, was stopped along a road on a Saturday afternoon by J. L. Harrell, a Caucasian farmer. Harrell said he was feeling good and just wanted to have a little fun. So he asked Roland to dance. As he asked him he pulled out his pistol and pointed it at Roland's feet, threatening to fire it to induce his request. Roland refused, allegedly saying that since Christmas was over, the time for such shenanigans was over, too. At that point he lunged for Harrell's gun. The gun went off, hitting Roland in the arm, while Harrell was hit in his abdomen and right hip and was later hospitalized. Roland fled the scene. News spread of the shooting. A group of Caucasians in the area formed a search party. When they found Roland between midnight and two in the morning near the public road between the towns of Camilla and Wigwham in next-door Mitchell County, they led him to the middle of the road and riddled him with bullets. Again it was concluded that this was a death that took place at the hands of unknown parties.

During this same period, forty-five miles northeast of Bainbridge, just outside of the town of Moultrie, a Negro preacher named F. A. White stepped to the pulpit of his small church and preached a revolutionary idea. He told his nervous congregation that it was time to show some backbone and stop waiting on "white folks," washing and scouring their clothes. As long as they were content to perform such menial tasks he said, they could expect to remain nothing more than Negroes. Someone in the congregation reported him to a "bossman." Later that week he was abducted by four Caucasian men who drove him three miles outside of town, stripped him, and tied him to a log. Then they proceeded to whip him into unconsciousness with a heavy leather trace, after which they returned to their cars and left him naked, shivering, stranded in the cold. As a result, he fled the county.

With such methods Caucasians in the area trained most of the large number of Negroes in the region to remain their nannies, cooks, maids, drivers, fieldhands, menial laborers, and clandestine female lovers. They conditioned each other to keep their eyes out for criminal activity among Negroes, while remaining paranoid about the sexuality of their males. Negroes humbly suffered it all, then on Sunday prayed for eventual deliverance through eternal life. From the depths of their church sanctuaries, shouts of congregational ecstasy pierced the air, alternating with interludes of moving gospel music and spirituals. In Bainbridge, once a month they queued along the banks of the Flint River, then ventured into its waters up to their waists so that their preachers could baptize a new one among them, usually a youth, in the name of the Father, the Son, and the Holy Spirit. Satisfied with such humbleness, Caucasians allowed Negroes to roam their mental space in other acceptable ways as well. On weekends in venues such as the immaculate Callahan Theater downtown, traveling minstrel shows featured Caucasian men in blackface performing what were known as "coon songs" while they "buck-danced," then told jokes in Negro dialect, all of it to gales of laughter.

Negroes remained integral to life elsewhere in the state, too, as when Georgia played host to the nation's elite. Every winter, two hundred miles east of town, the wealthiest of America with names like Rockefeller and Morgan gathered on the state's Sea Islands to frolic in elegant understated mansions they called cottages. Forty miles to the east of Bainbridge, some of the same millionaires built winter retreats outside of Thomasville, which they referred to as plantations, though they were really large tracts of real estate where they hunted the game raised and running wild for their pleasure—quail, pheasant, deer, boar. . . . From both colonies of wealth some of the most important decisions on the country's future were made while invisible Negroes arranged sumptuous meals for their enjoyment, then at night turned down their sheets, then in the morning cleaned their sheets. . . .

And there were the numerous vehicles with northern license plates passing down highways lined with Negro shanties, carrying Caucasian passengers on their way to the real estate boom that was Florida. Some made fortunes, others went belly-up after purchasing property sight unseen, only to eventually discover that what they had really bought was swampland, or land that didn't even exist, or land that had been sold several times over. The frenzy even spread to north Florida, in the woods south of Tallahassee where tracts were sold to the gullible for inflated prices. Trains heading for the state passed by Negroes as well. One day the St. Louis Express derailed four miles outside of Bainbridge, its cargo including several cars of some of the finest race horses in America en route to Florida for the racing season. Those most injured were shot on site.

And there were the times when a Negro's presence allowed what was really going on to pass unnoticed. Such as the opportunities presented by the prohibition of liquor. Raymond Powell, a Caucasian bootlegger, always hired a Negro boy from Bainbridge to ride with him to the Florida Gulf Coast. After the two of them loaded down his vehicle with illegal bounty for the return trip, he'd handcuff the boy so that if anyone stopped them he'd identify himself as a deputy sheriff transporting a prisoner. That said, his car was never searched.

In the midst of it all, a Negro woman from Blakely arrived one day in Joe Griffin's office seeking treatment. Upon examining her he determined he would need to take her to Florida A&M Hospital.

Her husband was disappointed to learn that they would have to travel forty miles farther south. After that Joe Griffin began planning to build his first infirmary. It would open in 1930, during the Depression. It would be a wooden structure on Water Street. The same Negro churches from which shouts of ecstasy could be heard contributed pictures and bedsteads. But Joe Griffin financed its construction all by himself. It contained eighteen beds, an operating room, a delivery room, a kitchen, and a dining hall. He named it for his wife's parents—the J. W. F. Johnson Memorial Hospital. After it opened his medical practice soared. After it opened he confronted the first instance where he risked stepping on local Caucasian toes.

A Negro female was brought to Dr. A. B. Alford, a Caucasian physician in town, for a diagnosis of what ailed her. He performed exploratory surgery and told her that she had cancer and only a few months to live. As often happened after being dissatisfied with what a Caucasian physician said, the woman was taken to Joe Griffin for a second opinion. Upon examining her his diagnosis was that she suffered from a uterine tumor with intestines adhered to the tumor. The situation was dangerous. Rather than attempt to do something about it, Dr. Alford had simply sewn her back up and sent her on her way. Joe Griffin sought a second opinion from a Negro colleague, Dr. T. V. McCoo, who practiced eighty miles away in Eufaula, Alabama. McCoo came to Bainbridge, confirmed his diagnosis, and suggested he operate soon because her condition was getting worse. And McCoo agreed to assist in the procedure. But when the time came to perform it he said he was unable to return to Bainbridge. A Negro physician in Thomasville and one in Tallahassee made themselves scarce as well.

Joe Griffin's nurse started to cry. "Dr. Alford told you the girl is gonna die and you just gonna ruin yourself," she sobbed. His wife agreed. "Dr. Alford said she is going to die and I wouldn't touch her." The situation had stirred up quite a bit of attention and emotion all over town. If she died it would mean that Joe Griffin had the audacity to consider his expertise above that of a Caucasian physician, and then sacrificed his patient's life on the operating table, proving that he was arrogantly wrong. It was a possible outcome that perhaps accounted for the unavailability of the other Negro physicians. For such a transgression he could be driven from town, maybe even lynched. He chose to go ahead with the procedure. It was a success. The girl lived. After performing it he was so exhausted that he got in his car, drove out into the country, parked under a tree, fell asleep, and didn't wake up until the next morning. From that point on, whenever Dr. Alford encountered him in town he crossed the street and looked the other way.

Long ago I had discovered that this was the atmosphere in which my great-uncle built his medical practice. But now I was mixing it with new information. This was the first I had heard about the role of Julian Ehrlich in bringing him to Bainbridge. It was also the first I had heard about anyone Jewish living comfortably on the Caucasian side of the racial divide in the Deep South, as Mr. Ehrlich insisted was the experience of his family. If his family had comfortably been on that side of the divide, I reasoned, then could I trust everything else Bertram Ehrlich would say? The investigative and curious sides to me said keep an open mind. Don't allow family sentiment to interfere. As we continued our conversation I tried not to.

CHAPTER 6

Still, as I sat in his apartment and thought back to the front-page column in the *Atlanta Journal-Constitution* published by the South's venerable Ralph McGill on Sunday, August 6, 1950, I couldn't resist feeling the same sense of pride I'd felt when I was fourteen and first read an old clipping of that column. McGill was editor of the *Constitution*. Along with luminaries such as newspaper owner Hodding Carter of Greenville, Mississippi, he had become the pride of liberal Caucasians in the South, the voice of moderation in that ocean of racial apartheid, serfdom, ignorance, insecurity, and caricature that had resulted in its inhabitants becoming the laughingstock of the rest of the country.

"Deep in southwest rural Georgia, not far from Florida's capital city of Tallahassee, I found a meaningful American story," he wrote. He went on to describe that story as the opening of Joseph Griffin's second and larger, more modern hospital, three days earlier. McGill had traveled to Bainbridge to give the keynote address at the dedication ceremony in the town square. Sitting with him on the dais along with Uncle Joe were Bainbridge's mayor (the Caucasian Cheney Griffin), the chairman of its city commission, and the county health commissioner. In the audience that hot sunny day were hundreds of people from the Georgia-Florida-Alabama tristate area.

Things had changed since the 1930s. There were far fewer lynchings. Joe Griffin's importance to the local economy was secure. Respected Caucasians in the region viewed the opening of his new hospital as proof that segregation could work—a belief they were eager to reinforce, due to fear that changes in their way of life would soon be ordered by the U.S. Supreme Court. The court was beginning to hear cases challenging Jim Crow in the region's schools, since the South hadn't lived up to the "equal" part in its separate provisions for Negroes. McGill, too, viewed the opening as a way to prove critics in the North wrong about the way of life practiced in the region. He hadn't yet reached the point where he supported integration. At that time no Caucasian in the South who expected to hold a position of authority for very long supported integration. Support for separate equality *was* the liberal position. And that was the point of McGill's column, which marveled that my great-uncle had managed to build a well-equipped hospital using a then fabulous quarter of a million dollars of his own money—a facility where he would invite Caucasian physicians to treat their Negro patients as well.*

Nationally syndicated columnist Elmer Wheeler also highlighted the opening in his column entitled "Success Secrets." He wrote:

> Recently a friend of mine brought up the old-fashioned philosophical teaser. Does man have free will, or is his will so conditioned by heredity and environment it is all decided for him what he can and cannot do? I did not waste time. I just told him the story of Joseph H. Griffin M.D., Bainbridge, Georgia. Dr. Griffin recently opened his quarter-of-a-million-dollar hospital. He built it himself. No one knows what put the idea in this Negro boy's head that he could rise above the limitations of his environment. Maybe it was because nobody told him about the limitations of heredity and environment and the condition of the human will.

It was those words and the wealth of my great-uncle, and the fact that on that day he opened the largest private hospital for Negroes in the state, and my father's assurances that the racists down there used to say, "Don't bother those Pearsons, they're crazy," and the prestige of the M.D.s after Uncle Joe's, Uncle David's, and my father's names that told me, given a lineage like that, I wasn't supposed to hang out on street corners, I wasn't supposed to speak jive, which by the late '60s, early '70s I had been trying my best to blend in with the rest of the boys in my neighborhood and the inner-city kids bused to our school, as we promoted Black Power in our own misdirected manner.

In the process I ignored the validation of segregation seen in my great-uncle's accomplishment by southern Caucasians of the early

---

*McGill's column and one other source acutally reported the cost to be "about $225,000," while other sources put it at about $250,000.

1950s. What mattered more to me was that he had overcome daunting obstacles during a period of what were, from my vantage point, unfathomable racial nightmares. It seemed that even among men in my family with little money, the determination to rise above the circumstances of their environment flamed so intensely you would have suffered first-degree burns if you tried touching it. Every summer our invalid mother took me and my sisters, Carol and Jennifer, by train at first and then by air to Jacksonville, Florida. There at dawn we could hear her father, Crawford Richardson, firing up the engines of his large trucks as he and his crew of men prepared to rise above the circumstances in Jacksonville, and go out and cut down the tall long-leaf pines in north Florida and south Georgia, load the logs on his trucks, and sell them to the pulpwood factories in town. Crawford Richardson, the entrepreneur, dreamed of owning the same type of lumber company Henry Ehrlich owned; for a little while he owned his own sawmill, but was forced to close it before I was born.

Joe Griffin hadn't wanted his kid sister to marry my grandfather, who hailed from the same town where T. V. McCoo practiced medicine, Eufaula, Alabama, just down the road and across the Chattahoochee River from Great-grandfather Griffin's farm in Stewart County, Georgia. Beginning in 1923 Grandmother left the farm every school year and headed for Bainbridge, where she lived with her oldest brother and his wife and newborn daughter, Mary Louise, and attended Hutto High School.

My grandmother watched him get up early in the morning, wash, shave, dress, eat, and trek to his office, then return home in the evening, only to answer patients' telephone calls, after which he ventured out to their homes to treat them, only to return home late at night, retire, and start the process all over again the next morning. She watched one night from her bedroom window as the local Klan burned a cross on his front lawn, necessitating one of the many negotiation sessions that for one reason or another became necessary to maintain that delicate balance in race relations. During the last years of high school in the summers when she returned to the family farm, she began dating Grandfather, who was six years older than she was. He was in the process of stealing her heart from the clutches of a young man in the area named Cornelius Ford, whose older brother had already married her sister Agnes.

In 1927, upon her graduation from high school, Uncle Joe enrolled her in Spelman College in Atlanta, while Grandfather made his way to New York City with one of his two brothers, their intention being to make a go of it far away from the clutches of their cruel father, who used to hang them by their hands from meat hooks and beat them with a leather whip for their teenage transgressions. One day Grandfather finally refused to take it anymore. He grabbed the whip from his father and threatened to kill the man who allegedly had been born to a Negro prostitute in Eufaula, and a Creek Native American she enjoyed regular relations with—a man whose family had decided not to join the seven-hundred-mile Trail of Tears transporting other Creeks to what became Oklahoma.

Grandfather's mother died while he and his four siblings were young. He was the second oldest and never learned much about her except that she, too, was of mixed heritage, a light-brown-skinned woman whose portrait indicated her black African and Caucasian lineage. Their father supported the family as a sharecropper and then, when the boys became old enough, expected them to get jobs to help support the family, which they did, until that day in 1927 when Crawford and Hartus decided to try making a go of it in distant New York City. Upon arriving they settled in a roominghouse in Harlem. It was the height of the Harlem Renaissance. The neighborhood's streets were packed with Negro migrants from the South—primarily Virginia, North Carolina, and South Carolina—and the West Indies. Jazz bands dazzled Caucasians who ventured to the neighborhood after dark, engaging in what was known as "slumming" at venues such as the Cotton Club (which didn't admit Negro patrons) where café-au-lait showgirls shimmied their hips and shook their fannies to syncopated music. Poets such as Langston Hughes and Countee Cullen and writers such as Jean Toomer and James Weldon Johnson wrote the first significant body of Negro literature. But Grandfather soon left the city. To him its freedom, relative to what he left in the South, wasn't worth a jammed-together existence in packed tenements, or the frigid winter climate, or the menial jobs, or the hustler's rackets necessary for making a living if you had no talent for use in the entertainment industry, or future as a writer, or credentials to pursue what few opportunities there were for Negroes with college and professional degrees.

He soon returned to Eufaula, then headed for Atlanta to propose marriage to Grandmother. To the dismay of her family—brother Joe in particular—she accepted his offer, while they pleaded with her to ask herself what kind of future was possible with a man who hadn't attended college and had no plans to do so. She dropped out of Spelman and eloped with Grandfather, after which they settled in Jacksonville. Grandfather, who had learned how to work on automobiles during the brief time he had lived in Troy, New York, found a job as a mechanic. Their first child, Edith, my mother, was born Christmas Eve 1930. After her there would be four more—Crawford Jr. in 1932, Elaine in 1937, Barbara and her twin sister, who would die shortly after birth, in 1940.

As so often happens in families, with the arrival of the first child, so, too, arrived the mending of relations between Grandmother and her oldest brother and the rest of her family. As her shy oldest daughter, mischievous son, and soon-to-be-mischievous second daughter grew, Grandmother brought them west to visit their Griffin side, including Uncle Joe in Bainbridge. On one visit in 1939 the two families attended church at Nelson Chapel A.M.E. By then, her oldest brother had weathered other racial incidents through the years, besides the cross burning she had seen on his front lawn when she was a teenager. Two years earlier there had been the Willie Reid incident, in which Reid was killed in jail under mysterious circumstances while awaiting trial for allegedly raping, then murdering a Caucasian woman, after which a mob spirited his remains from a local Negro funeral home, burned them in the local high school football field, and dragged his charred corpse past the Griffin home under threat of violence to all the town's "uppity nigras." After tempers cooled, Uncle Joe helped patch things up.

As part of the delicate balance in race relations he helped work out, he sought donations periodically to Negro community groups from respected Caucasians in town. On one such occasion he approached the local sheriff, S. W. Martin, who also happened to be a member of the Klan. Martin told him that through the Klan he would be glad to see to it that a donation of $150 was made to Nelson Chapel (a then significant sum) if the congregation allowed one of their representatives to speak. "Give us an opportunity to express ourselves," Martin told him. "We aren't your enemies, we are your friends. We'll have one of our men come and read a prepared statement."

So that Sunday in 1939, while Grandmother and her children and her brother and his family sat in Nelson Chapel with the rest of the congregation, the Klan representatives, including the deputy sheriff and a local attorney, approached Uncle Joe, who spoke to them outside, then escorted them to the pulpit where they made their donation and read their "conciliatory statement" making it clear that as long as certain lines weren't crossed, everything between the "races" would be fine. Dazzled by the relative influence and opulence of his uncle's life, Crawford Jr. wished he could be his son. He had seen his real father struggle with his dreams. In a few years he would see him act on those dreams.

When the U.S. entered World War II, Grandfather obtained a job as an aircraft engine mechanic at the large naval air base near Jacksonville. At the same time he launched his first entrepreneurial effort. He purchased two large flatbed trucks, nailed benches to them, and began transporting the Negro workers back and forth between their homes and the base. He also used the trucks on weekends to transport Negroes in Jacksonville back and forth between the city and the nearby Negro oceanfront resort at Fernandina Beach. The new enterprise resulted in his earning his first significant sum of money. When the war ended, he used the extra money he had earned to open a sawmill. In the mill he cut the lumber to be used to build the nightclub he intended to open.

A year later he opened the club. He named it the Rainbow Inn. He employed four people, including a cook. Because he couldn't obtain a liquor license he sold liquor under the table. To ensure he'd have no trouble doing so he paid the requisite bribes to two local police officers. At the Rainbow Inn customers could eat, drink, dance, or get romantic in one of two transient rooms he built on the side of the club. With his sawmill and club prospering he began making lots of money. But he was a poor money manager and was not callous enough to resist acquaintances who asked him for financial favors. As a result of his muscular, sculpted physical form, handsome face, and charismatic personality, he was popular—especially with the women. He had his affairs, just like Grandmother's brothers, including Uncle Joe, had their affairs. But he and Grandmother stayed together. Crawford Richardson was a very generous man. Every Christmas season he'd go to the farmers' market, purchase bags of fruit, then go door-to-door in his neighborhood giving the fruit away.

He was a proud man, too. One day he was heading home from his sawmill when he came upon one of his trucks stranded on the highway with a flat tire, its driver standing by helplessly. He stopped, got out, gave his employee the keys to his car, and told him to go back to the mill and retrieve a replacement tire. In the meantime he would sit there with the truck waiting for his return. While he waited two police officers drove up. They told him to move the truck off the highway. He replied that he couldn't do so until the replacement tire arrived, because if he tried moving the heavy truck with the flat tire still on it, the truck's weight would ruin the tire rim. The officers considered that answer to be too uppity for a Negro. He continued to make his case. So they handcuffed and arrested him.

On the way to the station house they pummeled him with racial insults. After arriving, they booked him and threw him in a cell with another Negro, at which point they decided to have some fun by placing bets on which one of the big muscular "coons" was the better fighter. They unlocked the cell door and took the two prisoners to a fenced-in yard in the back. With guns drawn to prevent their escape, on their signal they made the other prisoner lunge for Grandfather. The two men struggled. They wrestled. They beat each other with fists. First one got the upper hand, then the other. Finally Grandfather won. The losing officers didn't like it that the uppity troublemaker had gotten the better of the other "coon"—the other "rooster" they had placed their bets on. They decided to teach him a lesson. They put the handcuffs back on Grandfather and proceeded to beat and kick him so severely that they split his left jaw open all the way up to his ear. The next day after an employee paid his fine he was released. His jaw was sewn up. When he returned home, the sight of him traumatized his family. He assured them he was fine.

But things weren't fine. Grandfather soon lost his right to police protection assuring his ability to sell liquor under the table at his nightclub. As a result the club began losing patrons. His sawmill business started experiencing difficulties. Simultaneously, Mother was finishing Stanton High School. By the time she graduated in

1949 her father's finances were in such disarray he was unable to send her to Hampton Institute in Virginia, the college of her choice. Instead, upon graduating from Stanton she enrolled in nursing school in Augusta, Georgia, at the Medical College of Georgia's nursing school division for Negroes. Augusta sits along the banks of the Savannah River, about 125 miles upstream from the city of Savannah, which Mother periodically visited to have fun with her Griffin family cousins Mary Agnes and Robie; they were attending the same college Uncle Joe had attended, now called Savannah State.

By the time Mother graduated from nursing school in 1951, R.N. degree in hand, both her father's sawmill and nightclub had closed and he was using his trucks to cut and haul timber to sell to the pulpwood factories in Jacksonville. By then her rebellious brother Crawford Jr. had left home before finishing high school. To the consternation of Grandfather, he lied about his age and enlisted in the air force. Mother obtained a job at University Hospital of what was the Western Reserve University in Cleveland. It would be her first experience traveling north. It would also be her first experience tending the needs of Caucasian patients. Late one night a dying woman signaled the nurses' station. Being the only on-duty nurse who was free, Mother went to see what she could do for her. When she arrived, the woman responded, "I want a real nurse!" as in a Caucasian one. Offended, but not knowing what else to do, Mother swallowed the insult and tended to the needs of the dying woman anyway.

Two years later she found a nursing position with more opportunity. It was at Hubbard Hospital in Nashville. By that time Hubbard was a far different place from the days when Joseph Griffin attended medical school there. In 1931, using money donated primarily by the General Education Board of the Rockefeller Foundation, the Julius Rosenwald philanthropic fund, and Mrs. George Eastman, both the hospital and Meharry were moved to a new physical plant on the north side of Nashville, across the street from Fisk University. The new Hubbard was twice as large as the original hospital, but still small with only 180 beds. Upon arriving on its wards Mother met Father, who, as a third-year medical student at Meharry, had just begun his clinical rotations. Prior to gaining admission, he left Grandfather Pearson's farm outside of Glenwood,

Georgia, to attend the nearest Negro high school, which was thirty-five miles away in the town of Dublin. He boarded with relatives while attending. Upon graduating valedictorian of his class he returned to the family farm for a year to help Grandfather. Then he headed for Paine College in Augusta. Shortly after he enrolled, the U.S. entered World War II. Father was drafted into the army but soon received a medical deferment because he had flat feet. He returned to Paine. By contrast his older brother Nathan saw combat duty, including landing on the beaches of Normandy on D day in 1944, the year Father graduated from Paine.

After earning his bachelor's degree with honors, Father taught science courses at Boggs Academy, a private Negro high school outside of Augusta, and later at another Negro high school in the town of Perry. Wearing his restless ambition everywhere he went, he demonstrated a baffling frugality to his friends, while simultaneously cultivating a reputation as something of a lady's man. To take women out on dates, he borrowed cars—from his sister Lavester's husband who taught college in nearby Fort Valley, from friends who wondered why he wouldn't just buy one since by then Negro teachers—in fact, the bulk of the Negro middle class in the South—certainly earned enough money to afford homes and automobiles.

He'd tell all who asked that he refused to buy a car because he was saving his money so that he could one day attend medical school. What a pipe dream, plenty told him. In some ways it was. The college he had attended was of poor quality. He had been ill-informed about where to go, the blame falling not only on himself for lack of thorough investigation of college choices, but also on the shoulders of the postman who delivered mail to the family farm. With each report of high school excellence the postman urged Father to attend Paine College, a school supported by his church denomination. For plenty of people in the rural South *any college* was a good place to go. But Paine hardly measured up to Howard, or Morehouse, or Fisk, or Talladega (where sister Lavester had gone), or Tugaloo, or Lincoln University in Pennsylvania—the Negro colleges with the best premedical programs, their graduates making up disproportionate shares of the medical students at Howard and Meharry. Things were much different from when Joseph Griffin attended medical school. Given the explosion in medical knowledge that had taken place over the intervening forty years, entry requirements were much stiffer and course loads much heavier. In an average year Meharry accepted only one in five applicants to its medical school (at a time when the national average for acceptance of medical school applicants in all medical schools was a little better than one in four applicants [3.7], all due to dramatically increased competition with World War II veterans). Each summer between teaching high school science, Father traveled to Atlanta to take summer courses at Atlanta University to bolster his qualifications for admission.

People in his vicinity detected the scent of his upward mobility before even seeing or hearing him. Then upon seeing him, they noticed a man who dressed and groomed himself immaculately. When he spoke they noticed that he had ridded himself of all vestiges of a southern accent. He mastered the King's English: not a trace of a double negative or an "I axed" or the improper use of plurals expected of Negroes flew off his vocal cords. Short of the most blatant violations, such as venturing where Jim Crow didn't allow Negroes, he found other ways to circumvent the etiquette of Negro subordination—for instance, as mentioned earlier, forgoing the hats men usually wore daily back then so that he didn't have to remove his, as Negroes were expected to do in the presence of Caucasians, or after being asked a question by a Caucasian, just as his sister Lavester did, answering with "I did," or "I did not," rather than finishing statements off with the usual "Suhs" and "Ma'ams." When he presented himself to the Caucasian administrator of the Perry, Georgia, schools who made all final decisions on hiring teachers, the man didn't know what to make of him. After the interview he asked Father to leave the room. Then he addressed the Negro principal who had suggested Father for employment: "Well, if you want him, I'll hire him. But he's not going to stay. Little towns like this don't keep fellas like him for very long."

The statement was prophetic. Within five years, Perry bid him farewell because he was finally headed for Meharry. The medical school was in the same precarious financial situation it had been in since its founding. By then it trained almost half of all Negro medical doctors, and the majority of Negro physicians who practiced in the South. By the latter half of the 1920s Howard's medical school had caught up to equal the number of M.D.s Meharry awarded each year, and in many years it graduated even more, in a Washington, D.C., setting where things weren't as good as they could be but better than the obstacles faced by Meharry in Nashville. And more Caucasian medical schools had opened their doors to Negroes, admitting a token one or two per year. By the end of the 1940s they were training 10 percent of all Negro physicians, though most still admitted none. A total of between 130 and 150 Negro physicians were graduating among the 6,000 M.D.s awarded annually, leading to a national average of one Negro physician for every 3,500 Negroes, compared to one Caucasian physician for every 1,100 Caucasians. Below the Potomac and Ohio rivers, Meharry was the only medical school a Negro could attend. Besides 180-bed Hubbard Hospital, its clinical facilities included the 400-bed Waverly Hills Sanatorium near Louisville (where students observed TB cases, an arrangement that by 1953 would change when they would be sent to the 400-bed West Tennessee Tuberculosis Hospital in Memphis); the surgical service at the 52-bed Taborian Hospital in Mount Bayou, Mississippi; the surgical service at 165-bed John A. Andrew Memorial Hospital in Tuskegee; and the neuropsychiatric service at 685-bed Homer G. Phillips Hospital in St. Louis. Such were the precarious conditions under which the school operated, necessitating that it send its students far afield to acquire a decent level of clinical exposure.

In 1948 it had teetered on the brink of closing. A near $500,000 gap between its income and operating expenses had been amassed the previous fiscal year. This was a larger gap than philanthropic organizations such as the Rockefeller and Kellogg foundations were willing to continue closing. A number of options were entertained for how to keep the school open. One was to move it to Texas to serve Negroes of that state from a new facility built at Prairie View A&M University, a Negro college in a town of that same name near Houston. Another proposal was to move the school to St. Louis from which all of the departments at Homer G. Phillips Hospital would serve as a clinical teaching facility for the medical school. A third proposal was to move the school to Oakland, California, under the auspices of the Kaiser Foundation. And the fourth proposal was to build a new 400- to 600-bed Veterans Administration hospital for Negro veterans next to the campus, bolstering its clinical facilities and adding federal funding to defray the school's expenses. All four of the proposals would go nowhere.

The best solution, it was decided, was direct state or federal support to the existing facility. But federal support was blocked by congressmen in nonsouthern states who felt that it would be unfair to their taxpayers to support Meharry since Negro students could apply to their state medical schools, albeit with poor chances of admission. Besides that, Howard was still federally supported. And they saw no need for the federal government to support two predominantly Negro medical schools. The only alternative left for Meharry was to obtain support from a consortium of fourteen southern states that barred entry of Negroes into their medical schools. The board of trustees of Meharry voted to offer the school to those states as their training facility for Negro physicians, but with the stipulation that the board continue to control policy at the school. In February 1948 the governors of the southern states met in Tallahassee and agreed to the plan. It called for every Negro student from each state accepted at Meharry to be reimbursed the difference between the cost of tuition, room, and board at Meharry and the same costs at their state-supported medical schools. The funds Meharry received from the arrangement helped save the school.

At the same time it continued practices such as hiring Caucasian adjunct faculty members from crosstown Vanderbilt University Medical School to augment its skeletal staff and bolster its creditability. By contrast, Vanderbilt's medical school hired no Negro physicians. And many of the Vanderbilt adjuncts were paid more than Negro faculty who were teaching at Meharry full-time. This caused resentment, rage, and decreased morale among Negro faculty, many of whom took their anger out on the medical students by subjecting them to stiff unrelenting exams, and educational exercises in the clinical settings that were far more rigid and authoritarian than they needed to be. It wasn't unusual for Meharry students to be flunked out by unnecessarily harsh exams featuring minutiae that wouldn't be seen on national board tests. The same occurred at Howard. By contrast, most Caucasian medical schools did their best to graduate all of their matriculants. It was as though Meharry faculty were saying to their students, "Somebody's going to respect me fully, damn it. And that somebody is going to be you!" Though to some extent most medical schools suffered and still suffer from a boot-camp atmosphere, "boot camp" tended to be worst of all at Meharry and Howard.

In addition, many medical professors at Meharry compensated

for their lower salaries and esteem in the American medical community by pursuing economic gain through seeing as many patients as they could in their private practices, which had the added side effect of causing research activity to suffer. Of course greed was hardly the exclusive preserve of a handful of Negro professors in the academic medical establishment or Negro physicians as a whole. But the desire for money and the relative independence and prestige money could bring often took on a higher relative importance among Negro physicians than others. The material things money could buy were a salve to place on the psychic wounds inflicted by a segregated, racist world. Upon graduating, then fulfilling internships and residencies at Hubbard or elsewhere, Meharry students could either buy into this obsession or ignore it. A large number would choose to buy into it.

By the time he was to receive his M.D. in May 1955, Father was engaged to marry Mother. Every commencement season, as at other institutions, alumni attended to celebrate the anniversary of their graduation year. And as at most other schools the highest alumni class attendance usually took place in five-year intervals from the date of graduation. That same year was the occasion of Uncle Joe's fortieth reunion. It was also the year in which Marvin Griffin, the scion of Bainbridge's political and newspaper publishing family, the Caucasian Griffins, became governor of Georgia.

Griffin had been elected on a platform calling for all-out war on the Supreme Court's 1954 *Brown* v. *Board of Education* school desegregation decision. He promised that rather than integrate Georgia schools he would pursue a policy of upgrading the racially separate facilities to make the equal part in "separate but equal" have real meaning. In line with such thinking Meharry was committed to ensuring the financial support of the consortium of southern states that had met and agreed to support the school in 1948 in order to avoid integration of their respective medical schools. In the eyes of Meharrians it wasn't a matter of supporting segregation. It was a matter of pragmatism and survival. They hoped to see segregation end one day. But knowing the resistance of southern Caucasians to the idea and the need for Negro physicians to be educated somewhere other than Howard, they took support for the survival of their school from anywhere it was available.

Strange bedfellows scratched each other's backs. For the 1955 Meharry commencement Governor Griffin sent a letter to the president of Meharry, Harold D. West, praising the work being done in the recently built fifty-bed hospital owned and operated by the Negro Griffin in his hometown, a letter that was read at the alumni banquet. West wrote back to Governor Griffin: "Dr. Griffin's work is typical of the kind of thing Meharry graduates are doing throughout the South. . . . I am sure this points up the importance of this institution to the southern area in particular and to the nation in general."

Uncle Joe couldn't have been happier to have the letter read in front of his classmates and others. It was all part of the preening they did in front of one another, showing up in expensive sharkskin suits, driving Cadillac Fleetwoods and Lincoln Continentals and Buick Roadmasters. He preened most of all. Mother introduced him to her fiancé. He heartily shook Father's hand and asked him what he planned to do after completing his internship at St. Lawrence Hospital in Lansing, Michigan. Father told him he didn't know, but that in any case he planned to take the Georgia State Medical Board so that he could practice in his home state if he chose to do so. And even if he didn't return to Georgia, having the license would enable him to prescribe medication for relatives who became ill.

Uncle Joe told him to consider coming to Bainbridge. He also told him that since he, Joe Griffin, was such an influential man he could make a few phone calls and see about ensuring that Father would pass the state medical board. Mother advised Father to decline the invitation because the last thing he needed was to be beholden to her uncle. A classmate of his, Carl Gordon, who was from Albany, revealed to him a good reason to decline the invitation to practice with Uncle Joe, too. So did Uncle Joe's brother, Uncle David. After his younger brother graduated from Hutto High School in Bainbridge, Joe had sent David to Morehouse College, then on to Meharry, where he received his M.D. in 1942. After that he completed an internship at Hubbard Hospital, then a residency in obstetrics and gynecology, at which point he served in the Army Medical Corps, caring for the gynecological problems of the wives of army personnel and delivering their babies. Then he returned to Bainbridge to practice with his older brother, who allowed him almost no breathing room. This eventually resulted in his striking out on his own, first to nearby Thomasville, then to Brunswick,

Georgia. "Joe's too autocratic," he told Father about the possibility of coming to Bainbridge. "You'll never be your own man." Father took all of the advice he received from Mother, Carl Gordon, and Uncle David.

He and Mother married on June 22, 1955, in the living room of her parents' Jacksonville home. Mother's sister Elaine was maid of honor and her only attendant. Mother and Father honeymooned in Atlanta. Then they were off to Lansing in their new '55 Chevrolet Bel Air, Father's first automobile, which he purchased upon graduating at the age of thirty-four. After completing his internship Father passed the Indiana State Medical Board, then settled temporarily in Seymour, Indiana, to replace a physician on vacation. It was there that on August 24, 1956, their first child, Carol, was born. Then it was on to Butlerville, Indiana, for a temporary job as staff physician at Muscatatuk School, then on to Fort Wayne to replace Dr. Caesar Marshall while he and his family vacationed. And when Dr. Marshall returned, he helped Father set up a permanent practice in Fort Wayne, then aided Mother on September 25, 1957, in the delivery room of St. Joseph's Hospital, when I was ushered into the world.

Meanwhile, Mother's sister Elaine had finished high school the same year Mother and Father were married. Later that summer, before attending Florida A&M, she went to Bainbridge to work at Griffin Hospital and Clinic where she began training as a nurse under Blanche Campbell, who was responsible for training all of the hospital's nurses under a specified program. Then after attending Florida A&M for one year she returned to Griffin Hospital and Clinic where she worked from 1956 to 1958, after which she entered a formal training program for her R.N. degree at Lincoln Hospital in Durham, North Carolina. Aunt Barbara graduated from high school months after I was born and went off to attend college at Florida A&M, then later earn an E.D.D. degree with a concentration in history from Carnegie Mellon University in Pittsburgh, only to return to Florida A&M to teach history and eventually chair its history department.

Many years later, after interviewing people for her book about Uncle Joe and Griffin Hospital, this is what she wrote about his rise to influence and what he did for his patients. When it came to how he financed the construction and equipping of the quarter-of-a-million-dollar Griffin Hospital and Clinic with his own money, Uncle Joe told her: "I invested in government bonds over a period of years. And as we needed the bonds to finance construction, we got them." As for how he acquired the numerous homes and other extensive real estate holdings he amassed over the years, that was said to have been done simply through wise investing of what money his patients could afford to pay him. "During the summer months, he would rise early, put on his overalls, brogan shoes, and flop hat, and work with his crew, painting houses and mending roofs until 7:00 P.M. Then he would go home, take a bath and go to the office," Uncle David attested. The houses were then rented out to local residents. They included a row of small dwellings right across the street from the Griffin home that under local law Uncle Joe was allowed to rent only to Caucasians.

Uncle Joe was described as always kind and generous. He was described as extremely capable, and willing to treat patients' ailments that other physicians refused to touch. By the 1950s the Caucasian-owned Bainbridge Memorial Hospital had opened only its basement to Negro patients, and at Riverside Hospital, Negroes were consigned to an old house next to the regular hospital (from where, if they needed surgery they were carried to the main building in a stretcher, up the fire escape to the second floor where the operating room was located). By contrast, at Griffin Hospital they entered a facility that treated them with respect on spacious first- and second-floor wards. In addition, on the second floor there were two private suites, one with a terrace.

"You felt Dr. Griffin was your friend," recalled patient Ira Dean Long. "He made rounds three times a day," attested patient Susan Mention. "And even though he was busy, he would sit for a few minutes and talk to you." "If you were dissatisfied with the service of a member of the staff, you would only have to tell him and your problem would be solved," stated patient Josie Williams. Reported Uncle David: "He displayed the same kind of attitude and rendered the same kind of services to the 'little man,' the downtrodden, and the abused as he rendered to his more refined, more educated patients. He made no distinction between rich and poor. It was nothing to see him hugging, kissing, and flattering someone he knew in the lobby, even if the person had a mouth full of snuff or tobacco."

Aunt Elaine recalled accompanying him on Wednesdays, his house call days. Once she went along for a visit to a local woman known as Granny: "The road didn't extend all the way to Granny's house. We had to park the car and walk across a field. I was completely unaware of the patient's condition. I thought we had come to administer some routine medication. But when we got there, [he] gave Granny an intravenous infusion, a process which is normally performed in a hospital. Obviously he had planned to do this when he left. All of the equipment that he needed was there. She had an IV pole in her house that he had placed there for that purpose. I soon found out that this was one of his weekly visits."

And he continued to be daring with regard to challenging the social mores of the region if he thought it was medically necessary. Since he knew his surgical limitations, he would call in the appropriate specialist if the medical skills of others were required. One such case involved an elderly woman at the hospital who fell and broke her femur, necessitating that a Caucasian orthopedic surgeon from Tallahassee come to Griffin Hospital and operate on her. During the operation the orthopedist experienced difficulty in placing a pin in the patient's thigh to secure the broken bone. Uncle Joe, who was assisting him, became irritated, grabbed the instruments from the other surgeon, and inserted the pin himself.

Throughout his practice Uncle Joe was said to continue to allow his patients to pay whatever they could afford to pay. He was said to have continued to accept gifts in lieu of cash, gifts that he divided among the needy. He was said to have hired many Negroes to work for him, allowing them to perform intelligent rather than demeaning work. He was said to have once provided employment to a woman who had suffered a brain injury as a result of an automobile accident, allowing her to work in the hospital kitchen and live for free in the nurses' quarters he had constructed in back of the hospital. Aunt Elaine attested that she saw him "turn what were considered to be helpless drug addicts, alcoholics, and other outcasts into clean-shaven and respectable hospital orderlies, maintenance workers, chauffeurs, and cooks." The book contained the stories of his paying off the $18,000 mortgage on the Negro-owned farm that was to be foreclosed on and his making a $91,000 loan to the Negro farmer whom Caucasian businessmen didn't want to purchase strategically located property. Uncle Joe was said to have made it possible for numerous Negroes to purchase land, then demonstrated tremendous tolerance for those who were slow to pay him back, only occasionally foreclosing. The book stated that at one time he owned the liens on all the Negro-owned taxis in town; it stated that he purchased new cars for individuals and allowed them to pay him back rather than the dealer. It stated that he paid the mortgages on the homes of two Negro teachers who lost their jobs and in addition provided them and their families with food and clothing until they found new jobs.

He was said to have kept up with the latest medical developments even as he tended his busy medical practice and the other needs of Negroes in Bainbridge. This included attending the annual John A. Andrew Clinical Seminars at Tuskegee. The Andrew Seminars in the various medical specialties, held each April beginning in 1921, were perhaps the most impressive of any Negro medical body in the country, bringing together for one week experts in medical specialties of all races to discuss a range of difficult medical cases for the benefit of Negro physicians throughout the South and some from around the country. In 1937 Uncle Joe served as president of the society that sponsored the annual clinics. In 1950, while traveling with three other physicians with the intention of driving all night to attend and present a paper at the clinic, Dr. Charles Drew, chairman of the Department of Surgery at Howard University Medical School, the most prominent Negro surgeon of his generation, and the first person to successfully preserve blood plasma, was killed in an auto accident along a highway in Allamance County, North Carolina. Besides attending the Andrews Clinics, in 1943 Uncle Joe cofounded the Southwestern Medical Association, composed of Negro physicians in the southwestern Georgia, southeastern Alabama, and north Florida tristate area, and invited prominent physicians to address the society, including at Johnson Memorial Hospital, then Griffin Hospital and Clinic.

In November 1961 the renowned Negro newspaper the *Pittsburgh Courier* assigned its noted reporter Trezzvant W. Anderson to write an article on Griffin Hospital and Clinic. The *Courier* had a national circulation of over 100,000. From the beginning of the twentieth century, along with the *Chicago Defender,* it had smoked out countless cases of injustices committed against Negroes across the country. The *Courier* piece was the second major article on the hospital. Several months after it opened there had been a large photo spread commemorating it in a magazine called *Our World.* It showed

Uncle Joe in action in the wards of the hospital. It showed him meeting with architect Julian Kwilecki, Bertram Ehrlich's first cousin, about the layout of the hospital. It showed him in his living room with Great-grandmother Griffin, noting how proud she was of her oldest son.

Anderson and a *Courier* photographer gave the hospital similar treatment. On the cover of the November 4, 1961, issue of the *Courier* was a small photo of Uncle Joe, along with two larger photos about other subjects of that issue, which featured a tabloid layout. One was of four five-year-old Negro boys in armed services uniforms, winners of a contest at the Texas State Fair. The other was of the winner of a beauty contest in New York City presented for the benefit of the United Negro College Fund. Headlines read "Courier Reporter, Arrested and Jailed on Route 40, Writes: 'I Died a Little'"; "Westley W. Law Is Back on Job!"; and next to Uncle Joe's photo, the words "Courier Exclusives: A Giant of a Man Is Dr. Joseph Griffin, Georgia's Legendary Miracle Medico." To read about him you were directed to turn to pages 16 and 17 of the second section. The other exclusive was the story "Berlin and the Negro G.I.'s."

Inside this issue was also an article about the legal issues surrounding the student lunch counter civil rights sit-ins challenging segregation. The following week the case was to be heard by the U.S. Supreme Court. There was also an article detailing the use of violence by Caucasians in Mississippi to prevent Negroes from registering to vote. The article on the arrest of a *Courier* reporter told of the arrest of Evelyn Cunningham, who joined a group of prominent Negroes in their decision to emulate the Negro students who had started the Freedom Rides seeking to integrate interstate travel throughout the South. Cunningham and four NAACP officials, including New York City attorney Percy Sutton, headed out of New York City and stopped at a restaurant in Rosedale, Maryland, just north of Baltimore. Upon seeking service the waitress refused them, after which they were arrested and jailed. In the same issue, Anderson wrote about Martin Luther King, Jr., presenting President Kennedy with a detailed blueprint of how he could legally end segregation in the South. And on the editorial page columnist John McGray asked, "Should Negroes Leave the South?"

When you turned to the second section Uncle Joe provided his answer—a resounding no. "You can make it if you only try down here," he told Anderson. The article featured accompanying photos of Uncle Joe in the fifty-bed hospital and detailed its motorized beds, which at that time were "an unusual item in any hospital." It told of how there were TVs in every room, air-conditioned wards, anesthetic machines, top-flight X-ray equipment, a modern laboratory equipped with the finest equipment for blood chemistry, a blood bank, an EKG machine, an operating room, an obstetrical delivery room. . . . The top-flight medical equipment was bought between the time the hospital opened and the appearance of the *Courier* article. Uncle Joe purchased it with his own money, raising the value of the hospital to half a million dollars, which confirmed what Aunt Elaine later said in Aunt Barbara's book. The article noted that some of the equipment in Griffin Hospital and Clinic was more advanced than that in the Caucasian hospitals in town. A machine called an autoclave sometimes broke down at Bainbridge Memorial Hospital, necessitating that Bainbridge personnel bring their instruments over to Griffin Hospital to be sterilized.

All of this was quite amazing, considering the difficulty a handful of other Negro physicians in the South had during those days of segregation equipping their own small hospitals. There was, for example, the McClendon Medical Clinic in Atlanta, owned by Dr. F. Earl McClendon. In 1948 he approached a number of Atlanta philanthropists, including Robert W. Woodruff, the chairman of the board of Coca-Cola, with the goal of obtaining contributions for $5,000 worth of equipment for his hospital. By the fall of 1950, the same year Griffin Hospital and Clinic opened two hundred miles to the south, McClendon was still seeking ways to finance the purchase of equipment for his hospital. During that period the Atlanta area had only 391 hospital beds available to its 142,855 Negroes (compared to 1,459 hospital beds for its 356,254 Caucasians). Of those beds, 304 were in the segregated Negro wards of city-owned Grady Memorial Hospital where, given the quality of city hospital wards, no middle-class or well-to-do Negro wanted to go. And at that time no Negro physicians could practice at Grady, leaving only eighty-seven available hospital beds spread among three private hospitals for Atlanta's thirty-seven Negro physicians and its middle-class Negro populace. (A few years later the city decided to construct 120-bed Hughes Spaulding Pavilion for use by Negro physicians, a facility that would never live up to plans.) At the time

CHAPTER 7

After telling me about the property deeds and abortions, Mr. Ehrlich told me about the good civic deeds performed by Joe Griffin; gestures such as, once segregation came to an end, helping see to it that the town's schools were quietly integrated, and some of the other acts I was familiar with. He confirmed that overall he started out a good physician whose reputation in southwest Georgia was established during the 1918 influenza epidemic. But he said that as the years wore on, J.H., as he was called by plenty of locals, became money-hungry, and that as he became old he refused to give up his practice when he should have (though he stated that last characteristic was also demonstrated by some other Bainbridge physicians when they grew old). I asked him who else it might be good for me to talk to. He gave me the names of a couple of old-timers in Bainbridge, the only ones he felt were old enough to remember what was really going on in town during the heyday of my great-uncle's practice: Ecky Parker, a man who had owned a tailoring business in town, and Cheney Griffin, the town's former mayor and brother of the late and former governor Marvin Griffin. Mr. Ehrlich recounted how he had been good friends with the Marvin Griffin family, who lived next door to him. He told me that when Marvin ran for lieutenant governor of Georgia in 1948 he told him personally that he wasn't going to raise the race issue because Negroes were beginning to get the vote. (By 1946 the all-Caucasion Democratic primary in Georgia had been ruled illegal.) Then he turned right around and raised it anyway. "I asked him why he did it after saying he wouldn't, and he answered, 'Well, Bert, I figured there were more white than colored votes out there and I wanted to win.' And he did.

"He was just being pragmatic," Mr. Ehrlich assured me. That I took with a huge grain of salt.

As we parted I felt a mixture of emotions. The first had to do with the same thing I began wondering earlier in the interview.

Could I trust everything Bertram Ehrlich had to say? After all, he had been on the Caucasian side of the segregated world my great-uncle had been forced to operate in. And he didn't sound as though he personally conducted himself the way most people have been told American Jews acted toward Negroes in the era of Jim Crow—with a certain sense of empathy, because they had known so much oppression in Europe, having been that continent's niggers. Later on I uncovered solid evidence that he had been so thoroughly assimilated among other southerners who considered themselves white that the same year Griffin Hospital and Clinic opened he served as publicity chairman for a series of minstrel shows that were staged in the local Caucasian high school auditorium. The stage scene was a place the performers called "The Jig and Shuffle Cafe." Among the entertainers were a woman named Ophelia Prout, who called herself the "Queen of the Blues," and Dot Tonge, who gave the Fort Valley version of the infamous Negro caricature dance called "The Black Bottom." Cheney Griffin was also an eager participant, penning quite a few jokes. Enthusiastic participation in such shenanigans became a tradition on both Mr. Ehrlich's mother's and father's sides of the family. In 1920 two of his mother's brothers smeared themselves in blackface to play the roles of waiters in a minstrel production in which everyone was described as having had fun watching the fifty performers, including a "trio of buck-and-wing dancers" frolic and get in a few good local jokes. Then again, maybe such behavior was not surprising since Al Jolson, too, was Jewish.

I knew that it was all characteristic of the times. As Mr. Ehrlich said during the interview when discussing that era, they hadn't known anything else but abiding by the attitudes and traditions of segregation, which apparently meant Negroes were never far from their minds but in certain set ways. Given such a reality I wondered if there were elements of jealousy in his account of my great-uncle's life. Were the things he said colored by a belief that an ambitious Negro man like Joseph Griffin hadn't known his place, even though it seemed that inadvertently his place ultimately became, in the eyes of Caucasians in the region, that of a credit to their notion that the "races" could live successfully in separate worlds (except when it came to Negro women caring for their children, and cooking for and cleaning up after them, and serving as their discreet lovers)?

Dr. John V. de Grasse in 1854. He became one of the first Negro physicians in the country after graduating in 1849 from the now-defunct medical school at Maine's Bowdoin College. (Courtesy of the Schomburg Center for Research in Black Culture)

George W. Hubbard, M.D., first dean of Meharry Medical College, as he appeared in his later years. (Courtesy of Meharry Medical College)

Dr. Daniel Hale Williams, distinguished Negro surgeon, at the turn of the century. Credited as the first surgeon anywhere to successfully operate on the human heart, Williams played a major role in training Negro surgeons at Howard and at Meharry. (Courtesy of Corbis-Bettmann)

John H. Hale, M.D., pioneer surgeon at Meharry in the early twentieth century. Hale was the first chairman of the department of surgery at Meharry and mentor to Joseph H. Griffin. (Courtesy of Meharry Medical College)

The first George W. Hubbard Hospital, the official teaching hospital of Meharry Medical College, circa 1915, the year Joseph H. Griffin graduated. (Courtesy of Meharry Medical College)

Dr. Louis T. Wright, an honor graduate of the Harvard Medical School, in the 1930s. (Courtesy of the Schomburg Center for Research in Black Culture)

Harlem Hospital in the 1940s, the first integrated medical facility in the United States where Negro physicians could receive postgraduate medical training. Dr. Louis T. Wright, a contemporary of Joseph Griffin's, pursued a surgical teaching career here rather than accumulate wealth as a businessman and an owner of private hospitals. (Courtesy of the Schomburg Center for Research in Black Culture)

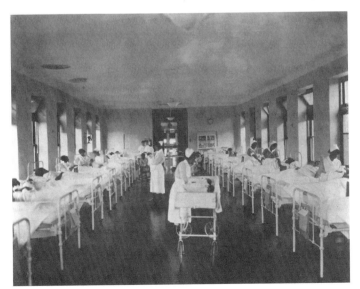

The obstetrics ward at Harlem Hospital, circa 1926, demonstrates the typical ward arrangement of hospitals through the 1950s. (Courtesy of the Schomburg Center for Research in Black Culture)

Freedmen's Hospital in the early 1970s, the final years of its use as the primary teaching hospital for the Howard University School of Medicine, the only other Negro medical school to survive during the Jim Crow years. (Courtesy of the Howard University School of Medicine)

The entrance to the second George W. Hubbard Hospital in 1931, the year it opened. This second facility was the teaching hospital for Meharry when my father was a medical student there from 1951 to 1955. (Courtesy of Meharry Medical College)

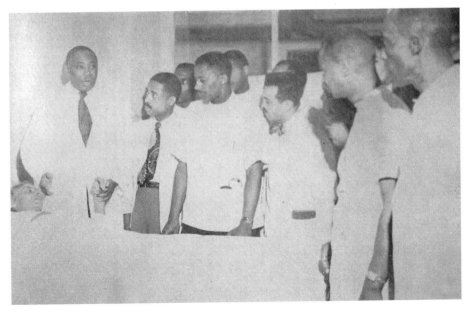

Dr. Matthew Walker, the second chairman of the department of surgery at Meharry, teaching students at a patient's bedside in 1954. Like Hale before him, Walker became a legend at Meharry. (Courtesy of Meharry Medical College)

ALFRED BLAIR JEFFERSON
PORTSMOUTH, OHIO
B.S., Ohio Univ.; Alpha Phi Alpha.

HAROLD RAY JOHNSON
BALTIMORE, MD.
B.S., Hampton Institute.

EDWARD ALLEN JONES, JR.
ATLANTA, GA.
B.S., Morehouse College; Alpha Phi Alpha.

ROBERT NELSON LEE
INKSTER, MICH.
B.S., Michigan State Normal; Alpha Phi Alpha.

PAUL HARGRAVE LOGAN
PETERSBURG, VA.
B.S., Virginia State College; Alpha Phi Alpha.

WILLIAM NELSON
LONDON
CHICAGO, ILL.
B.S., M.S., State Univ. of Iowa; Kappa Alpha Psi.

LUTHER WADE
McCASKILL
DETROIT, MICH.
B.S., Wayne Univ.; Omega Psi Phi.

ABRAHAM McINTOSH
TOWNSEND, GA.
Hampton Institute.

CHARLES BYRON
McINTOSH, JR.
JACKSONVILLE, FLA.
B.S., Florida A. & M. College; M.A., New York Univ.; Kappa Alpha Psi.

CLIFTON MALVIN MOORE
NORFOLK, VA.
B.S., Hampton Institute.

WILLIAM JOSEPH PARKER
MONTCLAIRE, N. J.
A.B., Upsala College.

HUEY LAWRENCE
PEARSON
GLENWOOD, GA.
A.B., Paine College; Alpha Phi Alpha.

Some of the sixty-five members of Meharry's Class of 1955, as seen in the 1954 yearbook. My father is in the lower right-hand corner. (Courtesy of Mrs. Lavester Pearson Rutland)

Portrait of Joseph H. Griffin, M.D., circa 1948, near the height of his influence as a businessman and surgeon. His second and larger hospital would open two years later. (Courtesy of Mrs. Mary Louise Griffin Perry)

Griffin Hospital and Clinic shortly after it opened. (Courtesy of Mrs. Mary Ford Grant)

Dr. Griffin conferring with senior nurses.

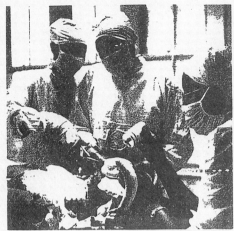

When a kerosene stove exploded in her home, this woman was rushed to the modern-equipped, Negro-owned Griffin clinic for treatment of severe burns.

Local civic leader H. D. McIver (l) compliments Dr. Joseph Griffin on his clinic's value to the community. White doctors send Negro patients here.

GEORGIA PIONEER

From a tenant farm to a respected citizen is the story of Dr. Joseph Griffin, who spent $225,000 to erect a hospital.

"THE KKK can't long exist in such an atmosphere of friendliness and understanding." The Atlanta *Constitution* made these editorial remarks when a Georgia-born Negro doctor opened his own 50-bed hospital at Bainbridge, Ga.

Attended by top white city and state officials, its opening last July ceremonies made big local history. The $225,000 project, financed entirely by Dr. Joseph Griffin, will serve patients in Florida, Alabama and Georgia. One of 17 children, the Meharry graduate is the son of uneducated tenant farmers. The modern building replaced a wooden clinic he built years ago. Dr. Griffin views it as a symbol of the Negro's confidence in the South.

When Moses Jones' leg was fractured by his car motor, he was treated by others.

Dr. Griffin, a World War I veteran practiced medicine 35 years. Wise investments in real estate brought him profits.

Dr. Griffin's wife, Eleanor, with their grandson. She's a first lady.

His mother, Mrs. Mary Griffin, at...

George Woodson, brought...

Architect ...

This photo essay on Griffin Hospital and Clinic appeared in the March 1951 issue of *Our World,* which competed headlong with *Ebony* magazine, achieving a circulation of 175,000 before ceasing publication in the mid-fifties. The article stated the cost of constructing the hospital was $225,000 (other articles and family put the price tag at $250,000) and embellished Uncle Joe's humble beginnings. (Courtesy of the Schomburg Center for Research in Black Culture and Johnson Publications)

My mother's family, circa 1943. She's standing between her parents, Mary Griffin Richardson, who was Joseph Griffin's youngest sister, and my grandfather, Crawford Richardson, who Uncle Joe didn't want grandmother to marry.

My sisters Carol (left) and Jennifer (right) and me, cutting up for our uncle in the driveway of our Fort Wayne, Indiana, home, September 1966. The house sat directly across the road from our elementary school, on the first block of an enclave of middle-class Afro-American homes surrounded by a lower-middle-class Caucasian community.

The extended Pearson family right after my grandmother Pearson's funeral in June 1968. My grandfather is in the center, my mother is standing directly behind him. He is flanked by three of his daughters. (Courtesy of Mrs. Thomaseanor Dudley Pearson)

Louis Sullivan, M.D., being sworn in as Secretary of Health and Human Services in 1989 by Judge A. Leon Higginbotham as his wife Ginger and President and Mrs. Bush look on. The childhood experience of riding with his father in an ambulance to take the sick and injured to Joseph Griffin's first hospital was what made Sullivan decide to become a physician. (Courtesy of Corbis-Bettmann)

Attorney Donald Hollowell, who earned the nickname "Georgia's Mr. Civil Rights" because he spearheaded so many legal battles during the civil rights era, talking to future governor of Georgia Lester Maddox during a break from a hearing. (Courtesy of Corbis-Bettmann)

Dr. LaSalle Leffall, distinguished cancer surgeon and the first Afro-American president of the American Cancer Society, who grew up near Bainbridge and was inspired by Joseph Griffin to pursue the study of medicine. (Copyright Bachrach)

Hosea Williams, a key aide, conferring with Dr. Martin Luther King, Jr. Williams grew up on a farm near Bainbridge and went to Dr. Griffin as a boy. Walking past the impressive Griffin home inspired him to want to be someone important. (Courtesy of Corbis-Bettman)

During the course of the interview he also told me stories about the Negro woman who worked for his family. A note of frustration entered his voice, mixed with fondness for her cooking recipes—frustration that she had been so thoroughly conditioned by segregation that even after it came to an end, upon being invited to sit and eat at the same table as the Ehrlichs, she couldn't bring herself to do it. Of how when she traveled with the family and they went to desegregated restaurants she refused to sit with them, preferring to take her meals in the restaurant's kitchen. I wondered if her reaction was learned subordination, or revulsion for a family who had so quickly and eagerly assimilated southern mores, or both.

Still pondering complexity, I wondered, too, why no Afro-Americans in Bainbridge answered my ad, which had been placed in the *Post-Searchlight*, the local weekly newspaper that most people in town, including plenty of Afro-Americans, bought or had delivered to their homes. Had they just missed it or was there something they didn't want to go on record about? Was there dirty laundry that they didn't want aired in public, an attitude that I encountered from plenty of Afro-Americans reacting to my Panther book? What was it?

Then I thought of the way families tend to create legends about their loved ones that amount to half-truths—tales of sweetness and light, of how they engaged in genuine honest hard work to make their marks. "Granddaddy walked five miles a day, every day, on his way to overcoming all the adversity life threw his way, to become the success he was. . . ." Usually, there is no hint that our family members were anything like the people we hear about and encounter in the cold, cruel, real world—those who took shortcuts, or swindled people out of what was rightfully theirs, or gratuitously engaged in mind games and/or expected to have their asses kissed for the simple pleasure of it. Our mothers, our fathers, our aunts, our uncles are always there to assure us that none of our ancestors could have possibly been like that.

I was reminded of the famous lines in my favorite play, *Death of a Salesman*, written by playwright Arthur Miller, who is Jewish. After a spate of hallucinating as his mind further degenerates, Willie Loman addresses his son Happy, who tries to lead him upstairs to bed. He tells Happy that his uncle Ben walked into the African jungle at age seventeen and by the time he was twenty-one he came out rich, after which Happy replies, "Someday I'd like to know how he did it." Yet maybe in real life most of us don't really want to know the answer to such a question. Maybe our love for those in our families who came before us, who paved our way, is unalterably connected to the ideal of goodness. So we tell ourselves that the people who made and continue to make the world so hard were and continue to be complete strangers to our genes.

All of those thoughts went through my mind after talking to Bertram Ehrlich. But at the same time neither was I ashamed of my great-uncle. Rather, I was even more intrigued by him. Was it true what Mr. Ehrlich said about the Caucasian coeds going to Griffin Hospital and Clinic to get abortions? And as for how Uncle Joe accumulated so much land, Mr. Ehrlich's explanation made sense to me. The *Pittsburgh Courier* stated that Joseph Griffin paid more property taxes than anyone else in Decatur County, Georgia. How else could he have gone from accepting chickens, turkeys, fruit, and vegetables as compensation for his medical services to accumulating so much real estate?

Other things began to fall into place as well. I knew that prior to legalization in 1973, it was hardly unusual for women to obtain criminal abortions (as opposed to the therapeutic variety, which were legal and performed only in cases where the mother's life was threatened). But it was always in secret, through back-alley, frequently nonmedically trained abortionists with whom they risked death, or through a local physician who occasionally agreed to perform one for a regular patient in utmost secrecy. If what Mr. Ehrlich said was true, then Uncle Joe had to have had a wide-ranging reputation as an abortionist, since Tallahassee, where Florida State is located, is forty miles from Bainbridge.

But back then one of the things most physicians did their best to avoid was a reputation for performing abortions. Plenty of women wanted the service. But to get it they went by assumed names, and were driven up those back alleys by mothers or fathers, husbands or boyfriends late at night. And the level of hypocrisy was such that people wouldn't want it known that for their general medical needs they saw a physician who performed them. But Uncle Joe could avoid that problem because he had a fifty-bed hospital in a small town—a facility that for quite some time was the best in the state for the hospitalization of Negroes. And a hospital was also the perfect setup for performing abortions when the patients were Negro (as plenty of his abortion patients were). Having a hospital made it easy to admit women for presumed legitimate medical conditions requiring overnight stay, an asset back then since the methods for safely aborting a pregnancy weren't as fast and efficient as they are today. And he was one of the few Negro physicians in that area, meaning that even if Negroes there didn't want to go to him because of the abortions, their alternatives were few unless they wished to endure second-class treatment from Caucasian physicians.

Now I began to wonder if it was his reputation for performing abortions that kept Uncle Joe's name from being mentioned in the same breath with the greats of the Negro medical world—those whose biographies intrigued me while I was growing up. Yes, in 1950 he was in McGill's Sunday *Atlanta Journal-Constitution* column, in Elmer Wheeler's syndicated piece, and several months later there was a spread on him in *Our World;* yes, in 1950 he was listed by the *Pittsburgh Courier* as one of its Top Ten Georgia Leaders, and there was the 1961 *Courier* article on him. And the following year he was featured in a book entitled *Distinguished Negro Georgians.* But when the *Journal of the National Medical Association* wrote about prominent Negro physicians, or I researched other articles about the pioneers in the history of the Negro medical world, Uncle Joe's name was nowhere to be found.

Instead there were names like Louis T. Wright, a Negro surgeon also from Georgia who was his exact contemporary. Wright's stepfather was Dr. William Fletcher Penn, who was among the Negro leaders of Atlanta who negotiated with the Caucasian power structure after the horrifying race riot of 1906. Wright's step-uncle was Garland Penn, who presided over Negro physicians organizing themselves into a representative body in 1895 during the Cotton States and International Exposition in Atlanta, and who convinced the exposition organizers to allow Booker T. Washington to speak.

From 1907 to 1911, while Joseph Griffin was breezing through Georgia State Industrial College in Savannah, Louis Wright was breezing through Clark University in Atlanta, a Negro institution with higher academic standards (later renamed Clark College and today called Clark Atlanta University). Prior to entering their respective colleges, while Joe Griffin spent his youth struggling to get past the severe racial limitations and relative hardships in rural southwest Georgia, Wright at least had the relative comfort of living in the midst of the Negro bourgeoisie in Atlanta. That city had begun distancing itself from the rest of Georgia in temperament and goals as soon as it began rebuilding after the Civil War, and it was as bitterly resented by the rest of the state as Atlantans looked down their noses upon the rest of Georgia.

From such a perch Wright's mother and stepfather, a graduate of Yale Medical School, could provide him with far better educational and financial assets than my great-grandparents provided Uncle Joe. Still Wright was no stranger to racial adversity. Like my great-uncle would later do, he faced down a racially violent mob, but at an earlier age. In his memoirs he vividly recalled the Atlanta riot of 1906:

> It was a moonlit night. And I and several others were given loaded Winchester rifles. . . . My instructions from my stepfather, who was covering the front and rear of the house, were to shoot and kill any man who opened our front gate. . . . All night long white men passed our house going to south Atlanta, and in the morning machine guns came out to supplement the activity in the area. At seven o'clock in the morning a group of white men came in the front gate of our home led by a white man who lived two doors above us and whose wife my father had delivered of three children. . . . My father stated, "What are you doing here? Do you know?" He said, "No, I don't know. Well, there's trouble." My father said, "Yes, there's trouble and you come to my house." The white men left after that. We learned indirectly that several white men had been killed by Negroes in south Atlanta and that martial law had been declared. Finally a Mr. O'Neil, a white man, came and took . . . my family away to another section of the city . . . until the effects of the riot were over . . .

In the riot's aftermath Wright started at the body of a dead Negro man hanging from a tree. He never forgot that. Neither did he forget seeing during his youth Negro chain gangs being treated brutally as they built most of the roads and streets of Atlanta. Upon graduating from Clark valedictorian of his class, he left the city unable to stomach any longer life in the South the way his stepfather and stepuncle were able to, unwilling to negotiate and compromise in adulthood as they and their champion Booker T. Washington were willing to do, and as Joseph Griffin would learn to do as well.

Wright retained a burning ambition to become a physician. Though his real father, who died while he was a small boy, was a graduate of Meharry's class of 1881, his destination wouldn't be Meharry or Howard, but instead Boston, where he intended to take the admission test for entry into Harvard Medical School. He spent the summer prior to taking the test as a bellboy in a local hotel. And when he presented himself to the director of admissions, initially he was graciously received because the director thought he was a graduate of Clark University in Worcester, Massachusetts. Upon discovering that he was from the Negro Clark University in Atlanta, he expressed amazement that the graduate of such a school would have the audacity to take the admission test for Harvard Medical School.

Wright was promptly referred to Dr. Otto Folin, an internationally famous biochemist on the faculty. The interview grew heated. In a voice dripping with superiority and condescension, Folin asked, "Mr. Wright, have you any sporting blood in your veins?"

"Yes," Wright responded.

"Will you agree if I ask you a few questions here today that I will never be bothered with you again in life?"

"Yes," Wright said once more.

To Folin's astonishment Wright passed the oral exam with flying colors.

He received his M.D. from Harvard in 1915, cum laude, ranking fourth in a graduating class of eighty-seven students. His average for the entire four years was a mere 0.27 percentage points behind the class leader. But because he received one blackball from a Jewish student from Memphis he wasn't elected to Alpha Omega Alpha, the honorary medical society. This, despite the fact that while a student he also conducted research that would serve as the basis for his first published paper (on the effect of alcohol on the rate of discharge from the stomach). Such academic excellence also meant nothing when it was time to apply for an internship. Wright was unable to obtain one at any of the reputable hospitals in Boston. So he applied to Freedmen's in Washington and was successful. Upon arriving he encountered resentment from fellow interns and faculty because he had gone to Harvard. It was not unlike the resentment encountered by his stepfather from fellow Negro physicians in Atlanta who had attended Meharry, jealous that he had gone to medical school at Yale (William Fletcher Penn was its first Negro graduate). For that reason they rarely referred patients to Dr. Penn, who had acquired some expertise in surgery, the same way most surgeons back then, especially Negro surgeons, acquired it—through retaining good knowledge of human anatomy and apprenticing with other physicians who did the same and, thus, had the courage and audacity to successfully attempt risky operations. At the turn of the century and the first two decades of the twentieth century, no other Negro physician in Atlanta had the surgical skill Penn had. As a result, the other Negro physicians feared that he might cause them permanent loss of their patients and thus damage their incomes. So instead they called in Caucasian physicians to perform their surgery.

Similarly, throughout his career Wright would experience problems. But for him it would be due to his refusal to play politics, even the politics of the day in which Negro physicians practiced their own brand of deference to important Caucasians. One day in the spring of 1916 President Woodrow Wilson ordered a huge peace parade as war raged in Europe; the U.S. had yet to enter the conflict. Since the hospital was federally funded, all of the physicians and nurses of Freedmen's were ordered to participate. Wright refused because he knew that any parade ordered by Wilson would relegate Negroes to the very rear of the participants. He was risking dismissal from his internship. And, of course, he was right about the position Negroes were relegated to in the parade. Wilson didn't even bother to stay long enough to watch them march by.

There were other indignities he was expected to swallow but didn't. One day he was sitting in a hospital laboratory in an operating gown when a Caucasian man and woman passed the door. "Sam, where can I find the superintendent?" asked the man.

"Charlie, you find him yourself," Wright responded.

"Why goddamnit, I'm a United States senator!" the man stated, shocked that a Negro would address him that way.

"Well, goddamnit, it's high time you learned to call a doctor a doctor!"

"I'll have you put out of here!" the senator replied, now even more livid.

Wright was reported. The hospital superintendent and medical chief gave him a severe dressing down. But he wasn't dismissed.

In another incident he refused to change on command the cause of death (alcoholism and kidney trouble) of the brother of a high government official who died after being rushed to Freedmen's emergency room because it was the nearest hospital. The official could make a lot of trouble for Freedmen's when budget time arrived. But Wright wouldn't bend. He survived that "indiscretion" as well. And while interning at the hospital he disproved the theory that the Schick test for the presence of diphtheria wasn't valid in Negroes because their skin was too dark. It was the first research paper published from Freedmen's and is believed to be the first scientific study based on work performed at a Negro hospital. But Wright was forced to carry out the study on his own because the National Vaccine and Antitoxin Institute wouldn't give him the necessary diphtheria toxin. Fellow interns shook their heads at his "arrogance" in believing he could carry out the study. But the hospital superintendent, William Warfield, the Negro surgeon who had learned so much from Daniel Hale Williams but hadn't been favorably disposed to Wright either when he first arrived, allowed him to conduct it. In addition he allowed Wright to conduct a study that introduced the medical world to the intradermal method of smallpox vaccination.

By the time Wright finished his internship, his stepfather was in dire financial straits due to continued organized antagonism by other Negro physicians in Atlanta. Wright reluctantly returned to town to help him out, easily passing the Georgia State Medical Board. Upon presenting himself at the Fulton County courthouse to register his license, he was reintroduced to the ways of the Deep South. The registrar, an elderly Caucasian man, told him to take a seat, which he did. After a while he heard the registrar call out, "Louie, Louie." Wright didn't answer. The registrar walked over to him, kicked his foot, and said, "I was talking to you."

"You weren't talking to me," Wright replied. "My name is Dr. Louis T. Wright." His mother and stepfather sat by nervously. His mother had always felt she had a strange son due to his unwillingness to live with the realities of racial etiquette that even most educated Negroes were willing to grit their teeth and bear. The registrar returned and after a while said, "Wright, Wright!" But Wright didn't answer. The registrar came over and kicked his foot again and stated, "I was talking to you."

Again, Wright answered, "You weren't talking to me; my name is Dr. Louis T. Wright."

"You aren't going to sell any dope are you, or do any abortions?" the registrar asked.

"Let me tell you something," Wright replied. "I'll choke you right here if you open your goddamn mouth again!" Wright's mother and stepfather couldn't believe his audacity or the audacity of the registrar in asking such a question. But Wright would get away with this seeming impudence, too. The registrar quickly gave him his medical certificate. And he entered medical practice with his stepfather, only to encounter more problems for being a maverick, as well as resentments similar to those he encountered from Negro physicians at Freedmen's. He tried to function with admitting privileges to the small clapboard Negro-owned Fairhaven Infirmary. But within a year he decided to leave Atlanta and join the Army Medical Corps, since the U.S. had just entered World War I. Unlike Joe Griffin he headed for the front and saw considerable action in France, including an engagement where he and his entire battalion were gassed with phosgene. Wright was hospitalized for three weeks, after which he returned to active duty but with permanent damage to his lungs. And he continued to fight the racial insults he constantly encountered, the only thing saving him being his medical acumen.

In 1919 he left active duty and settled in New York City, where he opened an office on Seventh Avenue in Harlem and was appointed an assistant physician in the New York City health department venereal disease clinic. His salary was forty dollars a month, which was less money than Joseph Griffin had made as a brick mason in Blakely, Georgia, the summer of 1911, prior to entering Meharry. He was also appointed clinical assistant visiting surgeon on the staff of Harlem Hospital, which meant that he worked in the clinic rather than in the actual hospital. As peculiar as it sounds today, Wright was the first Negro physician ever appointed to Harlem Hospital's staff. When the hospital opened at its second site in 1907 (the original was built elsewhere in Harlem in 1887), the neighborhood was still predominantly Caucasian. By the time Wright joined its staff, Negroes were flooding into the neighborhood. But the hospital personnel had yet to change their negative attitudes toward Negroes, which was one reason Wright had been hired to work in the clinic rather than the actual hospital, since Caucasian physicians wanted to minimize their contact with Negroes. Wright's permanent condition due to the wartime gassing he suffered placed some physical limitations on him. He couldn't climb stairs. In later years, his work in the operating room would be limited, due to his reduced ability to withstand anesthetic vapors. (He later was found to be suffering from TB.)

But he made landmark inroads at Harlem Hospital. First, he spearheaded protest by the few Negro physicians who were hired after him as adjunct visiting physicians at the hospital's clinic when one of their colleagues, Dr. Peter Murray, was turned down for promotion to a full-fledged staff physician. At two o'clock in the morning telegrams arrived at the homes of the city political machine bigwigs at Tammany Hall and the board members of Bellevue, the city's signature municipal hospital. The bold move resulted in Dr. Murray being appointed a full-fledged obstetrician on Harlem Hospital's staff, which allowed him to treat patients in the hospital proper (the year was 1925). That same year saw the appointment of Dr. Wright himself to the hospital's full-fledged staff, along with four other Negro physicians. The following year saw the appointment of the hospital's first Negro interns. In 1930, after the city reorganized its municipal hospital administration, nineteen Negro physicians were appointed to replace twenty-three Caucasian physicians at the hospital. The following year, as an active NAACP member and leader of the Manhattan Central Medical Society, a group of Negro physicians who had splintered off from a larger group of Negro physicians over the issue of more boldly challenging segregation in the city hospital system, Wright spearheaded a campaign to oppose efforts by the Julius Rosenwald Fund to erect a new segregated Negro hospital in New York City. It was all part of the fund's campaign to improve Negro health care facilities, right in line with its financing of the construction at that same time of a brand-new physical plant for Meharry, and in line with the spirit and philosophy of applauding Griffin Hospital and Clinic when it was constructed in 1950.

However, Wright opposed any plan that extended the segregation of Negroes in the field of medicine. This earned for him enmity from foundation sources important to the survival and prosperity of Howard, Meharry, and Negro hospitals throughout the South. In 1932 he organized protest of the construction of a second separate VA hospital for Negroes; the first had been the one in Tuskegee that

Robert Moton and John Kenney had fought so hard for. With the backing of the NAACP, of which he became board chairman in 1932, he was successful in preventing its construction and contributed mightily to the policy after World War II of full integration of all veterans' hospital facilities. As a result such stances placed him at odds with most Negro physicians of his era. Those active in the National Medical Association began to have little taste for him.

But no one could argue with his medical acumen. Like Daniel Hale Williams he was evolving into the type of Negro physician John A. Kenney, Sr., had once complained there weren't enough of. In 1929 he became the first Negro physician appointed a police surgeon for the city of New York, scoring higher than all but one other person on the medical exam. In 1936 he devised a splint for cervical fractures. Twelve years later he developed a plate for certain types of fractures of the femur. In 1934 he became the first Negro physician since Daniel Hale Williams to be admitted as a fellow of the American College of Surgeons. Four years later he became a diplomate of the American Board of Surgery, by examination rather than through appointment (appointment was a courtesy due to him, given his already proven expertise in the field, and a courtesy extended to two Caucasian junior Harlem Hospital staff members who were on medical school faculties Dr. Wright couldn't join due to his skin color). In 1938 he was appointed director of Harlem Hospital's Department of Surgery (which at that time was a non-salaried position, held on a rotating basis). In 1943 he became permanent chairman of the department. At the hospital he also initiated an uninterrupted flow of research papers on trauma cases that came through its busy emergency room and later established a cancer research foundation on its premises. By the early 1940s pharmaceutical companies supported numerous investigations by his medical team on the use of antibiotics, culminating in the distinction that his team was the first to use Aureomycin in human beings. In 1938 *Life* magazine called him the most eminent Negro physician in the U.S. (Charles Drew, who would soon earn similar distinction, was several years younger than Wright, and began his medical career much later.)

With such credentials, noted Dr. W. Montague Cobb, editor of the *Journal of the National Medical Association,* Wright could have easily become a wealthy man. But he chose not to, and lived only on the modest salary the city of New York paid him as a police surgeon. The most he was ever able to contribute to a medical school was a modest $100 contribution he once made to the one at Howard, at which at one point in his career he was offered the deanship but turned it down. Wright died of a heart attack in 1952 at the relatively young age of sixty-one, compared to fellow Georgia native Joseph Griffin, who died at ninety-two, almost thirty years later. Just before he died, Wright was preparing to attend the inauguration of his brother-in-law Harold D. West, who had just been named the first Negro president of Meharry—the same Harold West who three years later wrote back to Georgia governor Marvin Griffin, acknowledging the good deeds done by Meharry alumnus Joseph H. Griffin at Griffin Hospital and Clinic, which was in its third year of operation when Wright died.

While Wright fulfilled the scientific hopes of John Kenney that Negro physicians would prove they could hold their own against the best medical minds, Joe Griffin pursued the economic and political means of power available at that time in the South to an ambitious, financially hungry Negro man of medicine. He learned surgery by observing from afar at Cook County Hospital and the hospital of the University of Pennsylvania, and under the tutelage of a Meharry surgeon who learned most of what he knew on his own, since back then there were no surgical residencies for Negroes anywhere. Not to mention the fact that as late as 1930, there were only two specialty boards in all of medicine, period (ophthalmology and otolaryngology). When the specialty board for surgery was finally formed, Wright took the time to obtain board certification, while Joe Griffin, busy operating his own hospital, did not. Yet he was very good in the operating room (as, in later chapters, a very well-respected academic surgeon will also attest). During his career Joe Griffin also provided a safe, albeit illegal means for women to do what they probably would have done anyway to be rid of their unwanted pregnancies. And he became probably the most generous alumni benefactor of Meharry, providing the school not with a cash donation but, upon the death of the last of his three grandchildren, one-third of the dividends in perpetuity of blue-chip stocks worth $750,000 in 1972 (by the end of 1998, the value of the shares had increased to approximately $15,000,000). As I drove away from my meeting with Bertram Ehrlich I asked myself which contribution,

Wright's or Joseph Griffin's, ultimately was more important. I told myself, maybe it did take great crimes to amass fortunes. Maybe in order to become a man of wealth as well as influence, *especially a Negro man of wealth and influence,* it took a willingness to play some sort of elaborate game; a game that Louis Wright wouldn't play; a game Booker T. Washington did play with the powers-that-be in the South, as well as with rich northern philanthropists, in order to build Tuskegee and coerce donations to other Negro colleges out of such men; a game my great-uncle apparently played, too, at a different level, that in some ways looked like humiliation and cooperation with shame, but wasn't meant to be at all; that ultimately, perhaps, was pragmatism in the face of the certain impossibility at that time, of accomplishing the utopian goal of real integration—a point this country still hasn't reached, even though it no longer sanctions Jim Crow. Perhaps such men had no other choice, and the crippling effects of compromising with the system couldn't be avoided (though in Washington's case I'm convinced that political compromise was taken too far).

Still, there was, too, the flip side of the coin. While I could be proud of a man like my great-uncle, proud of my direct connection to such a man, must I also realize that he became what he was, in part, by blocking the ability of other Negroes to become all that they could be? And that after reaching such a plateau, he chose to reach backward with his wealth, with his image as a regional role model, and facilitate greater accomplishments on the part of ambitious Negroes of future generations, who, as time passed, wouldn't have to take the route he was forced to take in the Jim Crow South? Yet might it also have been that another reason he reached back with his philanthropy was because he was haunted by the same feelings of guilt that overcome plenty of wealthy men when, all alone with their consciences, they sift through the unsavory things they did to become wealthy, old age creeping upon them, forcing them to fear, after death, an accounting by a Creator? Were both influences working on him? Was it more one than the other?

I realized, too, that in temperament I was much closer to Wright than to my great-uncle. Evidence of my distaste for game-playing, for engaging in elaborate back-scratching and politics, has virtually defined the parameters of my career, as has my strong sense of what's right and what's wrong. Yet while growing up, after overcoming my fascination with black militancy and the misdirected belief that excelling academically meant "acting white," I wove what I read and was told about both Wright and my great-uncle into the stuff composing my sense of who I was and what I could do. Of course, I knew nothing of the kinds of things Mr. Ehrlich told me about my great-uncle, or of the complexities that I later learned defined Wright's life, and so was under the impression that both men simply, altruistically forged ahead to accomplish what they did. And I mixed pride for them with the pride I felt in my father. All of it came together to make up my definition of the ultimate that Afro-American men could accomplish in the cold, cruel world, even though at the time I had no true understanding of just how cold and cruel the world really was. At that particular point in my life, such an attitude was what made the difference between me and the other Afro-American boys I grew up with, even as I felt no direct interest in the sciences that all three men clearly loved, that all three of them had to have loved in order to become what they did.

And there was one more element to this burning ambition to do something important. It was traceable to what happened in December 1966: my mother's sudden mysterious illness. One night inexplicable pain pierced her limbs and her abdomen. In one fell swoop she was forced to alter her plans to return to nursing now that all three of her children were in school. That first night I called myself a brave nine-year-old, determined to sit up with his sick mother. When she went to one of my father's Caucasian colleagues for diagnosis he told her she had gouty arthritis and prescribed painkillers. The pain would go away for a little while. But it always returned, holding her within its grip for longer and longer stretches, slowly affecting her mental well-being, too. She began to feel as though she wasn't being a real mother to us because real mothers weren't forced to lie in bed sick for days at a time. As a result, any youthful transgression committed by us children set her off with a determination to prove her ability to still function properly as our mother. I committed most of the youthful transgressions. So she constantly grounded me, and she constantly whipped me when the drugs Demerol or Percodan or cortisone relieved her of enough pain to swing the long branch she made me walk out and cut from one of our backyard trees.

Eventually I concluded she would always be sick like that periodically. She would always be like that, but always around—for our graduations, for our weddings, for the birth of her grandchildren. She'd just have to make one more of her many trips to the hospital until she was well again. And she kept going to the hospital. She kept going to her physician, who periodically would send her to the experts at the Cleveland Clinic two hundred miles to the east, who would consult him and Father on her condition. Finally one day they came up with the correct diagnosis: systemic lupus erythematosus, now so far advanced that it was life-threatening. She and my father decided not to tell me and Carol and Jennifer. They felt it was best that way.

They may have been wrong. By the time I was fourteen I was sick and tired of my mother being sick. I was sick and tired of not being able to do the things other boys did: like staying out until a certain hour, beginning to date girls. . . . And even though my chores were far fewer than those performed by older sister Carol, who cooked dinner every night from the age of thirteen, I was sick and tired of what I thought were excessive chores, too. And I was sick and tired of the way my mother would send me to the neighborhood grocery store three or four times a day to get more items because she had forgotten everything she needed, due largely to the side effects of the painkillers she was taking and by then was addicted to. One day I decided I had had enough of her constantly grounding me, of her constantly sending me back and forth to the grocery store. I decided I had taken one grounding too many. This time I would tell her off. So one sunny Saturday, "You're a mother in name only!!!" cascaded out of my angry mouth.

It devastated her. It was as if I had kidney punched her. She cried. She plunged into a mild depression. I was punished for saying it. I apologized and soon regretted what I had said, convinced that I was worthy of the grounding I was sentenced to. Three years later, with her stays in the hospital slowly growing longer, my sister Carol came back for one week of spring break from her first year at Harvard. Mother kept getting up out of bed and walking to the family room without a word to anyone. She'd sit for a minute or two staring off into space, then rise and return to her bedroom, and start the process all over again, even after the rest of the family had gone to bed. Carol began to worry. My father decided that if Mother didn't stop after one more day, he'd take her to the hospital. She didn't stop and had to be taken.

For three months she lingered there while Carol returned to Harvard and I finished my final year of high school and our sister Jennifer completed the ninth grade. Periodically she'd return to a normal level of coherence. But within a day or two she'd be incoherent again. And it kept getting worse. I hoped she'd be out of the hospital in time to make my high school graduation. When I realized she wouldn't, I got the bright idea of going up to her hospital room on graduation day just before the ceremony, so she could see me in my sky blue cap and gown. I walked into her private room and immediately went to the bathroom to change. Then I presented myself in front of her. She was so disoriented by pain she didn't even know I was there. This time I was the one who was devastated. I walked back into the bathroom, changed, wiped away my tears, and tried to put on the best face mask of normality I could muster to walk past the nurses' station as if nothing had gone wrong. Then I drove off to my graduation. My sister Carol returned that evening from her first year in college. That night she told me our mother would soon die. In the back of my mind I wondered if my "telling her off" three years earlier had hastened her impending death.

It happened on July 16, 1975, while I was away in a pre-freshman summer program at Brown. Father had assured me that it was okay to go because she could linger for months. And by then I was eager to get away because every time she returned to a coherent state she would get after me about something, and my sister Carol was doing her best to take over so many helpful functions along with our grandmother, Joseph Griffin's kid sister, causing me feelings of uselessness. Yet after she died, not only did I feel guilty for telling her off three years earlier, but now also for not being there when she passed away. So while studying at Brown, when it was time to choose my career, not only was my choice informed by admiration for my father and my great-uncles and Louis T. Wright, and a budding belief that there was no better, more independent means of an Afro-American male making a living than being a physician. It was informed by my desire to make amends to my dead mother.

The effect of trying to master biology and chemistry and physics was like swallowing castor oil. Other than to reach my ultimate goal, I couldn't have cared less about what an antigen was, what chemical you could mix hydrochloric acid with in order to synthesize something new, or what it means that E = MC squared. I couldn't have cared less, not out of some presumed laziness—the stereotype Afro-American students at Brown constantly fought—but because science just didn't interest me. And I found it hard to stay interested in what seemed like the other dry disciplines, shocked that they were taught through lectures that were so different from the discussion groups I was engrossed in and often led in high school. Throughout my four years I kept trying to figure out if medicine was what I was really cut out for. I harbored no sense of mission to prove wrong the assumption that we Afro-American students—allegedly all affirmative action admittees—couldn't make the grade academically at Brown, as so many people expected all of us to disprove. I was too preoccupied with personal demons and struggles to even care.

And now as I drove away from Mr. Ehrlich's, I thought about how for Afro-Americans the mission of disproving stereotypes about us is constantly at war with our humanity in all its variety. Thus the pressure is always there to became one-dimensional, unmalleable, and impervious to reacting humanly to the affronts we've faced and/or still face: like the refusal of Caucasians during Jim Crow to address us as "mister" or "missus," or in the case of a Negro physician, as "doctor"; or the assumption that we really don't have intelligent minds; that all we can do that anyone would find useful is sing, dance, screw, or engage in athletics; the assumption that we're always up to something underhanded and/or always too emotional and irrational, traits that many of us have, no doubt, demonstrated, due to the circumstances we've been forced into; our expected strength in enduring all the adversity we've faced, warring with the just plain human urges within us, like the urge toward greed harbored by all people, or the desire to accumulate wealth and power by any means necessary, or to exercise power for the sake of power just because we're in a position to do it, or to express anger and seek revenge the way any person does after being affronted and disrespected, or the sensation of feeling lost just because we're confused and at the moment simply can't get it together academically or on the job—all human weaknesses that are expected to be straitjacketed out of Afro-Americans as part of the mission of "uplifting the race" and proving our adversaries wrong about us. The two urges—to embark on a mission, versus just being who I am, doing what I wish to as an individual—continue to war inside my own soul. Sometimes I understand why, collectively, we exhibit weaknesses, sometimes I don't. And always I'm thinking about how we can be free to be just plain human, yet, too, more accomplished.

In my class at Brown there was a Louis T. Wright equivalent among us. His name was Orlando Kirton. While the rest of us Afro-American students struggled with premed courses the same way most other premeds did, Orlando breezed right through them. Orlando was so good, so capable of holding his own with or surpassing the best Caucasian students, that he completed his premed courses in two years instead of the usual three. He was easily admitted to Harvard Medical School. Upon matriculating, he placed out of half of his first-year medical courses. We were proud of Orlando even as we envied him, even as we were thankful that we didn't have to be that good to get into a medical school, that the medical school admissions committees would cut us some slack and assure us that we didn't have to have grade-point averages as high as those of our Caucasian classmates.

With that assurance, and the knowledge that as a legacy I had an even greater edge, in addition to the fact that my great-uncle was the largest alumni benefactor in the history of Meharry, I applied to the school and was admitted, only to matriculate and run right smack into the realization that not only was I no Louis T. Wright, or Orlando Kirton, I was no Joseph Griffin, or David Griffin, or Huey L. Pearson, Sr., either; that going to medical school with no real interest in the science of medicine wasn't the way to make amends to my dead mother, that perhaps I owed her no amends at all and ultimately she understood why I did what I did.

And now as I made my way to my father's older sister's house in southwest Atlanta after talking to Bertram Ehrlich I realized, given what Mr. Ehrlich told me, I owed nothing to the memory of my great-uncle either—nothing except discovering to the extent I could the naked truth about his life, a naked truth that I could learn from, and which I was now more determined than ever to uncover.

CHAPTER 8

After leaving Atlanta I returned to Bainbridge. The first person I visited was Mary Louise. I decided not to tell her the details of my interview with Bertram Ehrlich, figuring it was best to assume that family would automatically, reflexively take issue with anything said by anyone who doesn't paint a rosy picture of loved ones. As she had when I visited several months earlier after attending Alice Hawthorne's funeral, she greeted me warmly and invited me inside. As happened then, too, I was treated with something close to reverence, which I concluded was probably due to the aura of family pride that still surrounded me after the publication of my first book. And now she knew about my desire to make the life of her father the centerpiece of this one. She gave me her approval but said she wouldn't contribute much of anything to it. She'd give me some assistance in talking to people who could. But she didn't say that with much enthusiasm. I realized that the reason was that my aunt's story of his life was supposed to be *it*. On the other hand, I sensed that there were two Mary Louises in front of me: the one who felt it would be too controversial to dig very deeply underneath the surface of her father's life, but didn't want to admit that, and a different Mary Louise, one who was intelligent and perceptive enough to respect the concept of attempting to place a person and what that person did in his life in the context of his times, no holds barred. Hence the support of my entire family, when I faced the controversy surrounding my Panther book, a controversy arising from the fact that I didn't romanticize Huey Newton and the Black Panthers. With them, too, I was determined to shed my mind of racial sensitivity, determined to observe as though I were a being from another planet, allowing the chips to fall where they may. And when the proverbial shit hit the fan with Panther romanticists, family was there with plenty of reassurance. What would happen now?

I wondered. Would they be there, too, when I applied objectivity to my own kin?

This time Mary Louise's son Joe, who was named after his maternal grandfather (and not with just his first and middle names, but his first, middle, and last names, as in Joseph Howard Griffin Perry), was there, too, still convalescing from his heart ailment. We had never met, since Joe is twelve years older than me and left Georgia by the time I was in grade school. After we shook hands we discovered that we had lived in the San Francisco Bay area at the same time. "I'll be damned!" he said. "I wish I had known you were out there." I discovered that he knew a few former Panthers. In fact, he was in his twenties during the heyday of the Panther movement and was an activist himself, not with the Black Panthers, but rather with a performing arts group called the Free Southern Theater. They used plays like Samuel Beckett's *Waiting for Godot* and improvisational dramas to enlighten poor Afro-Americans in Mississippi and Louisiana about their political and socioeconomic predicament in the South. After each play audience members would discuss what they saw, often rising and telling each other, "Don't you see what Beckett is saying? We just can't keep waiting. Are you gonna just keep waiting?" Joe joined the theater in 1964 in New Orleans, after leaving Morehouse College during his freshman year. The theater company was an integrated group with socialist leanings. Everyone was paid the same salary including the manager and artistic director. Most were from New York City. One night, almost like James Cheney, Andrew Goodman, and Mickey Schwerner, the three Mississippi Freedom Summer workers who were murdered, that same summer of 1964 Joe and two other troupe members faced the danger that they, too, could be killed.

It happened in a town called Jonesboro, Louisiana. They had been using improvisation to encourage local Negroes to protest the hiring practices of a local paper company. For their lodging they stayed at local Negro homes in a community about five miles from the town proper. One night Joe, along with the theater's artistic director, a Frenchman named Robert Cordier, and one other troupe member, a young Jewish guy from New York City named Billy Zucoff, decided to go into town, get something to eat, perhaps stop at a local tavern, then listen to some music. They hopped into one of the company cars to do so. They weren't in town for very long before they were stopped by a local police officer, allegedly for loitering. He got on the squad car radio and reported, "I got them right here." Then he arrested them and brought them to the jail. Once inside the sheriff confiscated their IDs. He looked at Cordier's, noticed he was from France, and told him, "Well, being from there I guess you don't know any better than to come down here and try to do things the way they might do them where you come from. But that's not how we do it down here. You should stay up in New York City."

Then he looked at Zucoff and said something most of us would expect, given the history of Afro-American and Jewish interaction during the civil rights movement and the South's reputation for anti-Semitism; "Hey, Jew boy! What are you doing down here?" He said that the theater troupe was an integrated company and they didn't like that. Then he looked at Joe's ID and said, "And you're from *Georgia?!?!?* You should know better!" He said that Joe must have been up in New York City. Then he went where all bigots hypocritically ventured when they criticized the movement and its ultimate goals. "What's it like, all of that white pussy up there that you've been gettin'?" Joe remained silent. At that point he figured he would soon be dead. He was all of nineteen years old and told himself, "I will just steel myself right now. I just hope I pass out first . . ."

When the three of them didn't return by 1:00 A.M. to where they were staying, the theater manager called the Jonesboro police station. Just like what happened in the case of Cheney, Goodman, and Schwerner, when their coworkers called the Philadelphia, Mississippi, police, the manager of the Free Southern Theater was told by the Jonesboro police that no one from the station house had seen Joe and the other two. He called the FBI. The FBI called the Jonesboro police and was told the same thing. Joe, Robert, and Billy stayed locked up in the jail until about 4:00 A.M. Then, again, just like events in the Cheney, Goodman, and Schwerner case, the sheriff told them he was letting them go. In front of the three he got on the phone and called someone and repeated, "I'm lettin' them go now." But he told them they couldn't take their car. They had to walk back. The three of them alighted into the fading darkness of the town just before dawn. They got their bearings and began walking along the highway back toward where their group was staying outside of town. After they began walking, cars suddenly began to turn off side streets onto the highway and follow them. They were certain they were done for. But when they got out into the country they got the bright idea of heading off the road into the woods and swampland. Zucoff broke into a little house and used the telephone to call for help. They hid out until the sunlight was bright enough. Then they were picked up by allies, avoiding what they assumed would be a tragic fate. Or maybe the sheriff and his friends had just tried to scare them. It worked because the theater company quickly left the area.

Not long after that Joe brought a group of his activist friends to Bainbridge. "I took them to Granddad's office in the hospital," he recounted as we sat in the family room drinking Cokes. "You have to imagine what that was like. Here were these dudes trying to blend in, but totally conspicuous, complete strangers to the area. I mean, these guys would stop traffic everywhere they went. So here they were sitting in Granddad's waiting room with everyone just staring at them silently. After a while Granddad walked in. He came straight up to me and said, 'Get these goddamn nuts outta my hospital! If there's any changing to be done in Bainbridge I'll be the one to do it!!!'"

After Joe told me this, I thought back to how throughout my elementary and teen years, as I eagerly read of the civil rights and Black Power movements, I hadn't given much thought to what my relatives were doing while they were taking place. In subsequent years I had not heard of a single one of those who remained in the South (most of the family) being involved in any major campaigns alongside King or anyone else. The closest level of involvement that I knew of was that of Herb Dudley, father-in-law of my father's youngest brother, who allowed King to stay at his motel in Dublin. I had no solid proof that my family weren't active supporters of the civil rights activists. In fact, after the movement, whenever the subject of someone like King came up, like most other Afro-Americans who were adults during his time, they talked about him with reverence, as if without question they supported what he was up to. But the truth was that most Negroes in the South didn't support King and the other activists, at least not publicly. They were too uneasy about such boldness. And in the North as well, hindsight has turned a man seen by most people—probably even most Negroes—as somewhat foolish in the last two years before his assassination (either for the way he focused attention on Vietnam as well as civil rights, or the seemingly outdated or useless nature of his nonviolent campaigns for social justice when he brought them north) into a hero. Not to mention the way they thought of the black militants, who weren't even granted the respect by most Negroes over thirty-five of being considered as intelligent as fools. Yet in their cases as well, as I discovered after my Panther book came out, in hindsight plenty of Afro-Americans remember them as heroes, even though it can be proven that most of these same people were mortified about the Panthers, for instance, in their heyday, demonstrating the degree to which for so many of us (most of us?) hindsight can put things in better perspective, but can also portray our past behavior in a manner at variance with the way it really was.

Given what Joe was telling me about his work in Louisiana and Mississippi in the mid-1960s, it appeared that he had been the only activist in my family. But did that mean the rest hadn't been responsible in some way for aiding and abetting Afro-American freedom? I decided that the answer is no. I decided that just as the encounter between Joe's friends and Uncle Joe implied, it was so much easier to be bolder when you didn't actually live in the towns and rural areas of the Deep South where you were attempting to bring about change. And it had been so much easier to be bolder, too, with the small victories such as the one registered by my aunt Lavester while interviewing for her first teaching job. It was the optimism and hubris of youth that brought so many like my cousin Joe and Billy Zucoff to different towns and counties to try to effect change. And the philanthropy of numerous northerners, particularly Jews, fueled it for a while. But such philanthropists were at a distance. They knew the responsibilities and usual disappointments learned by adults everywhere. But not in the Deep South, especially when you were a Negro. Negro adults, like most of my family, decided that the best alternative was to stay. They asked themselves, Did freedom truly constitute working in a factory in Chicago or Detroit or Pittsburgh, being susceptible to layoffs at the whims of the owners? Was that really freedom, as opposed to owning your own farm or timber company or funeral parlor or hospital in the Deep South, upon which you had built a reputation, and living in peace as long as you remained on your side of the real estate, and tried to compensate for the exclusions of Jim Crow to the best

of your ability? Wasn't freedom a concept inclusive of many different factors? Not to apologize for Jim Crow, but the stage had to be
set for change, the stage had to be set before change could come
about. And it appeared that in many ways my cousin Joe's grandfather, my great-uncle, had literally paved the way so that Joe could
afford to take things to a different level. Of course, Uncle Joe would
have preferred that his grandson hadn't done what he did in the
Free Southern Theater. He would have preferred that he stayed at
Morehouse, then gone on to medical school, then done postgraduate training and returned to Bainbridge to take over Griffin Hospital
and Clinic. But it was because he had done what he did to pave the
way for his grandson financially that Joe could afford to rebel. Uncle
Joe had wielded a certain degree of power in his role as a Negro
leader, sometimes compromising in ways that in hindsight look like
examples of shameful acquiescence. Then the moment he was confronted with a new order that would soon render his role as a Negro power broker a thing of the past, Uncle Joe couldn't see the
forest for the trees. He couldn't see he was a man who had facilitated his own obsolescence if only by helping hold down the fort
until the arrival of that new era, brought about by the changes in
Negro military stature during and after World War II, by the rise in
empathy for Negroes among American Jews due to the shocking
revelations of what Hitler had done to Jews in Europe. He couldn't
see that his obsolescence had been fueled by postwar prosperity, by
the slow progression of Supreme Court decisions chipping away at
the legitimacy of that same court's *Plessy v. Ferguson* decision in
1896, then the bravery of Martin Luther King, Jr., in leading Negro
residents who boycotted public buses in Montgomery, Alabama,
and all that eventually flowed from that, leading to grandson Joe
Perry's involvement in the Free Southern Theater. However, when
the new era arrived, Uncle Joe was still caught up in the way he had
been forced to do things. It was during this visit that Mary Louise
told me of the way he walked up to one of King's principal aides,
Hosea Williams, who grew up in the Bainbridge area, while
Williams was visiting one day during the civil rights movement,
and only half-jokingly told him never to return because Bainbridge
didn't need his kind of activism.

After a while Mary Louise left and went to another part of the
house. Then she returned, pardoned herself, and asked Joe if she

could speak to him in private. He left to speak with her. Then he returned and the two of us went out to lunch at a restaurant opened recently in town by a Nigerian immigrant. We both expressed surprise that anyone from Nigeria would want to come to Bainbridge. After ordering we continued to discuss his grandfather. He talked of how Uncle Joe once told him that he came to Bainbridge because he thought the town was going to grow rapidly. But it didn't, due to the small-mindedness of the city fathers. Had he known they wouldn't take advantage of the town's potential, he would have settled elsewhere. Joe told me of the times while growing up in the house, when he would hear the phone ring, and Uncle Joe would answer, "Good evening, Governor. . . ." It was Marvin Griffin calling. And they would discuss things that Joe wasn't privy to. He spoke of Uncle Joe's later years, when he had to visit the Mayo Clinic (where his great-niece, my sister Carol, would attend medical school) because of health problems, and how he loved the clinic, respected it, and loved medicine, and that once while he was being treated there, he needed someone to send in a payment for his property taxes. He wrote out a check for a six-figure sum and had Joe mail it.

"There's an elderly man, Bill Austin, a friend of the family that I think you'd enjoy talking to," Joe said in his deep bass voice as we drove back to the house. "He and Granddad worked together on Pullman porter issues. He would be very helpful. And there are a couple of other people I can think of. . . ." He said that he would call them and set everything up. As I prepared to leave, Joe and Mary Louise stood with me in the driveway talking some more. She volunteered that her father did perform abortions but said that it wasn't a very important part of what he did, that it was only occasional. "He figured, that's one less child who has to go through the hell of living in this world. . . ." Then we got into a conversation about the womanizing of Uncle David. Mary Louise told of how one day he mistakenly sent a letter to Uncle Joe, who was putting him through medical school at the time; the letter was intended for a young woman he was romancing. Uncle Joe wrote him back: "Dear Brother, I love you, too. But I'll be damned if I'm going to sleep with you. . . ." Then I said my farewells, got in my car, and visited our other cousin in town, Mary Agnes, then headed to Tallahassee to visit my aunt.

❖ ❖ ❖

Aunt Barbara had me meet her at her office at Florida A&M. As I sat there she got on the phone and called a Mr. Eaton, the man who went with her to conduct the series of interviews she had with Uncle Joe in 1978 and '79 in preparation for her book about him. Mr. Eaton was the curator of the college archives. "Yes, he's my nephew," she said into the telephone. "He's going to write a book that builds upon what I wrote. Can he come over to the archive? I see. I see. So it's not open right now. I see. Okay. I'll tell him." When she hung up she informed me that the archive at the university was being renovated and wouldn't be open until the fall, and that the items it had from Griffin Hospital and Clinic were few anyway. When we went to her house she gathered the rest of the material she had collected from Uncle Joe, so that I could add to what she had already given me and Aunt Elaine had mailed to me earlier. As she did so, I wondered how she really felt about my project. She had said I was going to build upon what she wrote. Was I? What if what I wrote made what she wrote look silly? Would we then become estranged? I certainly didn't want that. But neither would I shrink from the truth.

While sitting in her office she talked about how she had always loved to research things, but she hated writing. It had always been a chore. It was as if she was volunteering an explanation for why her short biography of Uncle Joe was the only book she had ever written. She had spent her entire career at Florida A&M. And now she was burned out from the politics of the place, engaged in a phased-in retirement from teaching students who, she said, didn't appear to want to learn history anyway. Then there was the prominent administrator who had called for closing the school of liberal arts. "Who ever heard of a university without a school of liberal arts?" Aunt Barbara asked rhetorically. It was an example of how things aren't always what they look like from the outside. Virtually everything that had been printed in recent years about Florida A&M made it seem that the university was on a mission where everyone was pointed in the same direction. It was as if every day everyone gathered and sang the school song, then went about disproving the stereotypes about Afro-Americans to the extent possible at such an institution, even as the school has become increasingly integrated in recent years thanks to state policies designed to eliminate the legacy

of segregation. Yet here was Aunt Barbara assuring me there had
been and still were petty politics at FAMU; professors and administrators who didn't like each other; jealousies. Life there had been as
complex as at any other university. Allegedly, certain people got high
off the heady fumes of esteem from the outside world, an esteem so
precious to the despised; an esteem that, when it comes, sets its re-
cipient apart from the loathed ordinary Negroes.

Now I wondered what part of my aunt's account of the politics
at FAMU corresponded with objective truth and what part
amounted to jealousy. If I went to the administrator who allegedly
called for closing the school of liberal arts, what would that person
have to say about my aunt? That she was a history department
chairman, yet hadn't written a single major tome? But then, wasn't
one of the criticisms of major universities that too often publishing
took precedence over teaching and that you couldn't both publish
and provide care and attention to student needs? So might it have
been that my aunt spent her career attempting to provide that attention at the price of not publishing a major volume of history?

I knew, too, that when acclaim from the larger world comes to
those of us labeled "black" it's as if we've been given honorary
"white" status—a pass for a while, meaning that we'll be presumed
intelligent, presumed a person of means. We tend to be very nou-
veau in our attitudes—quick to spend money on expensive clothes,
expensive cars, a nice home, because we latch on to even the small-
est opportunities for "honorary white" status. And if the opportunity presents itself career-wise, often we want to be the only one of
"us" to take advantage. We want to become the biggest fish possible in the small, pitiful Negro pond, which is a stereotype, but one
with a huge ring of truth, and one that is a logical human reaction
to what we've been through.

When I returned to Bainbridge, Bill Austin came over to Mary
Louise's house to talk with me about Uncle Joe. He told Joe that he
wanted to talk there instead of at his own house with me alone. He
said he wanted to talk in the presence of Joe and Mary Louise. As
this short, dark-skinned man, now in his eighties, took a seat in the
family room he acted extremely deferential toward them. It was as
if a serf had come to visit royalty. Every time I asked him a question
he turned to them and asked if it was okay for him to answer. Such

deference saddened me. It reminded me of what I had concluded a long time ago. It is often said among Afro-Americans that southern Afro-Americans are more family-oriented, less prone to commit crimes, more goal directed, etc., than those in the North. Yet every time I turn on the local news in the South someone's been shot, very often an Afro-American by another Afro-American. The region has the nation's highest murder rate. In no other section of the country is it easier to purchase a gun. And every time I enter a small southern town, the Afro-American locals tend to be the most docile people I've ever encountered in the country.

The romantic notion that they have it more together than Afro-Americans in the North seems to be part of a huge psycho-social cycle. In America, in the world, everyone dreams of a promised land. Then, when they reach it, quite often they become disappointed. And wherever they came from looks far better than it did while they were there. Hence Afro-Americans migrated North only to find out it wasn't all they hoped for, and now their descendants talk about the South as though their families were wrong to leave. Then when they return South they start the psycho-social process all over again. Time and time again I've encountered a new Afro-American arrival in Atlanta who came from somewhere in the North. Then after a year or two there, he or she starts complaining about how the Afro-Americans who seem to have the most initiative in the city are those from the North. They wonder if they really should have left New York City, or Chicago, or L.A., or wherever . . . where Afro-Americans are more together.

Which got me thinking once again about the difference between ambitious, educated Afro-Americans who remained in the South but abided by its rules, and the many who remained but appeared to be totally defeated. It appeared that at the level of ordinary Negroes who went no further than high school, most of the more ambitious left the South during Jim Crow. Those with ambition who stayed, as well as the educated Negroes who remained, appeared to have done so because they were able to provide some sort of niche service that would have been difficult to duplicate in the North, or because they owned something that would have been virtually impossible to rebuild in the North. Among Afro-Americans in the small-town and rural South, the more ambitious usually left for New York City, Chicago, L.A., Detroit, or closer to home—Atlanta,

Houston, Dallas, New Orleans. . . . Those with ambition who remained usually did so because they had taken advantage of a distinct economic reason for remaining. And in a peculiar way life became relatively easy for them as long as they abided by certain rules, since they could prosper among the Afro-American majority who remained but had little or no ambition to do much of anything—the Afro-Americans who had been taught their place by southern Caucasians most thoroughly of all.

After he left, Joe said that Mr. Austin wasn't himself because I was a stranger. But I sensed there was more to it than that. It reminded me of what I heard and read about Mississippi Freedom Summer as the SNCC volunteers attempted to effect change. There were those who reacted to the possibility for change in the way Joe and his fellow troupe members described. But more often than not the people they and the SNCC workers were trying to uplift would listen to what they had to say politely, deferentially, allowing it into one ear. Then after they left, the people would send it out the other ear and stay exactly where they were.

It was as if they had developed an impregnable façade. No doubt it was part of a defense mechanism against trouble, comparable to the shell covering a turtle, a hard psychological casing into which they retreated and that they passed from one generation to the next over the span of three hundred years, due to the terror visited on friends, family, any ancestors who showed initiative, drive, vigor, or receptivity to new ideas. And most of those who had much of that remaining after the onslaught migrated North or to Atlanta, while in the meantime relatives like Mr. Austin who stayed baked their defensive shells in the kiln of the broiling hot Deep South summers until they attained an impervious toughness.

Months later I would put all of this into perspective. Months later I would conclude that apparently, among such people, Afro-Americans like Uncle Joe quickly, shrewdly, cleverly obtained a lock on most of the opportunity down there that there was for Negroes. But Joe had said Mr. Austin had been like a son to Uncle Joe. I knew that somewhere along the way, a son rebels against his father. If a father has been a good father at all, the day eventually arrives where a growing son starts thinking for himself, starts questioning his father's wisdom, only to eventually return to his father and use his own wisdom to protect his father from the world the way his father once protected him. Maybe Joe was right about Mr. Austin virtually being a son to Uncle Joe. Thus he was also protecting the image of Uncle Joe, which accounted for his reticence. But maybe, too, most of the Afro-Americans who remained down there had remained like children, in that they grew up only to a certain degree. They could never experience all the options available to healthy adolescents and young adults, or make all the choices in full adulthood available to their Caucasian counterparts, especially Caucasian men. So for them Uncle Joe had turned into their dominating father figure to whom they gave license to do as he pleased. It was a conclusion I later drew. The evidence began accumulating first with Mr. Austin.

"Joe tells me you worked with my uncle on Pullman porter issues," I said after we exchanged pleasantries.

Joe quickly interjected, backtracking from what he had told me. "What I was saying was that Mr. Austin worked with the railroad and had a lot of experience during Jim Crow days and had seen many of the changes. But he wasn't actually involved in the union itself [the Brotherhood of Sleeping Car Porters]. He was telling me one time about some of the folks in Jacksonville, how nasty they were and how reluctant they were to let any black man get any kind of advancement or security in his job."

Then there was an awkward silence. Afterward Mr. Austin told me almost nothing new but rather the same legendary stories I was familiar with: about the burning of Willie Reid's corpse and the dragging of it past the homes of all the "uppity nigras" like Uncle Joe, but with the additional information that what was left of his corpse was then dumped in front of a local Negro Baptist church; about Uncle Joe saving the Negro farmer Emmet Thomas from foreclosure of his farm. And Mr. Austin kept saying he wanted to make sure everything he said was satisfactory with Joe and Mary Louise, a comment that raised my suspicions. "It's not an appeal to censorship," Joe assured me. "It's kind of a southern thing, a courtesy." Mary Louise was absent during most of the interview. I decided now that she was gone perhaps it was the time to test the winds of candor, because maybe Joe and Mr. Austin would have no problem with candor. Maybe it was a chauvinistic impulse on my part, an impulse precipitated by the fact that as she left the room Mary Louise stated, "I'll leave you menfolk to discuss things," rendering her departure somewhat in the tradition of all those old movies and old books where the men gathered together in the drawing room after the big meal, pulled out their cigars, and discussed serious matters while the women and children went off to indulge more frivolous concerns. So at that point I repeated Mr. Ehrlich's allegations about Florida State coeds coming to Griffin Hospital to have abortions.

"I don't want to get into any of that," Mr. Austin said.

"I rather doubt that FSU students came to Granddad for abortions," Joe stated with a slight testiness to his voice. At that point Mary Louise "coincidentally" returned to the room. She agreed. "In this particular setting that couldn't have happened for very long," she insisted. "That would never happen in that era. The powers that be were too racist." I explained why I thought the question was pertinent. Mary Louise and Joe accepted my explanation. Then there was another awkward silence, more awkward, more pregnant than the first one.

"Bill, are you all right?" Mary Louise asked. He said he was fine.

He was fine, I wasn't. I didn't like interviewing someone who was being so careful about what he said. Later on, his parting words to me were: "Now if there's anything else you need to know you just contact Mr. Perry [Joe] and he'll contact me and we'll get it to you." Yet he had told me he didn't want to address the issue of Uncle Joe and abortions. I knew that he had a telephone, so I wondered why I couldn't call him myself if he wasn't feeling pressure to censor himself. I guess his parting words meant if there was anything else I needed to know except anything on the issue of abortions, and probably the property issue as well, on which Joe could decide the validity of his speaking, to call Joe. I also wondered why he called Joe "Mr. Perry," when Joe was far younger than he was. Then again, Joe had called him "Mr. Austin." But that appeared to be out of respect for his greater age. In general, Mr. Austin was clearly the subordinate. When the also younger Mary Louise said, "Bill, are you all right?" it was as if she were a parent addressing a child who might have been psychologically wounded by precipitation of a bad recollection or the encouragement by someone else to do something his parents had told him would be quite naughty to do. I kept in mind that she and Joe were my family; that in the presence of nonfamily members a person is expected to make allowances for members of the family by avoiding harsh judgments he would otherwise make about them. I sensed that Mary Louise

and Joe were struggling to do the same with me, avoiding the conclusion that I was expressing ill will to the memory of my grandmother's oldest brother rather than all the best, keeping in mind
that at the same time I was interested in candid details about his
day-to-day life rather than just legendary stories about him. Thus,
Mary Louise tried to steer the conversation back to a certain level of
pleasantness and respectability with that added candor. She stated
that in the mid-thirties Uncle Joe had a lot of white patients. But
not for abortions. Rather, for a particular public health reason. But
after she told me she was adamant that I not mention that reason in
a book. "You had to keep a record of all those who came for [the
treatment] because the government checked once a month. It was
my responsibility to keep the records. I was about thirteen at the
time, and a lot of whites didn't want their white doctors to know
they were receiving [the treatments]—prominent whites, rich
whites. I was sworn under penalty of death not to tell anyone.
Daddy said he was telling me because I was the person he could
trust the most, that if I told any of it I could get us both killed. The
record book was kept under lock and key. From the superintendent
of schools at that time, to the millionaire who lived on the outskirts
of town with seven homes, all those folks came to him for [the
treatment]."

Of course, the astute reader can figure out what she was referring to. And I didn't have the heart to tell her that, ethically speaking, you can't contribute to an interview for a book or article, and
state that something you said is off the record after you've said it.
You must make that clear before saying what you have to say. And
anyway, why would anyone want to know the types of things they
wanted the world to know about Uncle Joe—the kind of things
written by my aunt Barbara—but not more interesting information
such as this that helped put into perspective his place in the
scheme of how the entire culture down there at that time func-
tioned? Obviously Mary Louise couldn't step back. Maybe if I were
in her shoes I wouldn't be able to either. Maybe it's a badge or
rather a sign of love, that you can't step back. Still, I was determined to step back.

They wanted me to talk with a woman named Eunice Hinds-
Adams. This time, aware of my suspicions about possible censor-

ship with regard to Mr. Austin, they assured me that Ms. Hinds-Adams would speak with me in her home alone. She was seventy-one, three years younger than Mary Louise. In recent years she had become virtually blind. She had been raised by her oldest sister, a woman much older than her, old enough to be her mother. In the 1930s and '40s her sister was principal of the segregated Negro high school, Hutto High, which my maternal grandmother had attended, a position which made her and her family part of the Negro bourgeoisie in Bainbridge. I saw that Ms. Hinds-Adams was a very light-brown-skinned woman with straight hair. In fact, she was so light-skinned that when she carried Joe and Jan around with her when they were small boys, people would stare, wondering what a Caucasian woman was doing taking care of Negro children. The reverse, of course—a Negro woman taking care of Caucasian children—had long been the norm. When they detected that a few drops of black African blood were in her ancestry, which rendered her a Negro in their book, everything was fine again.

Her family traced back one branch of their European mixture. I knew there had to be more, since what happened to them was so common among Afro-Americans, that what separated those who are like them—so much more light-skinned than the rest of us, with straight rather than kinky hair—was that the ancestor with black African heritage who bedded down with her Caucasian master was already mixed and simply further diluting her black African blood. And after slavery her offspring married someone whose family's black African blood had been similarly diluted. And maybe another one of those offspring bedded with a Caucasian man, and their offspring became so light in complexion that they called themselves olive-skinned Caucasians, and their descendants joined the ranks of Caucasian southerners who were able to cross the crucial barrier that made so much of a difference in fates and "passed for white."

The Caucasians in her family's ancestry that they had traced back came from the same country as the men who bequeathed the money to found the medical alma mater of my father and great-uncles: Ireland. They settled the Thomasville area after leaving that country during the potato famine. Eventually they became prosperous enough to purchase a few slaves. Upon growing up their son purchased a slave woman with whom he fell in love and lived with openly and had children. In those days such arrangements were common, as long as there was no marriage, as long as the children from such unions knew that there'd be an inferior place reserved for them—above that of the ordinary dark-skinned Negroes, but below that of the Caucasians, including the lowly Irish, even though in many ways such children were considered better than the poor Caucasians in the area who couldn't afford to own any slaves.

And then after freedom there came the decision to dilute no further their black African ancestry, and to join the ranks of the light-skinned Negro elite and face all the little things that they and their descendants had to deal with from others deemed "Negro." In elementary school the other children gave Eunice hell. By the time she was ten, during recess the other girls would grab her and hold her head underneath the water fountain outside to wet her hair and see if it would kink up, only to discover it wouldn't, causing them jealousy—jealousy that she didn't have to be subjected to the hot combs their mothers ran through their hair to "tame the kinks"; jealousy, because they knew Eunice would be among the most sought-after, the most courted women, receiving the good graces of all manner of men. If they hadn't broken it down to the particulars yet, they would discover later in life that she'd receive the inordinate attention of Negro men eager to possess café-au-lait women, especially those without kinky hair, because, like most men, they found women with hair that wasn't kinky more beautiful, and she'd receive the good graces of Caucasian men looking for mistresses who had that alluring exotic hint of black African sexuality that rendered such women more attractive in the eyes of plenty of men than most Caucasian women as well as most dark-skinned Negro women. And the girls Eunice attended school with were in the beginning stages of the realization of how much different Eunice's fate would be from theirs because of that. So they let Eunice know—the way all Negro women in her situation were made to know beginning in their childhoods—that they burned with envy and worshiped her just like everyone else did. They let her know by giving her what amounted to a backhanded compliment, not only brutally yanking her by her hair to run water on it from the fountain only to discover it wouldn't kink up, but by calling that hair the same thing such hair has always been called by coloreds, Negroes, blacks, African Americans, Afro-Americans: "good hair."

And Eunice and her family took their places at the head of the Negro subculture down there, a notch below Uncle Joe—who was dark-skinned due to the strong, barely diluted black African ancestry of Great-grandmother Griffin—a position that dark-skinned Negro men were able to achieve if they had the will and the drive to overcome the color caste system of the Negro bourgeoisie. And like most other dark-skinned Negro men who reached that level, he married a light-skinned woman, Elaine Johnson, whose hair wasn't straight, but whose father was a prominent dentist in town.

"We called Dr. Griffin 'Dr. Godfather,'" Ms. Hinds-Adams recalled. "Dr. Godfather" was able to protect Mary Louise from so many of the racial slights while she was growing up, just as Eunice's family was able to protect her. Whenever either girl traveled north by train their families purchased roomettes so that they didn't have to ride in the Jim Crow car. Turner's Dress Shop, a Caucasian-owned store in Bainbridge that their families and most Caucasians in Bainbridge shopped in, allowed the two families to try on dresses in a small room in the back, a courtesy allowed no other Negro girls or women in town.

When it was time to register to vote, the adults in Eunice's family, Uncle Joe's family, and a handful of other Negro families in town could pass the reading test administered to Negroes and afford to pay their poll taxes. And when it was time to cast their ballots, they voted at the separate polling facility the town reserved for the few Negroes who voted, which was located in back of the town jail. Rather than fight to abolish the poll tax and the reading test and the separate voting booth in back of the town jail, Joe Griffin did his best to try to get other Negroes in town to become literate enough to pass the test and save their money and pay their poll taxes and register to vote. Every election season he would urge them in meetings he'd hold at the various Negro churches in the area. But he would only go so far at the meetings. Ms. Hinds-Adams recalled one of them. "I was about eighteen at the time, so this was about in 1944. It was at a little place called Macedonian Baptist, behind his house. The church is gone now. But anyway, he was telling the group of people who met that night—and by the way, most of our women did domestic work in these white homes. So he was telling the group of people who met that night, 'Now listen. When you go to work tomorrow, don't go tellin' those white folks that Dr. Griffin had this meeting last night and told us who to vote for, because I am not telling you who to vote for. What I am telling you to do is register and vote.'"

He would only go that far because there was a line that at that time it was felt a Negro, even an influential Negro in that particular area of the South, didn't cross; a line demarcated many years earlier by Booker T. Washington; a line he stayed behind, gritting his teeth, wearing the mask, playing a sophisticated game to ensure his prosperity among Georgia racists, the overwhelming majority of whom eagerly supported candidates who did nothing but address tobacco-chewing Caucasian farmers from courthouse squares every campaign season to see who could out-nigger-nigger-nigger each other, particularly during the Democratic primary since it didn't allow those Negroes who could afford to pay their poll taxes and pass literacy tests to vote. And the Democratic primary was tantamount to a general election since at that time the Republican Party in Georgia, as elsewhere in the South, was insignificant. So, though he could vote in the general election, he couldn't see his way clear to publicly supporting Democratic nominees like Eugene Talmadge, who had a lock on the minds of most Caucasians in all areas of Georgia, except the Atlanta area (especially in rural and small-town counties in which the state's county-unit voting system allowed for inordinate power relative to that of the larger urban areas). Neither could he see his way clear to publicly endorsing non–Democratic Party candidates, if they were on the general election ballot, even if they had more enlightened racial views, since they hadn't a ghost of a chance of winning office.

So Uncle Joe wore a mask the same way he told Herb Dudley in the 1930s that he once wore one as he drove his big new tan Packard through the town of Blakely on his way back to Bainbridge from Stewart County, a time before he became as well known throughout the region as he'd be by the '40s and '50s to Caucasians and Negroes alike. And perhaps he thought about the time he lived and worked in Blakely as a brick mason before going off to medical school, so he was proud to return through the town now, in a big, shiny, fancy Packard. And Mary Louise was at his side and he liked to drive fast, and she liked to encourage her father to drive fast. So he drove fast around the town square. And after they got past the town square a police officer stopped the car. And when the officer walked up to the driver's window he said, "Boy, what are you doin' speedin' through this town in such a nice car?"

"I was just takin' it back to Dr. Griffin in Bainbridge, sir," replied Uncle Joe, leading the officer to think Dr. Griffin was Caucasian.

"Well, you make sure you get it back to him in one piece," the officer told him. "And don't go joy ridin' with it, you hear?"

"Yes, sir, officer," Uncle Joe answered. And the officer let him move on, after which he turned to Mary Louise and said, "We sure fooled him, didn't we, darling?"

"Yes, we did, Daddy," she proudly responded.

But when the coast was clear and he spoke to a small clique he could trust, he'd register his palpable frustration, register the reality that he didn't like sometimes being forced to wear such a mask, like all the other Negroes wore when they left the house each morning. He'd register his frustration by making a joke out of their collective predicament; by using humor, the most readily available medicine to frustrated Negroes down through the years, enabling them to make light of the impossible predicament that being a Negro added up to.

Eunice watched as he did it the day after the voter registration meeting at Macedonian Baptist. She watched as he did it with a small clique of old people who didn't work in southern Caucasian homes.

He said, "I just don't understand my people. I declare, if they ever learn to work together and cooperate we could get a hell of a lot of things done. Now you take, for instance, that group we were meeting with last night. All of them mostly work in the white folks' homes." And you have to understand, back in those days the whites who ran the businesses in town, twelve o'clock every day, they'd hang a sign in the window saying, "Gone to lunch." So everything closed because the whites went to eat this hot lunch that these black women had fixed for them. So Dr. Griffin said, "I told them not to go tellin' those white folks that I told them who to vote for." But what we could do if we stuck together is say, "Okay, now tomorrow when everybody comes home to eat lunch after closing all the businesses at twelve o'clock, we have poison in the food. We'd poison them off. And that would eliminate a lot of our problems." But he said, "You know some nigga would go to work the next morning and just walk around and keep yawning and yawning till Miss Sally would ask, 'Suzy, what's wrong with you? You've just been mopin' around and yawning.' And Suzy would say, 'I'z just sleepy, Miss Sally.' Then Miss Sally would say, 'Why you so sleepy?' And Suzy'd say, 'Well, you see last night Dr. Griffin kept us up all night plannin' on how we gonna poison y'all when y'all eat lunch at twelve o'clock.'"

He probably got his sense of humor from his mother. Great-grandmother Griffin, known far and wide as "Ma Griffin," was infamous for it, known by numerous people in the region because of it. And she called everybody nigga. She was familiar with old-fashioned southern home remedies and during visits with her oldest son would sit in his office waiting room, asking people why they were seeking medical treatment. And after they told her she'd tell them, "Honey you don't need to be goin' to no docta fo' that, you just get yoself some wild root. . . ." Until her son came in and had her put out of the waiting room. One day while watching President Eisenhower on TV in her apartment in the nurses' quarters that Uncle Joe had constructed in back of Griffin Hospital and Clinic—the place she went to live after Great-grandfather died and her granddaughter, Mary Agnes, left Stewart County and moved to Bainbridge to teach school, only to have Great-grandmother decide she was moving down there with her—she convulsed everyone sitting there watching with her when she observed, "Look at that President Eisenhower. I tell you he looks *juuust* like a chicken! Now don't he look like a chicken?"

So from her, Uncle Joe probably inherited his sense of humor and his candor. But his ambition probably came from watching his father. Yet he took it far beyond anything Great-grandfather could have taught. And Ms. Hinds-Adams clearly admired him for that, saying he belonged up there with the greats, that he wasn't afraid of anyone, that he was just a big man in a little pond, that he was way ahead of his time. And she told me of the principal achievement on his part that she was qualified to discuss, one he registered after he became quite old and virtually retired.

Prior to 1971 no Afro-American children in Bainbridge attended preschool. And though she didn't say this, I later figured out why Joseph Griffin did what he did as a result of that, and only did so as late as 1971. By then he was eighty-three years old. He had had plenty of time and money to remedy the situation much earlier. But at that point he knew he was near the end of his life. And a lot of things had happened in Bainbridge. "Dr. Godfather" had registered a lot of triumphs. But he had a lot of skeletons, too. And they weren't in his closet. They were out in the open and well known to people in town. And he knew that it wasn't long before he'd die and discover if there was a heaven and a hell, or you became a free-floating spirit in nature, or you were reincarnated, or you became nothing at all and just no longer existed. So in case there was a heaven—and this happens so often with rich men whose consciences begin to bother them upon realizing they'll soon find out one way or the other—he started donating his wealth to worthy causes. No doubt he figured, "I'll buy my way into heaven." And as part of the buying at the ripe old age of eighty-three he decided to donate $20,000 of the $75,000 it cost to build a nursery school that all the children of Bainbridge could attend, and solicit federal matching funds to help get it built and qualified as an accredited preschool. Ms. Hinds-Adams's oldest sister, retired as high school principal by that time, served as its first director. And when she died in 1973, Eunice returned to Bainbridge after living in the North for twenty-three years teaching high school and took over administration of the preschool.

She took over what had been named the Joseph H. Griffin Educational Complex upon completion of the building, and existed under the auspices of Nelson Chapel A.M.E. church, where thirty-four years earlier the Klan had come and spoken after making its donation at the invitation of Joseph Griffin. Its preschool teachers were certified by Albany State College. They taught an enrollment of forty-three preschoolers, virtually all of them Afro-American. And she recalled how one day a group of people, believed to be local Afro-Americans, came one night and painted over "Joseph H. Griffin" on the sign. So they had to have the defacing removed and Joseph Griffin's name restored. And she recalled how his picture hung in the dining room of the complex. But some Afro-American took it down. "And every time I put it back up, someone would take it down again."

When he donated $20,000 to have the complex built, many congregants at Nelson Chapel said he was just doing it to get a write-off on his income taxes; these were the same people who had been among those who had gone to him as patients. And every time they said that, Ms. Hinds-Adams came to his defense, comparing his benevolence to that of Henry Ford, and Andrew Carnegie and John D. Rockefeller, who, of course, were men far wealthier than Joseph H. Griffin, and who had a lot of skeletons in their closets, too, though Ms. Hinds-Adams didn't refer to their skeletons or Uncle Joe's skeletons, and maybe didn't even think of them the way I did as a result of my interview with Mr. Ehrlich. Or maybe she did think of them, and was being like Mr. Austin and simply censoring herself.

"Why do you think they did that?" I insincerely asked her, thinking I probably already knew the answer to that question.

"Because they were jealous of the man. Sometimes we are our own worst enemies."

And I was thrown for a loop because at that point, considering everything I had learned in thirty-nine years of living, I couldn't figure out who might have been the worst enemy. I knew who she was saying was sometimes the worst enemy. But I wondered if the real enemy in that case was Uncle Joe, or the coloreds, Negroes, blacks, African Americans, Afro-Americans everywhere, in Bainbridge, Atlanta, New York City . . . who, we both were aware, act more helpless than they really are, or who become so jealous of anyone deemed black who tries to do anything constructive, or who so easily and commonly engage in self-defeating behavior like proposals to arm ourselves when, as Saul Alinsky once observed about the Black Panthers, they know damn well the other side has the vast majority of weapons; or the ones who speak English like they're stupid and try to find pride in it by calling it "ebonics"; or the ones who attend church and pray as though Jesus will work a magic in Afro-American lives that will forgo the need for an Afro-American commitment to intellectualism and confident self-development not tied to religious superstition; or the ones who deep down inside know how illogical it is to expect a people to organize themselves purely around skin color and the mutual revulsion of others due to the fact they have at least one noticeable drop of the ancestry of people from a subcontinent who were backward largely because they were separated from the rest of mankind by the vast Sahara desert, and along their coast didn't have protective ports, or navigable rivers coursing through the interior of the land, which would have facilitated the construction of ships and boats, causing trade both intracontinentally and across continents, enabling them to advance to the point where they coalasced into lasting, larger nations on their own; people who didn't even know they were one race and thought of themselves instead as a multitude of ethnicities, until European explorers told them they were "black," which was a lack of conceptualization that made it so easy for them to sell each other, one ethnicity against another, into slavery; their American descendants, the coloreds, Negroes, blacks, African Americans, Afro-Americans who know deep down that there isn't another "ethnicity" in the U.S. who thinks of itself as one, based on as flimsy a definition of ethnicity (without even a unique language such as Latinos have in the U.S.), and so who logically engage in self-defeating behavior, but do so subconsciously, causing those of us who like to believe we are progressive to shake our heads and make comments similar to the one Uncle Joe made the day after the voter registration meeting in the church behind his house in Bainbridge in 1944.

"It wasn't until I got older and more experienced with our people that I really understood what he was talking about when he said that," Ms. Hinds-Adams stated after telling me about the joke. And it wasn't until a few years before I reached the age I was during the interview with her that I was able to appreciate such a joke, too, and laugh very hard after she recalled it for me. And now, after telling me about some Afro-Americans in Bainbridge painting over Uncle Joe's name and refusing to allow his portrait to hang in the Joseph H. Griffin Educational Complex, and questioning his sincerity in spearheading its construction, given what, by then, I had been told by Mr. Ehrlich, I wondered: Was the worst enemy Uncle Joe with regard to them, or them with regard to him, or all of us with regard to ourselves and each other?

I decided that there was one man who might know the answer. Martin Luther King, Jr., had called him "my wild man, my Castro." And he had grown up thirteen miles from Bainbridge, near a smaller town called Attapulgus. He went on to serve his country in World

War II. And a few years later he attended college at Morris Brown in Atlanta, where my great-uncle was a trustee for many years, and where he donated significant sums of money—services that eventually resulted in Morris Brown naming a brand-new science building after him. The man who I thought might have the answer to my question had gone to college there, only to eventually become Martin Luther King's "wild man" after growing up on a large farm in Decatur County owned by his maternal grandfather, Turner Williams, one of the four Negroes in Decatur County with sizable farms. He took the name of his mother's side of the family because for his first twenty-eight years of life he didn't know who his father was. His mother had been blind and died while giving birth to him, after becoming pregnant by a fellow blind student in residence at the school for the blind that she had run away from. Which is why he was raised by his maternal grandparents. And when anyone in the Williams family got sick they went to Joseph Howard Griffin for treatment.

While serving his country in World War II, Hosea Williams received head wounds in Germany during combat with the all-Negro 41st Infantry. Then he returned to Bainbridge and worked for a while before going off to college. After college he obtained a master's degree in chemistry. He became a full-time chemist, one of the pioneer Negro scientists in the federal Department of Agriculture, where he tested pyrethrum and other pesticides. When he first came to Martin Luther King's attention in 1963 he was not only an Agriculture Department chemist but a local activist in Savannah, promoting voter registration. He also recruited students for King's citizenship schools located near Savannah, run by a noble, intelligent, brave woman named Septima Clark, who thoroughly inculcated within him the concept of nonviolence.

Hosea Williams—like Joe Griffin during every political campaign in the 1940s—had plenty of experience trying to arouse Negroes from church pulpits. But by then times had changed. In the 1940s there had been no Montgomery bus boycott, no Freedom Rides, no lunch counter sit-ins. There had been no Martin Luther King, Jr., conducting a searing anti–Jim Crow campaign for all the nation to see on television, only to be shocked by a cruel local sheriff's reaction in which he okayed the release of angry police dogs who dug into the flanks of Negro youths, while fire hoses sprayed clothes-ripping jets of water upon them as though they were nothing but a collection of unwanted vermin. But all of that had taken place by 1963. And that same year, a few months after the Birmingham campaign took place, Williams arose to speak from the pulpit of Savannah's historic First Baptist Church, from where, after William Tecumseh Sherman's army had devastated Georgia during his historic "march to the sea" and he presented the city of Savannah as a Christmas present to President Lincoln, the Union Army general first read of the federal government's proposed plan to provide the newly freed slaves with "forty acres and a mule" (a plan it never carried out). Nearly one hundred years later Williams arose in the pulpit at First Baptist and convinced a local Negro seaport gangster named "Big Lester" Hankerson to put down his two .38-caliber pistols on a collection table in front of Martin Luther King and embrace nonviolence; to finally join in pressuring the federal government to live up to its obligation to right the wrongs that had caused men like Hankerson and Joseph H. Griffin to often use individualized and ruthless methods to pursue their success. And that year Williams became the leader of the Savannah movement to end Jim Crow, after which he joined King's SCLC full-time. He was at King's side in April 1968 immediately after he was hit by an assassin's bullet in Memphis, and he pulled one of the mules harnessed to the rickety wagon that bore King's body during his historic funeral. I thought Hosea Williams might know the answer to my question. So I headed for Atlanta to see him.

He calls the organization he now runs "Feed the Hungry and Homeless." Its offices are in a mangy storefront on Peachtree Street in the shadows of Sun Trust Tower, one of the tallest buildings on the Atlanta skyline. Three blocks down the street is renowned architect John Portman's first hotel, the design of which kicked off the national craze for hostelries with atriums. As is typical in the city's downtown (as opposed to prosperous Buckhead), such architectural signs of progress are right around the corner from signs that for plenty of Atlantans economic prosperity has passed them by. And Hosea Williams has cast his lot among such people, forgoing the opportunities for wealth pursued by former King lieutenants such as Andrew Young and Jesse Jackson after King's death.

When you call his home and get his answering machine his recorded voice tells you that he is unbought. Upon meeting him you encounter a man much heavier now—on his body, beneath his eyes, and on his cheeks—than in the photos of him next to King. A hint of disappointment in the way things have turned out for poor people now that the movement is over seems to hang over him. He wears a large medallion around his neck with Martin Luther King, Jr., in profile. "I've always been, I guess, a peculiar person," he began as we sat in his office decorated with civil rights memorabilia. "I was always a standout, a leader." He recalled that in Decatur County, Bainbridge was the big cheese.

In the late '30s and early '40s all the country folks would come to town on Saturday. And back in those days we had what you call juke joints. They sold sandwiches—hot dogs and hamburgers—and pop and beer. And the picoloes [a term used back then for what's commonly known as jukeboxes] were very popular back in those days, they were at the peak of their popularity. And country folks would come to town on Saturday and go to these juke joints, have sandwiches, drink Cokes and beer and dance. Black people did a lot of dancing back in those days. And I can remember there was always something magnetic about Dr. Griffin's home. I tell this story a lot of times. I always wanted to be up. I never wanted to be down. And Saturday after Saturday, even though my grandfather had this farm out in the country, we were part of the masses. I can remember time and time again I was just inspired, and I would leave the juke joint—and I was one of the better dancers—and I'd leave the juke joint which was only about three blocks from the main street where blacks congregated, the main street that went through Bainbridge past the town square. And I used to sneak out—at least I didn't tell anybody I was going—I'd leave all the partying and I'd walk down to Dr. Griffin's home and one or two kids would be playing in that yard with all its beautiful grass, and all these swings and the big cars, which we didn't have even though we had a farm, and I would walk around that house and yard which covered a block, and my greatest desire in life was just to be invited inside that fence and sit down in some of those lawn chairs. And the kids would look at me funny like I didn't belong, and I'd walk around that house and then I would get some kind of feeling, then go on back down to the juke joint. For years that thing lingered with me. It inspired me to really want to be somebody. It really gave me a deep inspiration.

"Dr. Griffin was an icon," he assured me. "He was the most respected and I guess considered the top black leader in not only Bainbridge, but several counties surrounding Decatur. . . ."

When I first got in touch with him I sensed that Hosea Williams was under the impression that what I wanted to hear were such tales of glory and nothing else. Now that we were face-to-face I told him that ever since I was a little boy I'd heard all about Joe Griffin being an icon. I knew all of that. And I was genuinely proud to hear that my grandmother's oldest brother had been a catalyst for the ambition of one of our principal civil rights heroes to be somebody, just as he had been a catalyst for me years later. But I also wanted complete candor. So I told Williams that. "He was very economic-minded," Williams continued after I made that clear. "He certainly owned a lot of homes not only in Bainbridge but in that section of Georgia, period. He was accused of taking some homes from people he shouldn't have."

I encouraged more candor by revealing, "Some people have told me that he was one of the principal abortion doctors for that area."

"Back in that time, no question. That was one of the places you went to if you got a girl pregnant. You'd take her to Dr. Griffin. He was in control, I'll tell you that. And that black school superintendent was in control, too."

I realized he had to have been referring to Ms. Hinds-Adams's oldest sister.

"When you say he was in control, what do you mean?" I asked.

"Well, I would say everybody feared Dr. Griffin," he said.

I was telling some kids, I've been in jail. I was arrested in the civil rights movement as Dr. King's field general, 135 times as a leader of the front-line soldiers. But the first time I was ever arrested in life was when Dr. Griffin had me arrested. What we were doing, me and a buddy of mine, we were going with these two women who took care of Dr. Griffin's hospital at night. And we'd go up there, didn't raise no hell or nothin', but we would be hugging and kissing, and dancing, we weren't making any noise. We were wrong for going up in a hospital to court girls. And somehow Dr. Griffin found out we were going up there. And one night we went up there and he was waiting parked outside. But we didn't see him. He had us arrested. And that record is still in the books in Bainbridge. Now they didn't convict us, but the judge took us in there and gave us a tongue-lashing. The judge said that he wasn't going to fine us or keep us in jail. But just to satisfy Dr. Griffin the records show that we were convicted. The girls were doing their jobs, they weren't overlooking anybody, but that man sure had us put in jail. He had that kind of power. He was feared. He had that control, honest to God. A lot of people lost their homes to him. You didn't mess with Dr. Griffin. If you did you were going to lose. It was almost like getting in the ring with Muhammad Ali. You mess with Dr. Griffin, you were going to lose. And my thing was when I returned to town after the war I got a job with the white Griffins. But even being in with them you still feared Dr. Griffin. In my little town we were not allowed to meet white people on the sidewalk. In Attapulgus if whites were coming down the sidewalk you got off that sidewalk until white folks passed. And if you were a black male and had a hat on and there was a white woman, you took that damn hat off. Still, through all that oppression that man [Dr. Griffin] was powerful, brother.

When Williams said that, I felt that my instincts about why so many people had been reticent, about the lack of response from local Afro-Americans to my newspaper ad, the carefulness of Mary Louise and Joe and Mr. Austin, and possibly Ms. Hinds-Adams, had been right on the mark. Yet I also felt pride that in such an atmosphere a member of my family could find a way to become so powerful. But I was troubled, too. I had begun investigating the security deed records down at the Decatur County courthouse, looking into people who took them out on their homes and other property to pay their medical bills to my uncle. So I pressed Williams further about the issue.

"He owned homes everywhere," Williams answered. "But he took them homes. Dr. Griffin would wait on you, you signed your house up and that bill grew so fast and so large it was impossible to pay it off and he foreclosed just like that. That was the guy you looked up to. That was the guy you didn't oppose. But I can see people now, particularly my age, and I'm seventy-two, who would have some fear of saying anything negative about him."

CHAPTER 9

I searched underneath rocks and between crevices, figuratively speaking, to reconstruct what it could have possibly been like for a Negro man to wield such power in the Jim Crow South. Something inside of me was desperate to know, as if my genes were driving me to find the answer; as if some part of me, that which refused to surrender to defeat of ambition, the extremely aggressive part that prevented me from circumscribing my goals because of racism, depended on it. I asked myself, What if the answer meant writing another book where I was accused by some of vilifying a fellow Afro-American, this time my own relative? And something inside of me said it didn't matter because ultimately the issue didn't boil down to the artifice, the façade of race. It boiled down to discovering what a human being could be driven to do when he was cornered by race, but still harbored tenacious ambition. Which meant that race was a handicap. But the handicap didn't define the man. What defined the man was how he attempted to bypass the handicap, or abolish it as an obstacle to what he wanted to achieve. I felt that I had attempted a similar objective distance in my Panther book. So what if there were those who insisted on simply reducing the issue to one dimension, as if the dimension ruled everything? It went far beyond race. It went to the very marrow of the human condition. And no matter how many people try to deny it, so much of what Afro-Americans have ultimately been driven to do is central to the essence of being human. I told myself as I had so many times before that our predicament was/is the most genuinely American; our stories, no matter how comic or tragic, were/are the stories behind what has made American society what it is. To hell with those who can't see why telling the truth about our lives is so important, and why there is so much to be learned from our truths.

In the process of searching I discovered that as World War II began, indeed Joseph Griffin was one of Decatur County's biggest landlords. But contrary to the image my aunt Barbara's book paints of him as a benevolent man, as a landlord he demonstrated an eagerness to make as much money off the tenants he rented to as he could. In January 1942 the federal government passed an emergency rent control measure designed to hold down rents charged to working-class housing tenants because it had also passed an emergency wage freeze for the duration of the war. The Emergency Price Control Act of 1942 established certain maximum rents in locales designated Defense-Rental Areas. Joseph Griffin owned a number of houses in the sectors of Bainbridge designated as such. And by 1942 complaints about the rents he charged and the services he provided were common at the local rent director's office.

On March 1 of that year he rented a four-bedroom house at 611 Cemetery Street containing a kitchen, front and back porches, and one bathroom to a Mr. William Smith and seven other adults. He charged each of the adults different rents and apparently rented out the living room as well as the bedrooms. Mr. John Smith and his wife paid $1.25 per week for one room. Mr. Will Hayes and his wife paid $1.25 per week for their room. Ms. Winnie Scott paid fifty cents per week for her room. And Mrs. Herbert Slappet paid fifty cents per week for hers. But Uncle Joe charged William Smith and his wife a rent of $2.50 per week for their room.

When the Emergency Price Control measures went into effect, henceforth for the duration of the war the maximum rent William Smith and his wife could be charged was frozen at $2.50 per week. Yet that same week Joe Griffin demanded and collected from William Smith $4.00 per week, in effect increasing his rent by more than 60 percent. William Smith reported him to the rent director's office. Such reports would become frequent.

Later that same month he rented a home to John W. Payne at 320 Calhoun Street, a six-room dwelling. The rent he charged was $30 per month, which Payne paid for the next three months. At the end of that time period, Uncle Joe increased the rent to $37.50 per month, collecting that amount from Payne until March 1, 1943. The rate was considerably higher than the rent charged for comparable dwellings in Bainbridge. Meanwhile, on his own initiative, Donald R. Bryan, the area rent director, investigated the maximum legal rent for 320 Calhoun Street and determined that when the Emergency Price Control measures went into effect, the maximum legal rent for the dwelling was $20 per month. Thus as of October 1, 1942, and thereafter, that was still the maximum legal rent Joe Griffin could charge a tenant for that dwelling. Allegedly Bryan informed him and his tenant, Mr. Payne. So when Payne paid his rent the following month he paid $20. Uncle Joe refused to accept that amount. Payne wouldn't pay him any more money than that. So on June 18, 1943, Uncle Joe moved to have Payne forcibly evicted. The warrant was served by Decatur County Sheriff W. J. Catledge. Payne had six days to leave.

This, too, was a violation of the legal statutes. According to the law any tenant being forcibly removed from a dwelling had to receive ten days' prior written notice before being evicted. And in the eyes of the law Uncle Joe had no legal grounds for removing Payne anyway. The area rent director immediately moved to have the eviction order stayed. He was successful. But Joe Griffin wouldn't budge from his position that he had a right to charge whatever rent he wanted in the cases of both Smith and Payne and anyone else he rented to. His rationale was that rent control was unconstitutional (my editor at the *Wall Street Journal*, Bob Bartley, would have loved that about him).

From the perspective of today, minus all the particulars, it's hard to determine everything that motivated Joe Griffin to act as he did or determine all the motives of Mr. Bryan, the area rent director. It appears that Joseph Howard Griffin, the allegedly benevolent, paternalistic sage of Afro-American Bainbridge, was simply being avaricious. But was Donald R. Bryan, who was also a local judge, giving a wealthy Negro a hard time because he was wealthy and a Negro? Of course that wouldn't excuse my uncle's behavior, which didn't warrant any excuse. It warranted corrective action by the aggrieved, which was exactly what happened.

Both Payne and Smith took him to federal court and tried to recover rental overcharges and penalties that could be levied on a landlord to the tune of fifty dollars per week for every week a tenant overpaid his rent. The lawyer my uncle hired to defend himself was a Caucasian man who would become mayor of Bainbridge later during this same Jim Crow era. And in his case, A. B. Conger did what defense lawyers often do. He tried to break the truth into so many confusing shards that the jury would call the shards "reasonable doubt." He claimed my uncle never received any notices from

Bryan's office telling him that he was overcharging his tenants. He tried to cast doubt that Bryan's secretary, Elizabeth Roberts, actually mailed my uncle the letters telling him that he had to abide by the dictates of rent control or face penalties.

"I'm sure I mailed the notice," Roberts insisted. She stated that her office sent out many letters each day and that the notice to Griffin was among them.

"Yes, I know you are sure," stated Conger. "But I'm talking about you don't remember independently this particular envelope, and particularly dropping it in the post office? You do not remember that, do you?"

"No, sir, but I know I did."

Conger accused Roberts's boss of being prejudiced against Griffin because of litigation Griffin was involved in over a number of years, and because of his wealth.

"Now, Judge [Area Rent Director], Dr. Griffin owns a number of houses in Bainbridge, doesn't he?" Conger asked.

"I imagine sixty or seventy-five," replied Bryan.

Conger alleged that Bryan had plenty of opportunities to tell Griffin in person that he was overcharging rent because Griffin was often in Bryan's office.

"He was there several times," agreed Bryan. "He came up there with you in response to one of these cases one time."

"You knew that I represented the doctor?"

"I did not know you represented him in all cases."

"You never made any mention to the doctor or me in this case about [the notice]?"

"I will be frank with you, in some cases where we have a great deal of trouble with a landlord, we feel that it is not expedient to notify them."

"Well, Judge, in good faith, don't you believe that where an order of yours would subject a man to a penalty of fifty dollars a week and him living right in your same town and coming to your office frequently, that it would have been your duty to have told him about it?"

"Ordinarily, but when we have a great deal of trouble with a landlord we do not feel it our duty to keep them out of trouble."

Then Conger attempted to establish that Bryan held animosity for Joe Griffin above and beyond any rental issue:

"Isn't your byword for him [Griffin] 'son-of-a-bitch'?"

"No, sir."

"You have never called him that?"

"I don't know whether I have or not. I might have."

"As a matter of fact, your feeling toward Dr. Griffin is not very good?"

"Just as good as toward any colored person."

"You have cursed him many, many times?"

"I might have."

"Not might have, but you have?"

"How do you know that?"

"I have heard you."

"It is nothing unusual."

"Would you say it is not unusual?"

"It is owing to what color he is."

The court decided against Joe Griffin, and he was forced to repay rental overcharges and penalties.

As for how he acquired so much property, one way was that as early as 1920 he convinced patients to sign over real estate they owned as collateral for paying the medical bills they owed him. Then he gave them a set monthly payment schedule on the bills, charging them 8 percent interest annually until they paid them off. He was thirty-two years old and had found his answer to the anger he often felt because he couldn't be remunerated the way he wished to be for the medical care he provided to a patient base that was generally much poorer than those his Caucasian counterparts cared for. That answer meant that patients who owned property were charged higher fees than poor patients, and would meet that payment schedule if they couldn't afford to pay right away, a policy that con-trasted with the benevolence allegedly advised by Great-grandfather, and described in my aunt's book. Or maybe it didn't contrast. "When a man comes to you with all he has, you accept it," Great-grandfather is supposed to have said. Apparently, Uncle Joe did ex-actly that.

No other physician in the county—and from 1919 to 1970 roughly twenty-nine physicians practiced in Decatur County—had patients deed their property as collateral on their bills to anywhere near the extent that Joseph Griffin did. According to Dr. Henry

Bridges, now the oldest living physician in Bainbridge, the only time other physicians ever did such a thing to any degree was during the Great Depression when money was scarce. And my investigations at the county courthouse confirmed that. Uncle Joe did it throughout his practice. Altogether I counted 129 security deeds in Decatur County alone taken out with him, along with numerous cases where people simply sold him their homes for "one dollar and other valuable considerations," most cases taking place in the 1920s, '30s, and '40s, in some years as many as two cases per month.

Bruce Kirbo is a local lawyer whose family has long been prominent in Bainbridge (his uncle Charles Kirbo, now deceased, was the lawyer advising many clients on legal matters regarding my great-uncle, until he moved to Atlanta to practice and eventually become President Jimmy Carter's most trusted adviser). According to Kirbo, when a person sold his home for "one dollar and other valuable considerations," often that meant he was satisfying a debt he owed by virtually giving his home to the person he owed money to. All told, over a fifty-year period there were 268 property purchases by or collateralizations to Joe Griffin in Decatur County, to say nothing of the surrounding counties, confirming something that had been noted in the 1961 *Pittsburgh Courier* article, though an overstatement—that his total real estate holdings were so vast that it was impossible to properly assess them (unless, of course, you had his assistance or were willing to track down every deed in every county in the Georgia-Florida-Alabama tristate area he could have possibly owned land in, as well as property outside of the area that he purchased, a process that would take quite a long time). But the *Courier* article made no mention of how he acquired so much property.

About one-third of the Decatur County transactions were real estate purchases for legitimate amounts of money, many involving property he successfully bid on at public auction. And within that third were also shrewd real estate deals involving commercial buildings he purchased, as well as one wedding gift of the lot his house was built on, from his father-in-law, J. W. F. Johnson, in 1920. But numerous were the transactions described as follows.

On April 18, 1923, Mack Humphrey placed in collateral a modest tract of land he owned in West Bainbridge to secure a $300 debt he owed to Joseph Griffin. He was to pay the debt plus 8 percent interest in six equal installments, starting on May 1, 1923, and ending with full payment by October 1 of that year. He never satisfied the debt and Uncle Joe acquired his property. On September 21, 1927, Ms. Lilla Sweet placed two acres of land in collateral to secure a $344.65 debt to Joe Griffin. The debt was payable in thirty-four monthly installments at an interest rate of 8 percent per year, meaning full payment was due in almost three years. Yet she didn't satisfy the debt until 1945, when she paid it to Uncle Joe's wife, who had paid off Ms. Sweet's debt to Uncle Joe on May 29, 1931, then held her property in collateral until Ms. Sweet was able to pay her back fourteen years later. In other words, the record of Joe Griffin's foreclosure on property due to the inability of patients to pay off their debts was quite mixed. Sometimes when they discovered they couldn't pay, it was apparent that they went to his wife, who interceded on their behalf and paid off their debt to him, after which he signed over their property to her and she allowed them to successfully meet a longer payment schedule. But in many cases he, too, allowed them to pay off their debt long after they were scheduled to. One debt incurred in 1927 was as high as $1,460, which was supposed to be paid over six years, but was actually paid in eight. In some cases he allowed patients to pay him several years later than they were supposed to. For instance, in January 1932 a man named Andrew A. L. Jackson placed property in collateral for a $200 debt that was to be paid by November of that year, which he didn't do. Uncle Joe allowed him eight more years to satisfy the debt with interest. In November 1933 I. S. Flugeon placed thirty-one acres in collateral on a $60 debt to be paid four months later. He didn't meet the obligation. Again, Uncle Joe didn't foreclose. Instead he allowed him to pay it off with interest twenty-two years down the road.

In plenty of cases, though, indeed as Mr. Ehrlich and Hosea Williams stated and is obvious in the first example, he foreclosed and acquired the property of those unable to meet their obligations. On August 28, 1929, Georgia Eubanks and Gurley Guy deeded their home to Uncle Joe to secure a debt of $168 with the understanding that if he foreclosed Ms. Eubanks could live in the house until she died. When they were unable to satisfy the debt he foreclosed, allowing her to stay in the home. On July 18, 1921, Annie and Clem Jackson collateralized one and a half acres of land, plus "one boy horse mule named Pete about twelve years old, one horse wagon bought of John Salow, one top buggy . . . and one black mare named

Daisy" to secure a $325 debt they ultimately were unable to pay. So all of the aforementioned were acquired by Uncle Joe. Perhaps the most interesting security deed was taken out by Clifton Burney in 1943. To secure a debt of $4,485 to Joe Griffin, he put up for collateral 125 acres of land, plus one four-year-old black mare mule named Maud; one six-year-old black mare mule named Emma; one eight-year-old brown horse mule named Dan; two four-year-old Jersey milk cows; two Jersey calves; five brown sows; a tractor; and all the farm tools, machinery, and equipment of every kind that he had placed in collateral with the Bainbridge Production and Credit Association, to which he satisfied his debt. But he never satisfied his debt to Uncle Joe and apparently Uncle Joe acquired all of the aforementioned.

So "economic-minded" was he that in April 1931, when Great-grandfather wanted his operating room set consisting of two cabinets and all of the instruments it contained, one office desk, two L. C. Smith typewriters, two hospital beds, eight chairs, medical books, and one Burroughs adding machine, Uncle Joe sold them to him in a purchase that included the same home formerly owned by Georgia Eubanks and Gurley Guy, all for the sum of $2,000, and in the midst of the Great Depression, when plenty of men, both Negro and Caucasian, roamed Decatur County searching for any work they could find.

It appeared that Joe Griffin was every bit as much the businessman as he was the physician—and maybe even more so. And what now amazed me was the apparently cunning manner in which he had discovered a way to prosper in a region rightfully characterized by others as an absolute living hell for Negroes. It was obvious that he had taken Booker T. Washington's philosophy to heart, his philosophy that nothing was more important for Negroes than property ownership, that with property ownership and the opening of businesses crucial to the southern economy the other massive problems they faced in the region would eventually melt away. And during a speech to students at Fort Valley State College in the spring of 1964, Joe Griffin revealed additional sources of his obsession with property ownership. "Several years ago I read an editorial in the *New York Evening Journal* by the late Arthur Brisbane, the famous Hearst editor, advising Americans: 'Purchase a corner on a busy street. Keep it and it will keep you,'" he told the students.

"Others have said that the best investment on earth is the earth itself. My father told us: 'The man who owns the land will control the community.'" That he was reading a New York City newspaper from his perch in south Georgia already set him apart not only from most Negroes but most people in the area, period. Continuing his speech, he told the Fort Valley students:

> Cheap land in south Georgia represents the last frontier in our state. New industry, something which every city and country is trying to obtain, must be built upon the land. We have water, power, labor, both skilled and unskilled, for converting crude material into the finished products. We must prepare ourselves to come forward as the progress of this frontier moves forward. The opportunities are here, but if we Negroes do not prepare we will not be able to participate in those opportunities.

Throughout his years in Bainbridge he had done his best to participate in the opportunities. And his efforts paid off with an entrée and privilege not enjoyed by other Negroes in the area. But as Paul Kwilecki, one of Bertram Ehrlich's first cousins, later assured me, that entrée also came at a heavy price: the development of a reputation among most people in the town as a physician obsessed with money, determined to amass as much of it as possible. And at the very least a perusal of available records revealed that he was quite stingy with money, quite attached to the notion that money was not a matter to be treated lightly. As a result his benevolence didn't extend nearly as far as my aunt's book made it seem, as the following case dramatizes.

In the summer of 1952 Pilgrim Life Insurance Company filed a civil suit against Joseph Griffin and H. G. Pughsley, a resident of Washington, D.C., because upon the death of Mr. Pughsley's mother, Lucy Pughsley, a resident of Bainbridge, on July 8, 1951, Mr. Pughsley was the written beneficiary of her life insurance policy paying $500. However, the insurance company didn't know who was the proper recipient of the money because Joe Griffin claimed he was the beneficiary instead, due to the fact that beginning in February 1933, Mr. Pughsley requested that he pay premiums on the policy since neither Mr. Pughsley nor his mother could

afford to. Uncle Joe stated that from that date until Lucy Pughsley's death, he had paid a total of $534.80 in premiums, meaning
that as a result there was a constructive change in the beneficiary
of the policy. Mr. Pughsley didn't agree. He expressed surprise that
Dr. Griffin would make a claim that he was the new effective beneficiary because he paid the premiums. Charles Kirbo represented
the insurance company. No record survives of how the case was ultimately decided. And at the very least it is obvious Joe Griffin was
trying to recover a financial loss, confirming once more that indeed
he was, as Hosea Williams stated, extremely interested in the economic bottom line.

But the question remains: Why did so many people still go to
Joseph Griffin as a physician? For twenty-five years there was one
other Negro physician in town, Dr. E. A. R. Lord. Dr. Lord opened
his own small clinic in Bainbridge, though it was much smaller
than Griffin Hospital and Clinic. And Mr. Ehrlich stated that in his
opinion as a pharmacist servicing all the physicians and patients in
town, Dr. Lord wasn't a very good physician. On October 30, 1960,
he was killed in an automobile accident. "His daughter came down
saying she was writing a book about him," Mr. Ehrlich recalled.
"But she didn't interview me, she interviewed my uncle, who was a
physician, too. He told her some things she didn't want to hear. She
was trying to prove that Dr. Lord was murdered, but there wasn't a
damn thing to it. I know exactly where it happened. He ran a stop
sign and he got hit. That's all there was to it. But his daughter was
trying to prove it was a black/white deal and the police got him. But
that didn't happen."

Sigo Ehrlich, Mr. Ehrlich's uncle who practiced as a pediatrician
in Bainbridge, told Dr. Lord's daughter some things she didn't want
to hear, obviously things that burst her family's bubble of legends
about him. *Webster's Dictionary* states that a legend is "a story coming down from the past; one popularly accepted as historical but
not verifiable." I had tried to verify the legends told by my family
about my great-uncle, and had heard stories buttressing those legends as well as accounts from Bertram Ehrlich and Hosea Williams
that contrasted with many of them. I searched available records,
finding that they confirmed much of what the two men said, proving that the family legends came up short, as most family legends

do to some extent. But I sensed there was another aspect of his life's story, one that was intangibly lost in the dustbin of history, a missing piece that renders records reliable only to a degree.

There had to be some magnetic something that kept patients returning to him, even after Bainbridge Memorial Hospital opened its basement to Negro patients and Riverside Hospital decided to open a neighboring house for their care. Perhaps it was his surgical skill and diagnostic acumen during the heyday of his career. Perhaps it was the spacious cleanliness of Griffin Hospital and Clinic (I uncovered plenty of evidence that this legend was true) and the relative respect with which they were treated by him and his staff compared to their treatment back then from Caucasian physicians and their support personnel. And what role did his services in the region as one of the principal abortionists play?

CHAPTER 10

As I continued investigating, I thought of how there are a few things we can be certain of besides death, taxes, and the need to eat, drink, and dispose of bodily wastes. We can also be certain that we will always find a way to enjoy ourselves by ingesting, inhaling, penetrating, or being penetrated by substances that will alter our moods and/or quench thirsts or hungers unrelated to staying alive. And the methods we will pursue principally include drinking alcoholic beverages, smoking some sort of plant, taking drugs, and having sex.

Sex is our most desired and universal means of enjoyment, often with more than one partner because often at some point having it with just one person becomes boring. Or the attraction to a second person is so strong that it can't be resisted. Or the pressure placed upon a woman to have sex with someone she otherwise wouldn't consider having it with is applied so strongly, then considered by the target of desire due to her need to put food on the table and keep a roof over her head and/or for her children's welfare, or due to her desire to advance her career, so that very often she surrenders to the request. And the ability to coerce a woman into having sex for reasons of job security, or because of the financial security the seeker can provide her, is a much-sought-after aphrodisiac that has ultimately been behind the actions of plenty of men who ruthlessly exploit and subordinate other people to their wills in order to amass the wealth that will enable them to enjoy sex with whomever they please. Yet the one overriding risk toyed with when a man penetrates a woman who hasn't yet reached menopause involves the body's not always controllable means of reproducing.

Almost as long as people have been having sex there has been someone around willing to try to terminate an unwanted pregnancy. The person providing abortions is probably engaging in a professional service older than prostitution. Prostitutes, abortionists, gambling hustlers, drug dealers, liquor distillers: In most societies all are assured of ready markets for their services. And the person willing to provide any of them need only have the mental where-withal to withstand the societal ostracism that at some point has accompanied or still accompanies the providers, as well as the means to pay for protection from law-enforcement officers and/or otherwise arrange for members of some other organized protective body to ensure their ability to do business.

As is true with so much of what is now legal or still illegal in American society, federal, state, and local governments initially recognized that there are certain services human beings are so desperate for that the desire cannot be adequately policed. At one point it was legal to consume cocaine, marijuana, and a variety of other drugs now illegal. Still, it is very easy to obtain such drugs from dealers who have no problem paying off law-enforcement officers throughout the country eager to pad their salaries. It was illegal for a short period of time to consume alcohol, after which the underground market for such beverages became so great that once more it had to be legalized. No one takes seriously antiprostitution laws except residents and merchants in neighborhoods that don't want prostitution flagrantly conducted where they are. Gambling has flourished legally in Nevada, Atlantic City, and now in a host of other locales desperate to cash in on the human urge for quick riches because their industrial or agricultural economies have withered away. And for even longer it has flourished illegally through numbers rackets and illegal casinos of all kinds throughout the country. And then there has been the history of abortion.

For most of the twentieth century it was illegal to abort an unborn child anywhere within the U.S. But the rush to make the practice illegal didn't begin until the mid-nineteenth century. Prior to that time anyone attempting to abort a fetus up to four months old had few problems with the law, and anyone attempting to do so after four months only encountered a few more difficulties in some places. In that era abortions were commonly performed and abortion services even advertised in newspapers, and offered by a wide variety of laymen and medical practitioners, who, as was made clear in an earlier chapter, were themselves very poorly regulated until the early part of the twentieth century. During that period of time women commonly attempted to induce abortions themselves with a variety of herbs and drugs they either purchased from an apothecary or ordered by mail. The drive to criminalize the procedure didn't reach full swing until the 1880s, when Anglo-Saxons felt threatened by the massive wave of new emigrants from Eastern Europe and the Mediterranean. If we abort our children, the thinking apparently went, then we will quicken the day when "the mongrels" will have overrun us in population.

But as was true in the campaign to regulate the practice of medicine, the most potent forces in the campaign to criminalize abortion were physicians educated at reputable medical institutions, engaged in trying to better shape the standards of the profession. In fact, the abortion issue was one of the key rallying points for better organizing the profession since abortion services were among the most lucrative means of making a living for anyone claiming a degree of competence and skill at operating on the human body. As a result, the American Medical Association, organized in 1847, made the anti-abortion crusade one of its highest priorities. It argued that not only was abortion immoral, it was dangerous.

That the procedure was dangerous in the hands of the wrong person cannot be argued. One of the most common ways young women died at that time was from botched abortions. Given the variety of foreign objects and solutions introduced through the cervix and into the uterus to abort an unwanted child, peritoneal infections easily developed, infections that, due to the rich vascular supply to the uterus, precipitated a septicemia that easily spread to the rest of a woman's body, causing a quick and very agonizing death in which the victim was conscious to the very end.

It seems that common sense would have told the physicians that given this reality, combined with the determination of so many women to be rid of their unwanted pregnancies, it would make far more sense to keep abortion legal but limit its practice to qualified physicians only. But a certain puritanical strain in the American psyche, combined with fear of mongrelization, drove the impetus in the opposite direction. Clean it up, eliminate it along with immoral sex and all the other vices far more readily associated with non-WASPs, polluting the very integrity of the nation. Popular was the notion that civilizing the heathens from Eastern Europe, the Mediterranean, Latin America, Africa, and Asia was the will of God, assigned to the WASPs, and also inscribed in the code of manifest destiny that had driven settlers across the frontier all the way to the

Pacific Ocean. Abortion was an evil, an abomination that no married woman should want anyway.

But what bigger hypocrites were there than Americans? In what nation were all the contradictions of human behavior greater? All men were created equal, yet there was slavery. Most people considered themselves Christian, which meant they should turn the other cheek and look out for the welfare of their fellow man. Yet life, liberty, and the pursuit of happiness meant that they also created a society where unregulated free enterprise meant opportunity for whoever was first and/or most clever, most often a Caucasian male, to make as much money as possible off a market idea and opportunity, precipitating oligopolies in a variety of industries. It was positively Darwinian, survival of the fittest in a nation where as long as you were WASP, having a lot of money rather than royal blood determined royalty. WASP men believed in family, God, and country, yet many wealthy ones kept concubines—particularly in the South—non-WASP women who inducted them into and continually indulged them in the pleasures of the female flesh so that WASP women could be saved for marriage and family. And if the concubines became pregnant in the process they were supposed to keep the children, accept them into the fold as the designated "other," never to receive the full riches and opportunity allegedly offered in a nation where all men, at least, were said to have been created equal.

In that same vein the contradiction of abortion flourished despite becoming illegal throughout the country by the end of the nineteenth century. It was a procedure people from all socioeconomic classes and ethnicities and all beliefs considered and had performed. And as the years passed and being WASP became less important than being not Negro, or Latino, or Asian, American puritanical hypocrisy was assimilated by the former outcasts from Europe who worked so hard to be accepted by the WASPs. Typical was the attitude of leading citizens such as ministers, bankers, and lawyers, publicly frowning on the abomination of abortion. Then one day they'd discover that a daughter wasn't chaste because she missed her period. She was only fifteen years old. There was high school to finish, debutante balls to choose from, finishing school to go off to, the proper introductions to be made to the proper men and the pretense of her virginity to maintain. Or the daughter was away in college having sex in an era when respectable women weren't supposed to have sex before marriage, though plenty of them did anyway, and pregnancy would embarrass her and her family and boyfriend. Or a mistress could use her pregnancy to embarrass a husband. Murdering her was a far riskier proposition than possibly murdering (terminating?) the unwanted and so far unseen child (or unseeable fetus). Or a wife was having an affair and there was no way she could explain her pregnancy to her husband since they had stopped having sex long ago, or he had been (or still was) away for a long stretch of time, at sea, or off to war, or on an ordinary peacetime military tour of duty, or in school, or on a job that took him away from home for long stretches of time. Or she was away from him for similar reasons. Or the wife and husband had been having sex and there had been a hole in the diaphragm and they already had as many mouths to feed as they could handle. One more would be too many. In all those cases something had to be done.

Maybe when the girl or woman found out, she panicked. Then she investigated possible ways to abort her pregnancy, ways other than the proverbial coat hanger, such as faking a miscarriage so she could go to a hospital emergency room and have an abortion completed for medical and thus legal reasons. To do that perhaps she went to the drugstore and purchased potassium permanganate tablets and inserted them directly into her vagina to induce bleeding and convince an emergency room staff that she was miscarrying. But that was dangerous because the tablets tended to erode the lining of the vagina and lacerate the cervix. Even more dangerous were instances where she would try to take the abortion entirely into her own hands by inserting a catheter through her vagina and cervix, then pour some sort of substance like turpentine through the catheter, which would literally cook the lining of her uterus, necessitating a hysterectomy at the very least, or worse, cause her death.

If she was smarter (not always smart, but smarter) she would go to someone else from the start. By the 1950s numerous hospitals had what were called "therapeutic abortion committees," composed of physicians and representative laymen who would hear cases of pregnant women who the petitioning physician felt simply couldn't have their babies either for physical or mental reasons.

Thus maybe the first attempt when approaching someone about an abortion involved trying to get her physician to find a psychiatrist willing to tell a therapeutic abortion committee she was mentally incapable of handling pregnancy. Or maybe her physician could come up with a convincing physical diagnosis for the committee that rendered her unable to go through with having her child.

If that didn't work or was useless to even try then it was time to approach the illegal provider. Where was the telephone number of that woman or man who knew someone who could fix it? What town was it in that so-and-so said there was this doctor who fixed it all the *right way*? Was it down in Florida? Georgia? Alabama? Over in Tennessee? Or was it Ohio or Maine? Now where was it I'd heard that everything could be taken care of where no one knew you, and there'd be no gossip since no one knew you and everything would be fine again?

A man named Frederick Taussig published a study in 1936 estimating that a half million illegal abortions took place in the U.S. every year. In 1953 the Kinsey Report concluded that nine out of ten premarital pregnancies among the women responding to their survey were aborted, and 20 percent of married women in the study reported that they had an abortion while being married. One estimate put the number of illegal abortions in the 1950s at 1.2 million per year. A police department estimated that in the early 1960s illegal abortion was the third biggest racket in the country, ranking behind only gambling and narcotics. If in the 1950s 1.2 million women per year were having abortions, that meant that somewhere in the country an average of 3,288 women were getting one every day. And that estimate is probably conservative.

The surest technique if the pregnancy wasn't too far along involved dilation and curettage (D&C), a procedure in which the cervix is dilated and the lining of the uterus scraped out (curettage). Normally a D&C is performed in legal medicine with regard to gynecological disorders. But it could also be used to eliminate an unwanted embryo embedded in the lining of the uterus. However, a D&C done the right way required that the abortionist have excellent clinical facilities available in order to place the pregnant woman under general anesthesia and the proper instruments with which to perform the surgery and a postoperative facility for her recovery. Plenty of abortionists couldn't afford that. Thus many of them—even those without the proper clinical facilities—attempted the procedure "blind," wherein they'd have the woman come into their office. They'd sterilize instruments, insert them through her vagina and cervix and attempt to scrape the uterus without a good view of what they were doing. It was tantamount to using a long instrument of some sort, groping around with it, feeling your way through scraping the inside of a thick, soft, nearly collapsed balloon. Which meant that you risked the possibility of puncturing your patient's uterus, causing her to die from massive hemorrhage. Or the possibility of puncturing her uterus and mistakenly removing a section of bowel that you thought was part of the unwanted fetus due to her being further along in the pregnancy than initially thought, which again meant a botched abortion and her possible death from septicemia, and ultimately your possible arrest.

Another technique, used particularly if a woman was far along in her pregnancy, was to introduce a foreign object of some sort— gauze, a rubber tube, etc.—through the cervix and leave it there in order to induce premature contractions of the uterus, causing the fetus to be expelled the same way it would have been in a normal delivery. This method was known as "packing" the uterus. Commonly, the procedure was started by the abortionist. The woman then left the facility and later went into premature labor and aborted, sometimes at home. Or she was taken to a local hospital emergency room where she was diagnosed as having a miscarriage. Then the abortion was no longer classifiable as criminal, but instead was now a therapeutic procedure, and a legal operation. And the emergency room physician would then complete the procedure. Sometimes you, the abortionist, might have already made arrangements with physicians who'd agree to look the other way when called down to the hospital to complete the "miscarriage," often for a share of your fee. But with such a procedure there was also the risk of septicemia due to improper sterilization of whatever had been introduced through the cervix. So again you risked the possible death of your patient and your arrest. The normal way to abort a pregnancy too far along for a D&C was to perform a hysterotomy in which you surgically incised the uterus, removed the fetus and placenta, then sutured up the uterus. But again, you'd need advanced facilities for that, so you could place the woman under general anesthesia, and all the other

And that person who asked about one will never show up again." He said he had to be that stern in order not to yield to temptation and not invite any others to come seek him out. You see, the temptation was so strong because since the procedure was illegal, it was unreported income and you could name your fee with the assurance that the abortion seeker would bring you whatever you asked for.

Despite making similar decisions to resist turning the performance of abortions into a regular practice, numerous doctors performed the very occasional procedure on a patient who had been with them for a very long time and simply had to have one. But that was to be done in utmost secrecy because, as Dr. Gordon explained, once word got out that you performed abortions, it was like having a genie released from a bottle. It would lead to a flood of requests. Then your regular patients would decide that they preferred not going to a physician whom everyone knew to provide such a service. And then you'd be left with nothing but an abortion practice that you could lose at any time through arrest, conviction, and loss of your license to practice medicine.

In 1940 a total of 1,407 illegal abortions resulted in death. Yet the difference between serious complications or death from abortion and serious complications or death from any other medical procedure *when performed by M.D.s* was that when a physician was responsible for other medical difficulties or deaths (something that back then and still today is not infrequently the case), at least he or she had going for him or herself the fact that it was legal to attempt whatever had been done, thus easy to cover up any responsibility for the death and keep his or her license. With illegal abortion, proof of the very fact that you attempted the procedure was enough to ruin you. So though the odds of success were overwhelmingly in a competent abortion provider's favor, just one difficulty or death could do her or him in, whereas one difficulty or death in any legal medical procedure often had no effect at all, not even on the willingness of patients to patronize you if your responsibility was properly concealed.

So you, the physician in private practice—the general practitioner, the general surgeon who also saw patients for general medical reasons, but especially the ob-gyn—had to decide what to do when you faced the pressure to perform an abortion, particularly because there were all kinds of abortionists women were eager to avoid. Like the non-M.D. who could appear at her door late at night with his collar turned up, and the grim expression of a mortician on his face, or lecherous eyes that gazed upon her body while he spoke. And he knew that he could get away with doing so because she was so desperate to take care of everything that she had no other choice. So she nervously allowed him inside and he performed the procedure on her kitchen table. Or there were alcoholics who operated out of filthy rooms off alleyways at night with a glass of whiskey in one hand and a blunt instrument in the other, who put their customers through intense pain, but before doing so made fun of them with comments like, "You can take your panties off now, but a month ago you should a' thought about keeping them on!"

To get to such an abortionist she might have been instructed to stand on a street corner reading a newspaper. Then someone would walk up to her and ask her if there was any interesting news inside, to which she was instructed what her precise reply should be. Then later she would be picked up by someone in a car, instructed to keep her head down, and driven out into the country or round about through streets to ensure that no one was following, then up the proper side street or road to where the procedure would be performed, sometimes with guards standing around with guns.

The variations were numerous. There were the seedy back-office performers. There were nurses confident that they were familiar enough with medical procedures to turn performing abortions into a lucrative sideline. There were the M.D.s who had lost their regular practices and did nothing else. But there were also competent small-town physicians who had clinics or private hospitals and simply integrated abortion patients into their larger patient population, drawing them from as far as a thousand miles away, or across the country. Everyone understood that sitting in such practitioners' waiting rooms would be the man who needed a hernia repair, a child who needed a vaccination, a woman complaining about back pains, and a young woman, perhaps with her boyfriend or mother and father who obviously didn't live in town and was there for some "unknown reason." The local police understood it. So did the mayor. So did everyone else. They may have found it good for the local economy that such people came and stayed at a local motel and dined at a local

restaurant while staying in town for the "mysterious consultation."
The local sheriff may have drawn a share of the physician's fee.

For many years, according to numerous people who lived in Bainbridge or the vicinity of Bainbridge at one time or another—including the town's two oldest living physicians—Joseph Howard Griffin was this last type of abortion doctor. "From the moment I came here in 1947, I heard about the abortions," recalled Dr. Henry Bridges. "In fact, there was another Dr. Griffin who practiced here for a while, besides J. H.'s brother. He's dead now. He was white. His name was Dr. Ed Griffin. He told me that quite often people would call him from Tallahassee, thinking he was the Dr. Griffin who performed abortions. He had to tell them they had the wrong Dr. Griffin."

"I heard about Dr. Griffin's reputation as an abortionist from the time I arrived here in 1951," said Dr. Frank Gibson. He also said that he occasionally saw patients for my great-uncle when he went out of town, but only for legitimate medical reasons.

"From what I heard whites liked to go to him [for abortions] because, first, no one would hear about it since they traveled in different social circles, and second, because he had his own hospital so you knew it was going to be done well," recalled Dr. LaSalle Leffall, chairman of the Department of Surgery at Howard University School of Medicine and the first Afro-American president of the American Cancer Society, who grew up in the town of Quincy, Florida, twenty-three miles from Bainbridge. "And then there would be the black girl in Quincy that you heard was supposed to have gotten pregnant. You heard that she went up to Bainbridge and Dr. Griffin took care of everything."

Abortions were only a part of the picture in the medicine Joseph Griffin practiced. That much is certain. "When I thought of him I didn't think about the abortions," Dr. Leffall continued. "I thought about the other medicine he practiced. I wondered where he learned to perform general surgery so well since back when he trained there were no surgical residencies *anywhere* for black physicians." But abortions were a big part of what he did since once word traveled around that you performed one, the genie was out of the bottle. It became an open secret to all seekers. With his own well-equipped hospital it was far easier to cover his tracks than if he had just a clinic or office. Thus there was no reason to worry about police officers hanging around his emergency room after receiving reports of a woman coming there under mysterious circumstances, since he and his staff were the only ones in the emergency room to possibly make any report. And forty miles away was a ready population of coeds in Tallahassee at both Florida A&M and Florida State University desperate for the service after a birth-control device failed.

"I remember students all the time at Florida A&M when I was an undergraduate who went up to Bainbridge and saw Uncle Joe when they got pregnant," admitted my aunt Barbara during another visit I made with her.

"Griffin Hospital was known all over the South as a place to take a girl to get an abortion," said her husband, William Cotton.

"It's true that a lot of FSU and FAMU students would go to Griffin Hospital for abortions," agreed Dr. A. D. Brickler, an Afro-American ob-gyn who has been practicing in Tallahassee since 1957. "I think that the profits from abortions were one of the financial supports behind his hospital. I think that the abortion part of his practice supported the hospital so that when he gave care to other patients he could afford it. Because back then there certainly wasn't any great deal of money made from his hospital in the legal forms of care."

The revelation about the abortions my great-uncle performed, told to him by Dr. Gordon, was the principal reason my father decided not to go to Bainbridge to practice medicine, something he didn't tell me until I began investigating the abortion issue.

"I can remember once while I worked there and we were preparing a patient for surgery," recalled my aunt Elaine. "After we finished preparing her the other nurses told me, 'Your uncle would like for you to leave now.' But then he walked in and said, 'No, she can stay. It's time for her to see this.' He was performing an abortion."

It may seem amazing that in the Jim Crow era a Negro physician could also perform the procedure on Caucasian women, that there were Caucasian men who had no problem with Negro physicians touching the genitals of Caucasian women. But considering the circumstances it wasn't as amazing as it at first appears. Indeed, it was an asset to have a Negro physician performing the procedure, as Dr. Leffall reasoned, for the same reason that Caucasians preferred going to a Negro physician for their VD shots. Which is why I found it hard to believe what Mary Louise said about the abortion issue. If Caucasians sought out Joseph Griffin because they were eager to keep one type of embarrassment safely away from their Caucasian friends and acquaintances, then why wouldn't they desperately seek him out to keep an even bigger embarrassment—getting an abortion—away from those same people? And while Bertram Ehrlich stated that there was something "suspicious" about Caucasian coeds going to Griffin Hospital overnight for abortions, he was referring to his own personal take on the matter. Yet even though he viewed it with suspicion, that didn't cause him to do anything about it. Because, as will be made clear later, no one in Bainbridge blew the whistle on Joseph Griffin. And when the whistle was blown it had nothing to do with the fact that he was performing abortions on Caucasian coeds, per se. It's impossible to calculate the percentage of abortion doctors who were Negro before *Roe v. Wade*. But in the years before legalization at least two Negro physicians in the Georgia-Florida-Alabama tristate area were routinely performing abortions on women of all colors. And before they became old it was better to have either of them do it than have happen what occurred to a Caucasian woman sixty miles away in Albany at the hands of a middle-aged Caucasian abortionist who wasn't a physician.

In December 1952 Ruby Jo Bryant Overart was eighteen years old, an Albany wife, and pregnant, it was believed, by a man who was not her husband. Rather, it was thought to be her husband's stepfather, whom she admitted having sex with while she and her husband were separated. Then they decided to get back together, with Mr. Overart, also eighteen, agreeing to the reconciliation on one condition—that she have an abortion. So they asked around and discovered that a middle-aged Caucasian registered nurse performed them, a woman whom Mr. Overart once delivered newspapers to as a boy on his paper route. Eula Conoly told the Overarts there was no danger at all in having her perform the abortion, that since she was a registered nurse she guaranteed her work. She assured them that she had successfully aborted several prominent women in Albany, which was easy to believe since she came highly recommended. So in the kitchen of a place called the Mecca Court Tourist Cabin where Mr. Overart worked, Mrs. Overart paid Mrs. Conoly eighty-five dollars to have the abortion.

After paying, Mrs. Overart lay down on a table in the kitchen. Her sister and husband were with her. As Mrs. Conoly began the procedure she assured them that if anything went wrong a physician in nearby Tifton would be available to handle any complications. She also assured them that if the first attempt wasn't successful she would try it a second time for no extra charge. Then she took "an aluminum-looking tube with a red ball on the end and another instrument" and attempted the abortion.

The first try wasn't successful. So on January 27, 1953, Mrs. Conoly picked Mrs. Overart up from the home of her sister. A few hours later she brought her back and Mrs. Overart collapsed on the bed after becoming very sick to her stomach. The following day a physician came to the house, examined her chest, and gave her a shot. The next night he came by again, examined her, and gave her another shot. The following day he arranged for her admission to a hospital. She was given oxygen as soon as she arrived. The nurses told her she was dying. They asked her who had performed the abortion. But she refused to tell. The physician who had been treating her had already told them it was Mrs. Conoly. While being administered a blood transfusion, Mrs. Overart died.

Imagine lying on a bed, in pain, struggling to breathe, being told you're about to die, all because you decided one night or one morning or one afternoon to have sex, to submit to your lust for someone. Or submit to his lust for you ("Why couldn't I have been stronger?"). But something went wrong with the birth control. You could have altered your life's plans and given birth to the life beginning to grow inside of you. But you didn't want that. There would have been too much trauma, too much shame, too many regrets, too many resentments. Even if you had given the baby up, there would be too many gnawing thoughts about where and with whom that child who grew inside of you ended up. Too much guilt about possibly causing another human being you helped create a nightmare from his life's very start. And if you had kept the child you may have had too much difficulty making ends meet and caring for a child possibly abandoned by the father. Then, too, the resentment that you had to alter your plans, welling up especially when the baby cried for what seemed like most of the night and wouldn't stop, but then you rocked him to sleep and as soon as you put him down he started crying all over again. Maybe you would have wanted to kill him then. So you chose to forgo any and all of that, have the fertilized egg removed from you before anything could reach that point. But you chose the wrong person to "take care of it." And now your life was about to end. That must be when it is realized most searingly of all that life is unfair. For the baby you could have had. For you. Your pain must be accompanied by the most inconceivably massive weight of guilt, a guilt that may even hasten your physical deterioration and death. Is that when you search for God if you never believed in a God before that? Is that when you start believing, start hoping that there was a Jesus who died for your sins?

Mrs. Conoly was arrested and three months later, based on the testimony of Mr. Overart and Mrs. Overart's sister, convicted of involuntary manslaughter and sentenced to two to four years in prison for the abortion death of Ruby Jo Bryant Overart. How many Caucasian physicians in the area Mrs. Overart could have gone to for her abortion is difficult to determine. But the Negro physicians with whom it would have been far safer at the time were Joseph Griffin in Bainbridge, and possibly Dr. William Reese, an osteopathic physician in Albany. At that same time, Dr. Reese, whose regular medical practice included a birthing clinic, was tried for performing an abortion on a Negro woman who *didn't* die or even become sick. He was acquitted of the charge, though, according to Dr. Gordon, it was an open secret that he performed abortions. And there was someone else she could have gone to, someone that another Caucasian woman saw two and a half years later.

Audrie Franich, a twenty-one-year-old mother of two from Jacksonville, Florida, was described as a perfect blonde. Her husband was away at sea on his job with the Swanee Steamship Company. While he was gone apparently she had been having an affair and got pregnant in March. She had family two hours away in the Tallahassee area, in the nearby town of Havana. Since discovering she was pregnant she had been asking around, trying to find someone who would perform an abortion. One of her aunts discovered someone. On Tuesday, July 26, Audrie went to him and paid $200 for the procedure. Then he placed her feet in the gynecological stirrups. Her cervix was dilated and she was "packed" with strips of gauze that had been dipped in chemicals to prevent an infection. By the next day she hadn't gone into labor. So she was "packed" once more and told not to return until she went into labor. Two nights later she went into labor, then the next morning returned to where she had been "packed." The fetus was delivered and disposed of. She was given shots of penicillin to prevent any adverse side effects. But infection set in anyway, causing septicemia. Three weeks later she was admitted to Tallahassee Memorial Hospital. Tubes were placed in her nose, she was gasping, her eyes rolled back frequently, she was very pale. Her children were brought to her. Her mother came to her side. She tried to tell her who performed the abortion.

"Let's not talk about that now," replied her mother. "Let's wait until after you get well and then you can sit down and tell me about it."

"No, Mother," Audrie said. "I'm not going to live to tell you about it."

The county sheriff came to see her and asked for a confession identifying the person who performed the abortion. She told him she had gone to the clinic of a Negro doctor in Tallahassee named Dr. Campbell, located near the A&P store. Three days later she died.

Dr. Alpha Omega Campbell was a short, bespectacled man, a year younger than Joseph Griffin. He was born in 1889. He began practicing medicine in Tallahassee in 1913 after graduating from a predominantly Caucasian medical school in Boston called the College of Physicians and Surgeons, now defunct. As a boy growing up in nearby Quincy he was the grandson of the much-loved maid to a Judge Love, who was, of course, Caucasian. "There weren't too many things a black boy could be back then," he'd tell patients. "Next to a preacher and lawyer, being a doctor was a big thing. That's what I wanted to be." Judge Love's brother, Herbert Love, was mayor of the town. He wrote Campbell a letter of introduction to the medical school. His tuition, room, and board were paid for by prominent Caucasians in Quincy who had employed his grandmother.

Upon setting up practice in Tallahassee he began seeing a variety of patients, including Caucasians, though most of those Caucasians were poor. He developed a reputation as a physician with a warm bedside manner. So popular was he with people in Tallahassee that to this day his legend has caused women to name their sons after him. In 1918 he married a woman of mixed Cherokee and Caucasian heritage. From his wife's Caucasian relatives they inherited a lot of real estate. In 1947 Dr. Campbell opened his own twenty-bed hospital next to his spacious home. It became the second hospital facility available to Negroes in Tallahassee after the sixty-bed Florida A&M Hospital.

Like Joseph Griffin, Campbell practiced legal medicine at his hospital and he performed abortions, including some for wealthy Caucasians in Tallahassee who paid him very well for doing so and keeping everything hush-hush. It was possible to keep things hush-hush except when a woman died. If she was Negro, then it was still possible to keep things hush-hush. But if she was Caucasian then it became impossible. When Audrie Franich died it was the beginning of the end for Dr. Campbell. Prior to that it was routine for potential abortion patients, including Caucasians, to visit him in the evening and schedule the abortion, then return later at night, circle the block his small hospital was located on, then drive into the alley and park. Then after the abortion was performed they would drive out of the alley with their lights off. After a couple of blocks they'd put their lights back on and drive off. A Caucasian teenage girl from Jacksonville whose boyfriend was about to start college at the University of Florida came to him that way.

A week after Audrey Franich came to him a Caucasian couple named the Pyles* approached Dr. Campbell. He told Mr. Pyle that he didn't perform abortions, but he knew someone in Georgia who did. (Was it Joe Griffin, with whom he was friends?) "No, I understand quite confidentially that you do that work," insisted Mr. Pyle. They talked some more and Dr. Campbell agreed to do it for $150. He estimated Mrs. Pyle was ten to twelve weeks pregnant. The Pyles told him they wanted the abortion immediately. Dr. Campbell took Mrs. Pyle into a back room and left the door open. He had a screen up. But Mr. Pyle could see through the screen. He watched as Dr. Campbell took an instrument, "something he put inside of her and separated somehow, and then he taken another instrument and went probing . . . and then he taken her and packed her with gauze and cotton and all these things he first dipped in chemicals." Then he gave her two penicillin shots and one of streptomycin. And then he told them to return the following night. He packed her again and the following day she aborted. But Dr. Campbell couldn't be found. So she was taken to Tallahassee Memorial where she claimed to be in the process of miscarrying and the procedure was successfully completed with no physical problems for her.

But Dr. Campbell had begun to lose his touch. In 1955 he was sixty-six years old. On February 3, 1956, for the abortion death of

*A pseudonym.

Audrie Franich and two other abortions, he was sentenced to four years in the state penitentiary at Starke. His small hospital was closed. He also lost his license to practice medicine. He emerged from prison in 1959, embittered. His hospital hadn't been as advanced as Griffin Hospital and Clinic, where Joseph Griffin was far more careful, even at the age of sixty-seven, in performing abortions. And he could monitor all of his patients from beginning to end, until they left his hospital and returned to the type of lives they had before discovering they were pregnant. Everything continued to go smoothly for him. He stubbornly refused to stop practicing medicine even though by then he was quite wealthy. In 1950 the *Pittsburgh Courier* had named him one of its Top Ten Georgia Leaders. In 1954 he received an honorary doctorate from Morris Brown. In 1961 it sent its famous reporter Trezzvant Anderson to write the story about him, headlined "A Giant of the Southland." In 1964 Bethune Cookman College, a Negro college in Daytona Beach, Florida, honored him for outstanding service in medicine and human relations. In 1965 the town of Bainbridge honored him at the National Guard Armory with "Joseph H. Griffin Appreciation Day." Everything rolled along nicely, even as he reached seventy-five, though by then many patients were concluding he was getting too old to practice. But he loved practicing medicine as much as he loved being a real estate tycoon whom many people feared, others were fond of, and still others had long viewed as an inspiration, some experiencing all three sentiments at the same time. So he kept practicing. Many patients continued to come to him for legitimate medicine, many continued to come to him for abortions. Coeds continued to come up from Tallahassee. By March 1967 he was seventy-nine years old when one particular Florida State University graduate student called him from Tallahassee seeking one.

Mary Louise had told me that he had no problem performing them. He had no problem because that meant one less child who had to go through the hell of living in this world. And what hell he had seen and knew of. Who would know more about the hell of living in this world than a Negro physician in the small-town Jim Crow Deep South? Who would know more than a Negro physician who had practiced medicine in his own hospital in the small-town Jim Crow Deep South? It was a hell that no doubt hardened him, made him cynical; a hell that drove him to do his best to protect his own with as much money as he could possibly accumulate; a hell that he had

*faced and beaten in so many ways with his bold daring in successfully per-
forming operations that he had only seen from the distance of the seats in
surgical amphitheaters because when he trained there were no surgical residencies anywhere for Negro physicians. Or operations he successfully performed after watching and assisting his surgical mentor John H. Hale,
procedures many of which Hale had learned from watching Daniel Hale
Williams who came from Chicago and performed surgery every winter at
Meharry. And Joseph Griffin had dared in the small-town Jim Crow Deep
South with a daring that had caused him to play plenty of sophisticated
games to get what he wanted, a daring that had caused him to collect plenty
of enemies, and cause other types of pain even as he alleviated medical pain.
And no doubt he became hardened by so many of the racial realities he was
forced to live with. So what was one less Caucasian child who would inevitably be taught how to make life difficult for Negroes? And even if he,
too, made life difficult, he may have reasoned that that was the way you
gained power. Either dominate or be dominated. And the only people he
could dominate during a life lived under Jim Crow were fellow Negroes. But
with Caucasians it was a different matter. Caucasians could dominate other
Caucasians, too. Or maybe when he was aborting a Caucasian pregnancy he
thought of the Caucasian mother. Maybe he thought that at least she, this
young desperate woman, will learn to appreciate this "colored" man who got
her out of her bind far more than she ever thought she would appreciate
someone of black African descent.*

*Or when the embryo or fetus he was aborting was a Negro mother's, upon
looking at the aborted "seedling" he may have thought, "You don't know how
wonderful it is that I have prevented you from coming into this world to fight
poverty and the ignorance of the family you would have been born into, which
you may not have even fought but simply accepted, simply embraced because
you would have known nothing else." Or if it was an ambitious Negro girl or
coed he was performing the abortion for, maybe he was only too glad to ensure
she could become something more than another embarrassing, depressing,
poverty statistic ending up with a little dirty, naked, potbellied Negro kid
among the many dirty, naked, potbellied Negro kids he had delivered and cyn-
ically watched grow out of infancy; the kind who were caricatured in the
movies, all teeth and bug eyes and hair sticking up all over their heads as they
dug into slices of watermelon; the kind made fun of in that same fashion for so
many years in the minstrels put on by people like Bertram Ehrlich, one of the
pharmacists who filled his prescriptions; Caucasians who would have laughed
at the kid and called her or him a pickanniny as they drove past the pitiful*

hovel the kid would have been forced to live in with a mama whose life had been unalterably changed when she had to leave college because she had become pregnant and the father, who also dropped out of college, found the going too difficult, so had abandoned the entire family. Maybe he was happy that he eliminated this possible scenario from the Negro coed's life by aborting her pregnancy so that she could finish college, then later on get married and have children she could raise the right way.

Perhaps all of those thoughts were his conscience-soothing rationalizations for performing abortions.

As 1967 began, Lois Brown* was a Caucasian Florida State University graduate student whose husband was in the army and on a tour of duty. She became pregnant and decided she had to do something about it. That March she called Dr. J. H. Griffin because someone told her quite confidentially that Dr. Griffin could "take care of everything." So she called him and he told her that he could. But it would cost her $400. He charged sliding-scale fees. There were plenty of Negro women who paid less. There were plenty whom he charged $200 to $250, women like Melissa Cain*, for whom he would perform one seven months later. Melissa went to him after four months of missing her menstrual period and noticing a mucous discharge from her vagina. So in October 1967 she went to him and he took his stethoscope and listened to her heart. Then he took her blood pressure. Then he listened to her abdomen to see if he could hear a fetal heartbeat. After finding out how much it would cost to have everything taken care of, she went down to the Liberty Loan Company in Bainbridge and told them she wanted to borrow $100. But she was told that since she already owed money she would have to borrow enough to pay off the balance of what she still owed. She borrowed $283, using part of the money to buy some things she needed. Then on Thursday morning, October 5, 1967, she went back to Griffin Hospital and Clinic and paid Joseph Griffin $250 for her abortion. He told her that the fee would probably take care of everything, and if not she could pay the balance later. She was washed and prepared for the procedure. Then once again he took his stethoscope and listened to her abdomen. He took her blood pressure. He placed her feet in gynecological stirrups. Then he "packed" her uterus, taking care to make sure he used the right chemicals in

*A pseudonym.

the process. He gave her shots to prevent infection. Then she was taken to a semi-private room. On Sunday morning she went into labor. Two employees took her to the emergency room. Her labor pains increased. Dr. Griffin came in and shortly afterward she expelled her fetus and the placenta. He disposed of them. She remained in the hospital until Wednesday, when she was discharged and successfully returned to her life prior to her pregnancy.

The previous March, Lois Brown had joined the long list of young women who came to Griffin Hospital and Clinic for abortions. She got her four hundred dollars together and traveled up from Tallahassee. When she arrived at the hospital she was prepared for the procedure. She placed her feet in the stirrups. Dr. Griffin "packed" her, then gave her the requisite shots to prevent infection. Then she was taken to a room in the hospital. When she went into labor she was returned to the emergency room, where she expelled the contents of her uterus and was given shots to prevent adverse side effects. The next day she was discharged and returned to Tallahassee. Soon she began suffering delayed side effects. Instead of returning to Bainbridge she went to Tallahassee Memorial where Dr. Evan Duces treated her. She admitted having an abortion. Dr. Duces notified the district attorney's office. They had an investigator come down and take a "dying confessional" from Mrs. Brown with regard to who had performed her abortion. She told him it was Dr. Joseph Griffin of Bainbridge, Georgia. But afterward something fortunate happened. Lois didn't die. She got well. Joseph Griffin was investigated anyway.

CHAPTER 11

One April day I went to see Paul Kwilecki, a serious and thoughtful looking, bespectacled documentary photographer of medium height living in Bainbridge. His most famous photograph is of three Afro-American men from Mount Zuma Baptist Church standing in the Flint River, which ambles through Decatur County, Georgia, with a little girl named Lisa Spear, after they've just baptized her. It's a photograph displayed in many photo-essay collections about the South. It's a photo I saw during my next-to-last-month as an editorial page writer for the *Wall Street Journal.* I had walked into Rizzoli's bookstore in the World Financial Center looking for material to prepare my second-to-last feature editorial for the *Journal,* and I purchased a book entitled *Picturing the South: 1860 to the Present.* It contained essays and riveting photographs taken over that span of time in various settings all over the region. At the time I didn't know who Paul Kwilecki was. He was seventy years old when I interviewed him nearly two years later. He is the son of Julian Kwilecki and first cousin of Bertram Ehrlich. He is the grandson of Isadore Kwilecki, who started the chain of hardware and building supply stores previously mentioned, and was one of the organizers and the first president of Temple Beth El, Bainbridge's only Jewish temple. Julian Sr., Paul's father, was mayor of Bainbridge from 1938 to 1942. He was also the bank president who allegedly advised Joseph Griffin to invest some of his budding wealth in government bonds. Julian Jr., Paul's brother, did architectural work on Griffin Hospital and Clinic. This is what Paul had to say:

> When you are telling a story about anything you have to give the downside as well as the upside if it's going to be credible. And if you report the hearsay, then just say it was hearsay but you were unable to find any evidence to support it. That's part of the story. And you couldn't give a complete picture of Dr. Griffin without all of these

things. But you have to have the intellectual equipment to absorb the negative as well as the positive things you find out, to take in the whole picture.

Let me point out something else. And I'm throwing this out more as a suggestion to which you can react any way you want to. But I think that probably you should take into consideration that when you talk to people like Bertram and to me who were on the scene when a lot of these things happened, that Bertram and I absorbed our impression of Dr. Griffin from a white community view at a time when segregation and isolation were the rule. There was a big gap between black and white. And so anything any white person says about him has to be sifted through the mesh of justice or fairness and the likelihood that it's exaggerated, tainted, or completely wrong. I'm making a disclaimer. Travel at your own risk, or take what seems right to you, and what seems wrong, throw it out.

There's a side to Dr. Griffin you have to admire if you're a person who recognizes and admires competence and ability. He was an extremely able man. He couldn't have done what he did if he wasn't. And obviously he was highly intelligent. He had a kind of intimidating personality. He came on strong. I don't know that he meant to. But he did. That was just his manner of speech. It was very strong and almost physical. If you were just an ordinary guy you kind of stepped back.

He'd come into our store and talk to Dad, he and Dad were good friends. Dad was president of one of the banks here. And Dr. Griffin was a customer of the banks and a lot of our businesses. I remember one time Dr. Griffin came in—and I saw this. In the early '40s we built an addition to the Griffin home. And he had impressive trust in my father. And he had him build this addition to the house. And when the addition was finished, I don't remember anymore the amount of money but it was probably twelve or fifteen or maybe twenty thousand dollars—back then that was a lot of money. And one day Dr. Griffin came into the store and into Dad's office. And he had a big brown paper sack with him. And he sat down and talked. And I was watching—Dad had glass around his office—so I could see what was going on. I was working in the bookkeeping department. And I didn't pay any attention. After a few minutes I looked up and I saw Dr. Griffin take that brown paper bag and turn it upside down on Dad's desk, and you never saw so much money come out. The whole amount of that bill for the addition to his home he paid for in cash. And after he left, Dad had about six of us counting it. And there were hundred-dollar bills. I bet there were more hundred-dollar bills than the bank had. And he pulled the whole thing out.

Dr. Griffin, he was respected, but because of his money. Now make no mistake about that. There are a lot of ways to get the respect of the unintelligent and people of average intelligence. And possession of power and money are two of them. And Dr. Griffin was respected. Dad and the rest of the bankers in town would roll out the red carpet for Dr. Griffin just like they would have for the king of England if he came to town.

He became powerful like that in a day of such horrible segregation because of his money. You make an exception in a case like that. One, he was a physician. And second, he was not overly encumbered with principle. Now that makes for a heady combination. There were the abortions, and the taking advantage of people. We're talking about human thinking and feeling. You don't say I want money. You're not conscious that that's motivating you. But it is. So when the opportunity arises to acquire it you find a way of getting your hands on it. And you don't think of yourself as being unfair or dishonest or anything. I don't think that Dr. Griffin considered that he was doing anything that to him was reproachful. But whether we like it or not, other people are watching. And they had their standards. And the moral Judeo-Christian standards he violated as easily as I'd cross the street.

An abortion at that time was worse than illegal. It was considered a very heinous, unscrupulous act for a man who had taken the Hippocratic Oath. And yes, I, too, heard for years that he was the person to go to if you wanted an abortion. I've heard that some whites went. And that's hearsay. I don't condemn Dr. Griffin in the same way a lot of people did. I try to understand.

Now I'm not certain what his point of view was. . . . But if you said, "Well, just freely, tell me what you think it might have been," I would say that probably he was raised with a lot of insecurities and that money seemed to be the answer to that. And he very single-mindedly set out to establish himself on a level that he could not be threatened by either poverty or the white community. If you got enough money you can shake your fist at the whole damn world. That's a sad fact but it's true. And in a way it relieves you of a certain kind of responsibility. I mean he didn't have to answer to anybody. And all of these churchgoing highfalutin Christians around here who condemned him over the supper table took his money when he spent it with them. In this town there were plenty of people who did that, who condemned him for doing things like taking out somebody's appendix two or three times. And for keeping a body in the hospital and not releasing it until the next of kin paid the bill. Or even keeping people who had gone to the hospital sick and then gotten well in there until they paid the bill. Here again, this is all hearsay. But it was so common that one is inclined to think that there was some truth to it.

Those people that you mentioned like Cheney and Sam [Griffin] and so forth who [are not saying what I'm saying] are partly motivated by fear. It isn't fashionable to go muckraking in the black community—especially if you're white. But I have very dear friends in the black community. And a great portion of my life's work is devoted to showing the black community as it really is. And there is tremendous beauty and durability there. I once got in trouble about that. The [Bainbridge Junior] college here had Black Awareness Week. And I had taken a lot of pictures of the shade tobacco industry around Attapulgus. And of a black ghetto here in Bainbridge called Battle's Quarters. And it showed, I thought, the nobility of blacks. And I thought, How can these people live like this in Battle's Quarters and get up every morning knowing that things aren't going to get any better? And these pictures I thought showed that nobility. And [Bainbridge Junior College] put the ones I selected up at an exhibition. And within three hours the president of the college was on the phone. He said he had a delegation from the black community who wanted those pictures taken down. They considered them to be humiliating. I said that if you want to take them down, you can take them down. I'll leave that up to you because that certainly wasn't my intention. My intention was to show the nobility and strength of these people. And that someday they would come to appreciate those pictures, because when they are light-years away from that condition, the pictures will show where they came from. They were in the best tradition of documentary photographs. And they took them down. Well, about six or seven years later, the *Atlanta Constitution* had an article in their Sunday magazine section about my work and a show displaying it at the High Museum in Atlanta. And it was a very laudatory piece. And I was walking down the street the next day after it appeared. And one of the women in that delegation that complained about the photographs being displayed at the junior college here was walking past me in the opposite direction and she called out to me. And she said she wanted to talk to me. And she told me, "I am so sorry we didn't understand your work. I read about you in the paper. And I see what you're trying to do. And I'm sorry we had this misunderstanding." Well, she really didn't understand any more about it then than she had before. But the *Atlanta Constitution* validated the work for her. She took their word for it and that changed her opinion. That's okay, but what I'm saying is my reverence for the Negro race, and especially those in Bainbridge, is genuine and consistent throughout. I try to admire what deserves to be admired.

The reason I went through this digression is to make the point that people in this town are playing social and political games when they brush you off when you ask them for a candid take on how Dr. Griffin was viewed around here. They don't want any trouble from the black community. For example, the people at Nelson Chapel where Dr. Griffin was very generous. And you know that preschool building is called the Joseph H. Griffin Educational Complex. That's what's written on there. I photographed extensively at that church and they are very grateful for what Dr. Griffin did. And this is the other side of Dr. Griffin. His genuine generosity. He didn't have to do that. But if you go play this tape or tell certain people what I have said, they might get angry with me. But it would be because they misunderstand or partially misunderstand what I am saying.

You must not judge him by our standards today. I'll give you an example of how wrongheaded that can be. You remember a few years ago when the VFW and American Legion got up in arms with the Smithsonian about the *Enola Gay* exhibit, and the way the exhibit was saying that the [atomic] bomb didn't have to be dropped? Well, the bombing critics were using hindsight to judge something that happened fifty years before. I lived through that, and the hatred of the Japanese was so intense in this country that I don't think anybody cared whether we nuked them or not. After Pearl Harbor, which was considered a stab in the back of the first magnitude, and the mistreatment of our prisoners of war they captured, the Bataan March, for example. All of those things just crystallized in this country the hatred of the Japanese. Now no small part of it, I'm sure, was racial. They were yellow and not white. But that was never discussed. What was discussed was what sneaky bastards they were. But to judge the

American people's hearts in 1945 by the standards of today is totally wrong because we're not in the same place.

Likewise, it would be wrong to judge Dr. Griffin by the standards of today. He was a man of great energy and resourcefulness. Why did Afro-Americans still go to him, given his practice of getting them to deed property? I heard that question asked all of my life. I think it was a matter of personality. There was a certain charisma about him. He was a man of power and authority. He would inspire confidence as a physician as well as something else. He didn't equivocate about anything. Even in the '40s and '50s. Now I don't mean that he was a troublemaker of any kind. But he was not deferential. Maybe he was walking a thin line, but he certainly walked it well.

Dr. Griffin's life poses a question, this business of ambition driven by insecurity, or whatever it was driven by, versus principles and so forth and how we maneuver and skirt around obstacles like right and wrong to reach our destination. All of the elements of classic Greek tragedy are involved in his life. I mean, a black man comes to the community and he's a doctor but he doesn't have much money. And little by little he is transformed into something else. And as he acquires wealth the wealth changes him. And those changes affect his goals and different things shift and intensify.

About his abortion troubles [in 1967–68]. I heard nothing about the circumstances surrounding why the charges were brought. But I do remember when the trial took place. And everybody said, "Oh, he'll be acquitted." But first they said it would never go to trial. And then when it went to trial they said he'd be acquitted. Because he had that reputation of being able to beat these things. And in his heyday he would have. But he was an old man by then. In his heyday he would have known who to talk to to get everything dropped. He would have managed it.

CHAPTER 12

After Lois Brown identified Joseph Howard Griffin as the physician who performed her abortion, the Tallahassee district attorney's office notified the Georgia Bureau of Investigation (GBI). The GBI, in turn, decided to place Griffin Hospital and Clinic under surveillance for four months. Its agents saw not only young women going in for abortions. Patients passed them by going in for such problems as gangrene of the right foot; cardiovascular complications; cerebrospinal infection; cerebral hemorrhage; stroke complicated by hypertension; malignant hypertension; an arthritic, dilated heart; acute inflammatory pelvic disease; a fractured femur; cancer; aortic disease; paralysis and hypertension; severe arteriosclerosis; muscular dystrophy; stroke; osteomyelitis; cancer of the stomach; and acute infection of the lower extremities.

Negro patients had been coming to Joseph Griffin for such problems for years. And plenty of them didn't stop even though by then he was seventy-nine. Plenty of them didn't stop even though by 1967 legal segregation had been outlawed for three years, so they no longer had to withstand the indignities of waiting in a segregated section of a Caucasian physician's office for an examination, or being confined to the house adjacent to Riverside Hospital or the basement of Bainbridge Memorial Hospital when they needed hospitalization. The population of the county at that time was estimated to be between 25,000 and 30,000. There were ten physicians to care for them. The Negro population was estimated to be between 10,000 and 15,000. Joseph Griffin was the only Negro physician in the county. So plenty kept coming to him, along with a mix of young women seeking abortions.

The GBI agents watched for four months, and they approached certain young women they saw who admitted having had an abortion, and they subpoenaed such young women, who joined Ms. Brown in appearing before a Decatur County grand jury convened to decide whether or not to indict Joseph Griffin for performing abortions. On November 8, 1967, five separate abortion indictments were handed down, along with one charge of murdering a newborn infant. After he was arrested and taken into custody he was so shocked and humiliated that the following day, while attending patients at his hospital under police escort, his blood pressure rose to a dangerous level. He was confined to the hospital for a few days. The following week he was driven to Thomasville to see a physician who examined him and gave him medication. He got better. There had been publicity not only from the local news weekly, but correspondents for the Tallahassee and Albany dailies covering his arrest, as well as television news stations from those same cities. Legally speaking, he knew what to do. He knew plenty of attorneys he could call. A man who operated at his level for so many years was quite familiar with attorneys, had to be familiar with them to accomplish all he accomplished. Two of the lawyers he called were Negro men who had grown to become legends in the recently concluded civil rights struggle.

In September 1952 Donald L. Hollowell was sitting in the living room of the home of Joseph Griffin when he received the news that he had passed the Georgia State Bar exam. His wife, Louise, had grown up in nearby Iron City. Dr. Griffin had been her family physician. Upon hearing the news, Joseph Griffin grabbed him and hugged him and celebrated with him. Over the years he became like a father to Donald Hollowell. From his base in Atlanta, Hollowell went on to represent so many activists during the civil rights movement that hit Georgia by the late 1950s that he became known as Georgia's "Mr. Civil Rights." When President Bill Clinton's "first friend" Vernon Jordan graduated from Howard University Law School in 1960 and eagerly sought his first job as a lawyer, Donald Hollowell hired him as his law clerk. Later that same year, when Charlayne Hunter and Hamilton Holmes attempted to become the first Negro students to attend the University of Georgia in Athens, only to encounter harassment and violence, Hollowell was there to successfully handle their case, resulting in integration of the school and ultimately for Hunter, now Hunter-Gault, a career as a reporter for PBS's *McNeil-Lehrer News Hour* and for NPR, and for Holmes a career as one of Georgia's most distinguished orthopedic surgeons. When Martin Luther King, Jr., was arrested in October 1960 while helping demonstrate for the integration of Atlanta's Rich's Department Store and was transferred to Georgia's infamous Reidsville prison while the entire nation held its breath in fear that he might be killed there, it was Donald Hollowell who filed the appropriate legal papers to get him out of there. When the civil rights movement hit Albany, Georgia, in 1961 like a hurricane, placing the city in the national spotlight, due to the nonviolent demonstrations staged by local leaders and SNCC activists and Martin Luther King, Jr., and his disciples, it was Donald Hollowell, along with C. B. King, southwest Georgia's only Negro lawyer at the time, who courageously and skillfully handled most of the arrest cases.

So, too, it would be Donald Hollowell and C. B. King who rushed to Joseph Griffin's side when he was arrested at the age of seventy-nine for performing abortions. Hollowell understood where he had been coming from all those years. Hollowell had become all too familiar with the ins and outs of the lives of the handful of Negro men in Georgia during the segregation era who wielded a great degree of power relative to other Negroes, including men such as Herbert Dudley in Dublin. He knew that meant they had led lives that were not always pretty. He knew it required in them drive, greed, the ability to manipulate, the ability to wear the right mask at the right time, the ability to be compassionate at the right time. He knew that if all of the same was necessary in Caucasian men who acquired money and power, it had to be ten times as necessary for Negro men who acquired money and power. "Even in the times when things were very, very dark for black people, there were always certain people with whom white folks would deal, and Doc [Joseph Griffin] was one of them," Hollowell explained to me. "He did a lot of things for people in power where they couldn't get him. Doc knew that money talked. And Doc always had some. It will carry you a long way, especially when you are in a position to know people's secrets."

There was a lot Joseph Griffin could do. But by then, as Paul Kwilecki said, he was old. Many people viewed the indictments as a convenient impetus to get him to realize he was too old to keep practicing medicine. By 1967 Hollowell no longer engaged in the private practice of law. In February 1966 he had been appointed regional director of the federal Equal Employment Opportunity Commission (EEOC). So when he heard the news about the indictments he came down, stayed at the Griffin home, dealt with the media, and offered legal advice to C. B. King and the other lawyers. Then, because King didn't have expertise in that particular area and didn't feel qualified to work out the appropriate deal, he left the case to Caucasian lawyer J. Willis Conger, who served as the local man, while Aaron Kravich and John Hendrix, Caucasian lawyers from Savannah, were the ones who ultimately negotiated with the prosecution.

All of the counts were to be tried separately. A motion for continuance of the case, meaning a postponement, was successfully filed and Joseph Griffin was released from prison on bail. The first case involving performing an abortion on Lois Brown was tried the following year. The date was November 12, 1968. Among the evidence heard was the testimony of former Griffin Hospital nurse Alice Faye Jackson, who told the court she had assisted Dr. Griffin in performing several abortions. He denied performing them, denied even having any contact with Lois Brown, because he had to deny it all, had to claim, as physicians caught performing abortions usually did, that in the cases where it could be proven the woman came to them for treatment, they were simply completing a miscarriage already in progress. But in the case of Brown, he claimed she had never been to his hospital, he had never heard of her, and that Alice Faye Jackson was a liar. But there was not only the testimony of Brown and Jackson, there were the telephone records proving Brown had called him. There was the testimony of the physician at Florida State who told her she was pregnant. There was the testimony of Dr. Duces, who treated her for complications after the abortion. The following day the all-male Caucasian jury returned a verdict of "Guilty." The second case got under way the day after that. It involved an abortion he allegedly performed on a Negro woman from Valdosta, seventy-six miles to the east. But there wasn't enough evidence to nail the case (or maybe the charge of performing an abortion on a Negro woman wasn't taken as seriously). So the following day he was found "Not guilty." The following week he was tried for the charge of murdering a newborn infant, an indictment handed down under the presumption that the aborted fetus could have lived. There was debate back and forth between physicians called by the prosecution and defense as expert witnesses, on the ability of a fetus at a certain stage to live outside of the womb. By the end of the week the defense prevailed and he was found "Not guilty." The three other cases were negotiated over a period of several months and eventually the prosecution and defense decided to proceed no further in the cases. In other words, J. H. Griffin's lawyers worked all the other cases out. And when sentencing time came in May 1969 for the abortion performed on Lois Brown, since she hadn't died, the judge saw no reason to be harsh. He fined Dr. Griffin $1,000 and sentenced him to a year's probation. And Uncle Joe kept his license to practice medicine, which he did until his official retirement in 1977, when he closed his practice as well as Griffin Hospital and Clinic at the age of eighty-eight. In effect, he survived his brush with disaster, not as cleanly as he might have in his heyday, but he survived only with his pride ruffled somewhat, and perhaps with a sense of contrition, and, as he would make clear in the years that followed, the desire to focus on what his legacy would be.

There would be the Joseph H. Griffin Educational Complex. He would be a driving force behind the orderly integration of Bainbridge's schools. There would be the three-way sharing among Meharry, Morris Brown, and Nelson Chapel of the dividends in perpetuity from stock he owned in Coca-Cola and other blue-chip companies, worth $750,000 in 1972, now worth about $15 million. There would be the honor of Morris Brown naming a science building after him. And after he died, if his daughter and grandchildren were to meet an early demise, a lot of real estate was to go to Meharry, the profits of which were to be used to train Negro men and women to become physicians. In addition, he had already made an impact that went beyond his financial contributions, or his direct contributions to medical care in the tristate area, as well as to women seeking abortions before abortions were legal.

After George Bush was elected President in 1988, he named Afro-American hematologist Louis Sullivan as his Secretary of Health and Human Services. Sullivan had already served as the first dean of the medical school opened at Morehouse College in 1975 and then as its first president in 1981, when it became independent. Sullivan received his bachelor's degree from Morehouse in 1954, then his M.D. from Boston University School of Medicine in 1958, after which he became the first Afro-American house staff member at New York Hospital–Cornell Medical Center (as a resident in internal medicine), then the first Afro-American fellow in hematology on the Harvard service of the Thorndike Laboratory at Boston City Hospital, then after that, a board-certified academic hematologist at Harvard, the College of Medicine and Dentistry of New Jersey, then Boston University School of Medicine.

His medical ambitions began while he was growing up in the town of Blakely, forty-three miles north of Bainbridge. His father was an insurance salesman and owner of a funeral home, who also ran an ambulance service. As a boy Louis would ride with him when he took emergency cases to the nearest place Negroes could get decent medical care—Joseph Griffin's hospital in Bainbridge. "Dr. Griffin was the first black physician I ever met," Sullivan recalled. "I believe my father purposely had me ride along to his hospital to motivate me. Watching Dr. Griffin was what made me decide to go into medicine."

And there was the young man from Quincy, Florida, twenty-five miles south of Bainbridge, who would go on to graduate valedictorian of his medical school class at Howard in 1952, and after completing his residency in surgery at Freedmen's Hospital, on to board certification and a fellowship in cancer surgery at Memorial Hospital for Cancer and Allied Diseases (now Memorial Sloan-Kettering Cancer Center) in New York City, become chairman of the Department of Surgery at Howard University School of Medicine and its first Charles R. Drew Professor of Surgery, and the first Afro-American president of the American Cancer Society.

"He was one of my best students," recalled Dr. W. Montague Cobb, former president of the NAACP and distinguished professor of anatomy at Howard University School of Medicine, who, after earning his bachelor's degree at Amherst, M.D. at Howard, then a Ph.D. in anatomy and physical anthropology at Western Reserve University (now Case Western Reserve), pioneered the "graphic" method of teaching anatomy, wherein students reasoned their way through learning parts of the human body rather than engaging in the usual rote memorization. "I had a little custom in my classes that I called "bustout." I'd say, 'Who's ready for "bustout" today?' A student would say, 'Come on, Doctor, try me.' Then I would try to stump him with questions on material being covered in the classes. At some point the student might be stumped—"bust out."

He would say, 'I'll be ready for you next time.' But [LaSalle] Leffall—
I could never bust him out."

"On a Sunday, Daddy would say, 'We're going up to Bainbridge
to see Dr. Griffin,'" recalls Dr. Leffall about his boyhood in Quincy.
His father was the principal of the Negro high school in the town,
his mother was the principal of the Negro elementary school. "That
was back when he had his first hospital. So as a kid I'd hear we were
going up to Bainbridge to have dinner with Dr. Griffin. We'd go up
and have dinner and it was just nice to talk with him and see what
was going on, to hear about things." Leffall's impressionability may
have been abetted by the fact that he was still very young when he
left home. He graduated from high school at the age of fifteen and
medical school at the age of twenty-two. "I went over to see [Dr.
Griffin] at his second hospital while I was in medical school," he
continued.

> And I remember him telling me that after I finished I could have
> something like that someday, or come there and work with him. And
> I was so impressed, because he had built what looked to me like a real
> hospital as opposed to the makeshift facilities that a few other black
> physicians had as hospitals in the days of segregation. And because
> not only did he operate on people, but his patients, as far as I was able
> to tell, did well. You see, word got around in little towns in particular,
> if your patients did well or not. People may not have known firsthand
> whether or not you were good. But if they saw that someone you op-
> erated on got better, did fine, then they had to say you were good.
> And Dr. Griffin had a reputation that his patients did well.

That he could be so many different things, good and bad, to so
many different people, and plant the seed that caused or further
spurred some of the most impressive Afro-American men in the
country to become important, provided the answer to why it was so
difficult to take the proper measure of him over the course of my
two years of research. Upon writing about the Black Panthers I
learned that no matter how self-destructive or harmful an Afro-
American had been to other Afro-Americans, if he made only one
major contribution that caused us to hold our heads collectively
just a little bit higher, or straighten out just a bit our backs that are
collectively bent, everything else he did will, in hindsight, be can-

celed out and he will be defended by most Afro-Americans as though all his life he had been a saint. I discovered it to be true with Huey Newton. I discovered it to be true with my great-uncle, whose contributions made Newton's pale by comparison, and whose negatives weren't nearly as great. The magnitude of the collective harm from racism is so profound that this is the case.

We tend to celebrate the last forty-five years of Afro-American life as though it is the most important phase of Afro-American history. The legal victory of *Brown* v. *Board of Education* in 1954 stands out virtually as the launch for the gaining of our civil rights. Then we tend to date the real driving force that got everything going really good as occurring in December 1955, with Rosa Parks's refusal to get up and move to the back of a public bus in Montgomery, Alabama. And it is right that we place so much significance on those dates and all that followed after them. But as I think back to the kinds of things that happened to us before then, as I think back to how easy it is to take for granted my freedom to go anywhere I please, associate with whomever I please, and pursue any dream my mind is capable of even though I might not achieve the goal, I wonder if I could have survived in the days when none of this was assured, or in the South, most of it not available, the way my forebears survived, to say nothing of wondering if I could have prospered.

As Paul Kwilecki said, Joseph Griffin should not be judged by the standards of today. I must not judge him, the rest of my generation and those younger than me must not judge him, or judge the troops or commanders who fought Japan in World War II, or judge anyone who lived through anything where there was, or still is, pain and hardship on scales unimaginable to us—a generation growing used to the rapid ease of E-mail and the other conveniences of cyberspace, while maxing out credit cards, who can't imagine compulsory military service or the fear of vigilante injustice coming to snatch away our lives in the middle of the night. . . . We mustn't judge since we are able to live the comfortable, frequently banal lives we so often lead today because of what they went through as they paved the way to this comfort and/or boredom we take for granted, even when they couldn't see the forest for the trees. It may be difficult to understand, it may sound ironic to ears like ours that Joseph Howard Griffin could motivate simply by

what he accomplished, then be the first person to have placed under arrest civil rights activist Hosea Williams, whom he later told
never to return to Bainbridge for good because the town didn't
need his kind of activism, while at the same time he served as a father figure to another icon of the civil rights movement. "He
wanted to see black folks able to do what any man or woman could
do," sums up Donald Hollowell. "He was willing to work for it, to
pay for it, to talk for it, to do whatever else was reasonably necessary and maybe even more, in order to see it brought about for his
people. I believe that with all my heart." In the end, combined with
all I found out about the life led by my maternal grandmother's oldest brother, I had no alternative but to accept that conviction from
an esteemed fighter who was there.

EPILOGUE

It is the Fourth of July 1998, and I am attending a family reunion in Atlanta on the Pearson side with my own family: Nancy; her son, five-year-old Jordan (whose father lives in Mexico), who is now our son; and our eight-month old twins, Francesca Edith Pearson and Nathaniel Griffin Pearson. Relatives are fascinated and delighted with the two latest additions to the fifth generation dating back from Law and Mary Pearson's marriage in 1869 and the fourteen children they had.

There are 198 family members in attendance, including doctors, lawyers, M.B.A.s, C.P.A.s, Ph.D.s, Ivy League graduates, alumni of Morehouse and Spelman and elsewhere, who spent the day on a tour of the city, then at a picnic held at a horse ranch south of the city. And now we're attending the evening banquet in the Comfort Inn ballroom, during which descendants of each of Law and Mary's children who married and had kids send a representative to the microphone set up in front of the banquet tables to tell what has happened in the last year within each extended family. My father always represents the Nathan Pearson branch. He is seventy-seven years old now, and a little slower than he used to be as he walks past all the tables with aunts, uncles, first cousins, second cousins, child third and fourth cousins, and cousin-in-laws, in their finest attire, past the buffet table to the right that was filled with enticing trays of food before everyone took their helpings, and onto the parquet floor that later in the evening will be filled with a band and dancers, primarily the teenagers of the family, gyrating to the latest r&b and rap hits. When he reaches there, using his formal tone of voice—one that contrasts with his informal person-to-person give-and-take only in that it is an octave deeper—he begins to enunciate with a precise diction that hints he may just as well have been an English teacher before attending medical school as a science teacher. And as he speaks, true to his nature, the first words to come out of his mouth are those designed to correct a relative who preceded him, on certain dates that other family events took place, after which he proceeds to give a report on the Nathan Pearson branch, including the "fact" that his first grandchildren were born on November 3, 1997, when they were actually born on November 4.

According to articles published recently in the major media, extended family reunions are now a big thing within Afro-American families. They are events where we tell and retell each other stories handed down about past family glory, each family convinced that they distinguished themselves above and beyond all the other Negro families down through the years because of what they have achieved, and because their families "didn't take any [or more colloquially, "no"] shit from the white man." Uncle or grandpa or cousin so-and-so told that white man to get outta his face or else. . . . I remember one more in a long line of such stories, told to me by my father after the film *Rosewood* premiered (about the Afro-American town in Florida that was burned down in 1923 and its residents massacred, based on the false report that a Caucasian woman in a nearby town had been raped by a Negro man). I called to tell him I had seen it, after which he replied, "Something similar happened, I forget which year, on a smaller scale somewhere else in Florida, where some of our relatives lived. And one of our cousins defended his family, then had to leave the town. And, wait now. He left the town and told the whites that if anything happened to anyone in his family he was coming back to do some harm. And do you know they never bothered anyone else in the family. . . ." True? True, but embellished? False? I can't tell.

And when so many family members tell such stories, they say that there was something about those times that made them better times (my father is an exception here), even though there was occasional violence and the ever-present Jim Crow. The neighbor, the elderly woman who acted like a mother to every child on the block, whose house was right down the street, who spanked any kid who got out of line and told his parents about it, after which the child received a second spanking from one of his parents. And they say that because of segregation, Afro-American businesses were booming, when in reality it was true that Afro-American commercial districts thrived just like in-town commercial districts everywhere thrived before suburbanization, but in most places most of those businesses were not Afro-American–owned. And yes, lamentably, there were many forward-thinking prosperous Afro-American businesspersons like Uncle Joe and Herb Dudley, whose enterprises died once segregation ended. Yet plenty of Afro-American tradesmen and businessmen in the South were decimated, too, upon the advent of Jim Crow in the late 1800s; 80 percent of Afro-Americans back then lived in relative poverty; and in fact, there is far more opportunity for Afro-American businesses today than there was during Jim Crow. Yet nostalgists overlook this complex reality and insist that people back then helped each other more. . . . On a day-to-day basis, that may have been true. Yet, overall, the truth is always more complex than we admit, and the real past is somewhere in an unfocused midpoint between where we insist it was and what we hate about the present.

The reunions where such stories are exchanged have become so important because, like Christianity, they have become a salve, a balm, a refreshment, an oasis in a nation that hasn't yet fully embraced Afro-Americans (will it ever?). And like all unwelcomed and collectively injured people, we tell uplifting stories to ourselves, to each other, to give us reasons to keep getting up every morning to face a new day. So, just like there is nothing like the bosom of Jesus, we tell each other at these reunions that there is nothing like the family we come from. "Don't listen to nobody [anyone] who tries to tell you different [differently]." And in this fashion we spin an improvised ethnicity, an improvised set of traditions, remaining typically American, reenergizing ourselves to the extent a people can be reenergized by the rudiments of an ethnicity in a society that disallows us any feeling of fully participating in, fully belonging to all that it's about.

At the reunion, one of my cousins, Amber, a member of the fifth generation (I am a member of the fourth) and, like me, from the Nathan Pearson branch and a graduate of Brown (in her case, class of 1995), who spent a year in the Philippines, compliments of the consulting firm she works for in Washington, walks up to me, sits down, and says, "I can't believe it! Hugh with kids!" I find the comment both amusing and galling since I can vividly recall when she was the same age as Nathaniel and Francesca (the year she was born was the same year I received my driver's license). Then she asks what I am writing about now. I tell her it's a book about family, but it doesn't focus that much attention on the Pearson side, only enough to tell the story the way I think it needs to be told. And true to what's to be expected, since with each generation family legends grow and become embellished just as the stories about Jesus grew and became embellished, having heard many of them, she replies with enthusiasm in her voice and a prideful glow, "Someone should write the story of the Pearsons!" I know exactly what she wants. And I know that what she wants is also what numerous families want and think everyone wants to read. And I know that before I began writing professionally, before I registered more years out in the real world, I would have wanted the same thing. Yet there is one story that she's never been told, a story told only to me. And I know that the only reason I was told it was because of an illness I had but recovered from in 1995.

My father, the most accomplished, the most defiant of Nathan Pearson's children, and the least likely to tell such stories, was sitting in my hospital room, when suddenly I looked up and saw that he was wiping away tears. He had been coming into that room like a proud hawk, resplendent in a beige sports jacket, white shirt, and brown tie, and on the lookout for any blows to his pride from all the hotshot M.D.s around there, blows that were supposed to be countered by the insignia of one of the medical societies he belongs to on his lapel. And, sure enough, on one visit he was meted out a dose of condescension from one of the hospital's resident physicians. "See this pin, young man," my father replied, pointing to his lapel as though he were instructing a small child. "What does that tell you? It tells you that I'm a physician, too." This time he came in and sat down next to my bed, rubbed his forehead with one of his hands, then tears welled up in his eyes and he took a hanky and wiped them away. Then he tried to make an intimate connection with his son. Yet, simultaneously, it felt as though I were a priest and he were a Catholic layman in the confessional. Because what he said was totally out of left, or, since I'm left-handed, right field.

"When I was a boy, I went into town one day and this white man saw me and he walked up to me and told me to dance. I said, 'Dance? But there's no music.' He said he knew that, but he wanted me to dance anyway. So I had to dance."

End of story, his composure during and after telling it successfully maintained. I knew how difficult, how excruciating it was for my father to tell me that story. How it was his effort, his own convoluted way of finally connecting with his son in a way he had never connected with him before, his way of admitting that the toughness he insisted all those years was the protoplasm composing the Pearson family had a few chinks in it.

And it was as close as we ever got to a heart-to-heart. Three years later as I drove through the hot, humid air of Mitchell County, Georgia, on the way back for my last visit to Bainbridge before finishing this book, as I gazed upon the fields, and the kudzu and Spanish moss covering the trees, and the pine forests and the red clay backroads coming off the highway, I thought about that story and imagined what it must have looked like in the early morning hours before dawn in January 1921, just days before my father was born, when Jim Roland, the forty-year-old proud Negro owner of a two-hundred-acre farm, was marched to the middle of a red clay road in that very county by a group of Caucasian men, then riddled with bullets until he was dead, because he had wrestled a gun away from J. L. Harrell the day before and wounded him in the process, after Harrell, brandishing that gun, demanded that he dance. But Roland refused. And I wondered if, like Roland, my father had refused, would I even be here?

I constantly remind myself that the world is tough and few things in life are as simple as we'd like to believe. I was shocked and angered that my father had to experience anything like that, and even more shocked that he would tell me (that is, at that particular moment). But the more I thought about it, the more I appreciated the sacrifices he and all the rest of my forebears made, and the more I marveled that they were able to transmit so much self-confidence to me. "We were responsible for your freedom!" the elderly Jewish man had told me at the 92nd Street Y. Now more than ever, I realized how flippant and incorrect he had been, and as a result, I felt a fresh anger that subsided into an acceptance of how elusive true understanding between people, between groups, can be. Once more I realized how, in essence, the racial problem boils down to a mutual refusal to deal with each other's individual humanity, to see how we all play the cards we are dealt, and when you don't appreciate the other fella's hand, then you can't appreciate his strategy. If you could appreciate it you might be able to see where he makes a wrong move. But you have to analyze the cards, not simply dismiss his game. I, too, have been guilty of such flippant dismissal—in the case of ghetto rappers, emotional churchgoing Afro-Americans. . . . Yet even here there is a certain complexity in what I feel, given the fact that a large part of my irritation derives from society's tendency to see, to highlight such Afro-Americans and grant short shrift to the rest of us. This nation's culture tends to act as though the rest of us aren't "truly black" unless we behave as they do (whatever "true blackness" is). And, given my pedigree, it has never been within me to behave either way. And what of my pedigree as it relates to Joseph Howard Griffin?

Some part of me was still proud of him, in fact, the lion's share of me. Maybe at a younger age I would have felt some sort of shame, given the security deeds. And if I hadn't researched what it was like for women before abortion was legalized, his abortion practice, too, may have been a source of shame. But not anymore. I felt bad for anyone who lost their land to my great-uncle. But the larger part of me thought of the robber barons and the legions of other millionaires who ruthlessly exploited or did something illegal on the way to their wealth, their descendants now sanitized into respectability (with names like Rockefeller, Kennedy, Bronfman, etc.). I concluded that there aren't too many ways to become very wealthy, minus a certain ruthlessness and willingness to bend the rules. Returning once more to my favorite play, *Death of a Salesman,* I recalled the scene where the teenage Biff Loman playfully boxes with his uncle Ben, the millionaire brother his father admires, whom Biff has never seen before, after which Uncle Ben offers Biff his hand for a handshake. Biff shakes his hand and Uncle Ben then takes his umbrella and shoves Biff to the ground with the umbrella across his neck, telling him, "Never fight fair with a stranger, boy, you'll never get out of the jungle that way." I pondered, too, the hunger, the desire to set yourself and your descendants up for life so that they can bypass most of the world's harsh realities. The older I get, the more I understand it. The more bubbles of idealism within me that are burst (particularly when I take into consideration race), the more I appreciate such drive, even as I grow increasingly convinced that it's not within me to be very ruthless.

And there was the additional revelation to consider, uncovered by my investigations: the fact that two southern Jewish families had played a very important role in his life. What did I make of that? Did this fact support any notion that Jews had been responsible for "my freedom" through being responsible for my great-uncle's success, and thus becoming responsible for providing me with a major portion of my self-esteem? I decided the answer is no. Even if Julian Ehrlich hadn't encouraged Joe Griffin to settle in Bainbridge, eventually my great-uncle would have found another town or city to settle down in and, given his energy and resourcefulness, he would have prospered. No doubt the precise route would have been different. But still he would have become the success he became because it was within him to become it. He had the will and the drive. And most of that will and drive had been instilled by his own family and the circumstances in which he was raised. That two southern Jewish families aided him more than others who considered themselves white cannot be denied. That it was a good thing that he had such "friends" to the extent a Negro man could have Caucasian friends in southwest Georgia in that day and age was a good thing, underscoring the tradition of Afro-American and Jewish cooperation even as we have been, to a tremendous extent, estranged. This I had to appreciate. This I had to factor positively into my peculiar, complicated feelings toward Jews as a whole, making it impossible for me to hate them as a group, still admiring them while feeling disappointed by the flippant racism so many of them demonstrate today toward Afro-Americans, as they leave us out in the cold and assimilate with the rest of America. As I factor this in I have to ask myself, If Afro-Americans had the opportunity to escape association with another group considered even more outcast than us, and run into the quasi-open embrace of the rest of America, would we do the same thing? I think the answer is yes. So, to me, in the final analysis Jews are only being human, which doesn't make it any easier to accept arrogance from a Jew when it rears its ugly head, but perhaps makes it easier to understand. Now it was time for me to attempt to reach a final understanding about the legacy left to me by Joseph Griffin.

I continued through Mitchell County and crossed into neighboring Decatur County, then into Bainbridge, to visit what is now PX Printing but used to be Griffin Hospital and Clinic. I hadn't been inside since I was a small boy in the early '60s and my father took us there to pick up his mother-in-law, my maternal grandmother, Mary Griffin Richardson, after she had surgery. Besides installing a new roof, I wondered what else the new owner had done to the building, this place that was one of the cornerstones of my sense of family pride, this place that was a foundation next to the grounding, the meshing my self-esteem was encased in, based on my father being a physician and, when I was a teenager, based on the way he gave me those answers about how the Caucasians in Jim Crow Georgia used to say "Don't bother those Pearsons, they're crazy!"

For the most part, the building was still laid out the same way Uncle Joe had it built. But the walls in the reception area had been painted blue and white. And there was a counter in front, and on that counter were the pamphlets that a congressman distributes periodically to his constituents, in this case, Stanford Bishop, an Afro-American. The headline on the pamphlets assured his constituents that he was "Taking Care of Business." The owner, a Caucasian man named Julian Braswell, came out to greet me and guide me through the building. We walked past the reception area, through the door, into a long corridor off which were several rooms, the rooms where once there were patients. At the end of the corridor was what used to be the emergency room entrance, and to the right, the emergency room. But I could get no farther and not at all to the second floor, due to renovations that Mr. Braswell was making to the building. He kept saying how amazing a man Dr. Griffin must have been, that he understood that the hospital was the largest private hospital built for blacks in the entire country. Another human embellishment registered over time. I told him it wasn't the largest in the country, but at one time it was the largest in the state.

Then I thanked him for the brief tour and made my way over to Water Street, a couple of blocks away, turned left, and walked over to a shop called Material Things, filled with sewing notions and fabric. Seated and standing in there were six women, all Caucasian.

"Don't you know how dangerous it is for a man to walk into a place like this by himself with all these women?" one of them said. We all laughed. Then she asked, "What can we do for you?"

"My name is Hugh Pearson. I came here because a woman who works over at Cynda's [the restaurant and bar in the town square] told me that on the second floor of this building was my great-uncle Joseph Griffin's first hospital. She said you can still see the room numbers over the doors."

"Yes, it's true. If you'd like we'll have someone take you up there."

When I and my two twenty-something escorts reached the top of the stairs, they told me that the new owners were renovating the floor into what they said would be apartments. And to my astonishment, there was plenty from the old days that was still intact. After a left turn, at the end of a corridor, was a large room with a door that read "Dr. Griffin. Private." Then when I turned right, down the next corridor, before me were several rooms with beautiful stained wooden facing composing the door frames just as he had them built, and metal numbers above the doors. There were eleven rooms in all, and a call box. "When we came up here for the first time," one of the women said, "we found old bottles of chloroform." Then she led me into what had been the old operating room, which was down another hallway that opened up to the right. "I did some wonderful surgery there," Uncle Joe had told my aunt Barbara. But there is little to see there now except an empty room and faucet outlets.

"All of this is too precious to tear down," I told them.

"They don't plan on doing that," one of them responded. "They're going to try to preserve as much as they can."

It was something I was relieved to hear but couldn't imagine being carried out while dividing the space up into apartments. And somehow I wished that I could have lifted the entire floor up and carted it off to a museum, the Smithsonian perhaps, or the new Afro-American museum in Detroit, anywhere to ensure that later generations could see what my grandmother's oldest brother had achieved in the middle of that age of horror for our people. Who would believe it? Here was the tangible evidence of accomplishment, something to buttress many of the family legends, something to sink your disbelieving eyes into, where you could imagine Joseph Griffin in the 1930s and '40s, going from room to room just blocks from the town square, the hospital and him abuzz with important activity well beyond the menial tasks and ghastly lynchings history records so effectively and to the exclusion of almost everything else about Negro life at that time in towns like this, as it tells us what the Jim Crow South was like. If I didn't cart it off to a museum, I wondered, what younger person listening to me if I reach the age of eighty—a jaded forty-year-old adult like myself—would believe my accounts of this, rather than give me a patronizing nod, uncertain of the accuracy of my aging mind, the kind of nod that all too often I am prone to give an elderly person when hearing him or her recall such places, unsure of the recollective ability of a mind, *any mind,* trying to think back forty or more years earlier.

I thought of how I had made a visit to the Caucasian R. A. "Cheney" Griffin, brother of former Georgia governor Marvin Griffin, the previous February, to try to get him to shake out the old memories. Slightly frail and nearing eighty, he greeted me, ushered me inside, and invited me to sit in his living room. He and Hosea Williams had been close in a way that seems peculiar to our current sensibilities, a way that indicated how both warmth and contempt could exist between Caucasians and Negroes in the Jim Crow South at the same time. Hosea Williams had recounted for me how upon returning to Bainbridge after World War II, he went to work at the Junior Chamber of Commerce Club headed by Cheney, a club where he alleged the two of them didn't always run a kosher operation, in that they'd run up the bills customers incurred in the club bar and restaurant and steal from the slot machines that had been installed. He alleged that eventually Cheney told him he should go to college because as a Negro the only chance he had to make anything important of himself was with a college education. And that when he told Cheney he couldn't afford to go, Cheney helped pay his way.*

But before going, he and Cheney were content to play out certain roles expected of them in order to thrive among the residents of Bainbridge. Cheney was mayor of the town from 1947 to 1964 (and sat on the dais and introduced Ralph McGill at the dedication ceremony for my great-uncle's second hospital). At the Caucasians-only Junior Chamber of Commerce Club, patrons would often come by because they wanted to fraternize with Cheney, the mayor, as he hung out there. And as they ordered food and drinks their bill would grow and grow, until they'd question it, leading Cheney to call Williams. "He'd say, 'Goddamn, you're [doing something] to these poor folks, nigger come here, nigger come here . . . ,'" recalled Williams. "And you know it was all a game, and one time he grabbed me and cut my tie off, I had this tie, and he said, 'Goddamnit nigger!' That made them crackers feel good, too. Then when they left we'd just bust out laughing."

*Cheney Griffin denies the allegation that he stole from slot machines or helped pay Hosea Williams's college expenses.

"I don't remember that, but it could be so," Cheney replied when I asked him about the incident and the antics. Then I asked the man who was alleged to have given new meaning to the term "spoils system" when he served as chief of staff for his brother Marvin when governor of Georgia about his interactions with my great-uncle. And as I recalled to Paul Kwilecki, he recounted the standard pleasantries, and of how my great-uncle had been friends with his father Pat Griffin, to which Kwilecki explained why, in his opinion, that was Cheney's response (as recorded in Chapter 11), a response similar to others I was getting. But there was one thing Cheney alleged that my great-uncle was quite instrumental in doing, which again was telling with regard to the peculiar relationship between Caucasians and Negroes down there at that time. "Back then, maybe some black associating with some white, that could cause some trouble. [Me and Dr. Griffin] would get together to keep anything from getting worse. He'd do his best to get the person out of circulation, up north to where he had relatives." To where *he* had relatives. In other words, he was referring to a Negro male being accused of "associating with some white." That could cause trouble. And of course we can guess what kind of "white" Cheney Griffin was referring to. Joseph Griffin was instrumental in getting a Negro male up north to avoid being killed for allegedly associating with a Caucasian female.

He walked a thin line, and, as Paul Kwilecki said, apparently he walked it well. Cheney agreed that "Doc was both a businessman and a physician." And he heard all about the abortions, and the deeding of property, and I could tell that he knew a lot more about what was going on in the town back then than he was telling, that older people all over town had their Dr. Griffin stories, and jokes, like the one I heard repeatedly from Cheney and every Caucasian interviewee. One year in the 1950s, Uncle Joe was under investigation by the IRS for possible tax evasion. He had bank accounts all over the area, in Bainbridge, Thomasville, and Dothan, Alabama, etc. So the IRS went searching for the accounts and tallied up all the money in the accounts and the federal taxes he needed to pay on the money. "How much do I owe you?" Uncle Joe is said to have asked. When he was presented a bill for a quarter of a million dollars, allegedly he pulled out a checkbook and wrote a check for the full amount on a bank account the IRS hadn't found (another legend, and one I was unable to confirm or disprove because the records of the case no longer exist).

"Yes, Daddy was something else," Mary Louise agreed as I sat in the family room of her house after touring the old hospital site above Material Things. I could tell that she knew that I knew a lot more about his past than she had been willing to tell me. She called me savvy. I recalled the joke Ms. Hinds-Adams told me Uncle Joe had made in the 1940s about the imaginary maid sabotaging the imaginary plans for poisoning the town's well-to-do Caucasians. "Yes," Mary Louise chuckled, adding, "Then the old maid would have said, 'He's just as bad as you all say he is.'" Then she told me of how once during a conversation he told her she could never accumulate wealth because she was unwilling to take risks, that only risk-takers became rich. Then she told me about an informal club that had been organized among the town's middle-class Negro men—the postmen, schoolteachers, preachers, undertakers, a club formed in the 1930s. "It was called the Stop Griffin Club. Daddy thought these men were his friends. But they had formed the club because they thought he was becoming too powerful and they wanted to stop him. After he found out about it he said, 'Okay, I'm sure enough gonna fix them now!'" And apparently he did, since he became more and more powerful not only through his bank account and stock and real estate holdings, but through holding the liens on all the taxis owned by the Negro taxi cab company in town that was used by so many people since most Negroes in town back then didn't own cars. He also developed a commercial district called Griffin Quarters where he rented out space to small Negro businesses, and an auditorium called Griffin Auditorium where community groups held meetings. I could tell that Mary Louise had been thinking about it all, reflecting on the true breadth of her father's life while I was gone, between the time I had last seen her and this visit, the times when I slipped into Bainbridge unannounced, and didn't visit her or anyone else in the family, staying for weeks at a time because I didn't want any of them to influence my research, or to have their sentiments and warmth, or possible suspicions and resulting anger cloud my efforts to uncover the real story of how my great-uncle was perceived and how he accomplished all that he did.

His life represented such an odd countervailing twist to Caucasians' expectations of Negroes, while corresponding to their
stereotypes of the same ethnic group that the elderly man I argued
with at the 92nd Street Y belongs to, the ethnic group they
accepted, unlike citizens in most other southern towns. Summing it
all up, Mary Louise reminisced, "People in this town used
to call Daddy the black Jew." Would that I had told that to my tor-
mentor.

"I'm glad you're doing this," a sixty-something Caucasian man
named Mayo Livingston, who wrote occasionally for the town
newspaper, told me during one of my visits. "For a long time I've
thought someone should do something on Dr. Griffin. To get the
black perspective you should talk to Luther Conyers. He knew a lot
about what was going on back then." Luther Conyers begged off,
then recommended that I talk to an elderly woman who begged off,
then recommended that I talk to someone else. And when I finally
got to speak to someone, usually that person would tell me the
same kind of story, confirming what Hosea Williams had predicted
about the reluctance of so many people to be completely candid.
"He'd take cases no other doctor would touch," said an Afro-American store clerk in Fowlstown, a small community just south of
Bainbridge. The clerk was about in his mid- to late sixties, and I just
stopped in the store to buy something on my way to interviewing a
woman who wasn't of much help, and I forgot to get the clerk's
name (and would be unsuccessful in locating him several months
later). "I remember going over to Memorial Hospital once when I
was sick," he recalled. "They were rude, didn't treat me with any respect. So I called up Dr. Griffin who told me to come over to Griffin
Hospital. He gave me this pink liquid he called 'Griffin Special.' I
took that and after a while I was fine." As to why people who
owned property deeded their property to him as collateral on their
medical bills, he said it was because Dr. Griffin was such a good
physician. How many accounts of the same type of stories can you
record in a book before it's no longer interesting? I wondered. How
many hints that a man was really more complex, combined with
outright candid assessments from a few sources detailing his true
complexity, and solid evidence of that complexity dug up from

court records and deed records and newspaper clips, will suffice when trying to reconstruct the true depth of such a man?

On the Sunday of my final visit I make my way over to Nelson Chapel A.M.E. church to see for myself the preschool building next to it launched and funded by Uncle Joe. I can tell when I've reached the Afro-American section of this part of Bainbridge because the sidewalk ends. During Jim Crow it was common for sidewalks to end once the Negro section of town began (though the sidewalk didn't end in front of Uncle Joe's house, on the other side of the center of town, but continued past his property). Above the doorway of the modern one-story addition, the sign reads: "The Dr. Joseph H. Griffin Educational Complex, erected 1971." There is no more defacing. I can't go inside because the doors are locked, but I'm assured that his portrait is hanging inside, unharmed. I walk inside the redbrick church, where a service is in progress. But on this Sunday there are few in attendance, only about thirty people, two-thirds women, two-thirds elderly. How many times have I heard such services? The preacher singsongs his sermon about Jesus, a style I'm familiar with, but not from my childhood since the A.M.E. congregation I grew up in frowned on such practices. Behind him sits the youth choir. The congregation sings the same old songs I heard while growing up, on those once-a-month Sundays when we did attend church. Outfitted in an elegant dress, Mary Louise sits in one of the front pews. Suddenly I think of the transcripts from one of my aunt's interviews of Uncle Joe twenty years earlier. On that particular visit my grandmother made the trip to Bainbridge with her, along with Mr. Eaton of Florida A&M. During the interview, in which she aided their efforts to reconstruct the past, Grandmother and Mr. Eaton tried to get Uncle Joe to acknowledge the role the Lord had played in his success. But he refused, telling them, "That may be the way you see it, but not me. I was the one who was responsible." Proof positive that he hadn't been very religious or sentimental, that he was more of a pragmatist who appeared not to think of God too much. But then how else would an abortion doctor—especially an abortion doctor back when he performed abortions—have behaved?

As I watch and listen, I wonder: Does Mary Louise feel a certain sense of contrition about her father's life and the way he amassed his wealth? Does she feel she must atone for it? Does she pray for his soul, under the belief that your offspring must pray for you, asking God's mercy for the sins you committed during your life? Is that task, along with a number of other things, what brings her here every Sunday? But I'm too chicken to broach the issue. After the service I tell her that I came to see the educational complex and that now I am on my way back to New York City. She wishes me well, we hug, and I depart.

I head east along four-laned U.S. highway 84. And about eighteen miles outside of Bainbridge, in neighboring Grady County, just before I reach the town of Cairo—where baseball great Jackie Robinson was born in 1919, after which his mother moved the family to California—upon driving over a hill, to the left, at the summit of another hill, an impressive off-white marble mausoleum comes into view. I turn onto the exit ramp, then onto the grounds in front of the black wrought-iron gate connected to white stucco walls on either side, with potted plants on top of the edge of each gate wall, and to one side a pink marble sign that reads "Dr. Joseph H. Griffin Memorial Gardens: In Honor of Dr. Joseph H. Griffin, Bainbridge, Georgia." I park and get out. I have been here before. It cost Uncle Joe fifty thousand dollars to build. I have stood in front of the impressive pink marble flowerpots flanking the doorway and gazed upon the engraving over the mausoleum with its ancient insignia of the physician, the wings and a rod with serpents coiled around the rod, then the words "South Georgia's First Negro Surgeon: Joseph H. Griffin, M.D., erected November 26, 1958." And I've peered inside the mausoleum, which contains the remains of my great-grandmother and great-grandfather Griffin, and Uncle Joe and his wife, Aunt Elaine, and Uncle David and Uncle Robert (Uncle Joe died on December 30, 1980, just short of the age of ninety-three, while his wife died just five days later).

On the grounds surrounding the mausoleum are the graves of other family members, and elsewhere in the cemetery are the graves of nonfamily members who purchased plots. Not all Griffin family members are here. Not, for instance, Joseph Griffin's youngest sister. Grandma chose to be buried next to Grandpa Richardson in Jacksonville. Still, there is something very regal about these grounds and the mausoleum, the way they flaunt their presence to all travelers making their way across south Georgia, from the outskirts of Savannah, southwestward to Waycross, Valdosta, then west and on into Thomasville, then Cairo, then Bainbridge, and destinations in between. Nothing else along this roughly two hundred miles of roadway through south Georgia rises up the same way (or maybe inadvertent family sentiment *causes me to think* that nothing else rises up the same way). It is enough to inflate the ego of any and every family member, as though this, along with celebrating himself in posterity, was Uncle Joe's intention. I linger here for a while, sit in one of the wrought-iron chairs in a lounge area in front of the mausoleum, and look out over the landscape of red clay fields and pine forests, and think about all I've been through, all I've learned, and imagine just a bit what Uncle Joe, my father, my grandfathers, my great-grandfathers, my other uncles, and others in my family went and have been through. And I wonder what really happens after you die. Are the Christians correct? Are there pearly gates, angels in white with wings waiting to greet true believers who will experience perpetual bliss, God presiding over it from a throne, Jesus at his side with flowing locks, Caucasian features, or with brown skin and Negroid features, and in either case, the flip side of all that, a place called hell for unrepentant sinners, with an abominable Satan, and fire and brimstone? I still doubt such a conception of an afterlife, and remain convinced that it would be in the best interest of Afro-Americans to expunge it from our minds. But I don't doubt the existence of a creative spirit, or the possibility of reincarnation, or the possibility that the dead are part of the wind and the rest of nature, observing those of us they've left behind. Of late I've developed a theory that all life is cyclical, like the seasons, or a woman's menstrual period, and that when we die it's like when we sleep but don't remember dreaming and don't realize we were asleep until we wake up the next day, the process after death being rebirth several billion or so years later, after man's stupidity destroys life, and then there is a gaseous nonexistence once more, then water, then the amoeba comes back, then the rest of sea life, etc., until our time comes once again, to emerge from our mothers' wombs, and fulfill an approximation of Santayana's infamous dictum: "Those who cannot remember the past are condemned to repeat it." But just in case I'm wrong and the dead are all around us I rise and step up to the mausoleum and pray to my great-uncle's memory. And in my prayer, this, more or less, is what I say:

Dear Uncle Joe,

We all want to believe that outside there is something called the cold, cruel real world, while inside is the shelter of our family no matter how exasperating our family can be. That no matter how much our family angers us, saddens us, irritates us, in the end family still isn't among those who contribute to the cruelty in the proverbial real world. How could they, since they are our family? The feeling goes somewhat in tandem with what almost always happens when someone dies. The survivors, friends, and acquaintances insist the deceased was the nicest person you'd ever want to meet, helping old ladies across the street, always there for the sick, always ready with a kind word and a kind deed for everyone.

At these moments we never stop to consider that, since everyone is a member of a family, and if everyone who dies was so sweet, then who are all those people who make the real world so cold and cruel? The lovers who cheated on us, or broke up with us because we lost a job, or because we turned unattractive or because they fell in love with someone else; the boss who pressured us into having sex, or overlooked us for a raise or promotion, or who fired us for no good reason; the landlord who didn't renew our lease because someone else would pay more, or there was a big real estate deal to cash in on, so he sold the building; the countless businesspersons who run their scams and cheat us out of our money. . . . If no one in our family is among them, if we aren't among them, if no one who dies is among them, then who are the ones out in the "real world" that our family warned us (usually when we were being obnoxious know-it-all teenagers) would at some point be waiting to do us harm? And if such cruel people never die, then, given the human instinct for survival, is it in our best interest to be cold, cruel, and heartless? I don't think so. Yet neither can I judge you and try to determine if, when you were being that way, you were or weren't justified, though I know that quite often, numerous times, countless times, you were a savior for so many people of all colors in this region.

Since you are deceased, I wasn't even supposed to get close to asking hard questions about your life. Since you are family I was doubly prohibited from even thinking about you in any way but the most al-truistic. Since you lived your life as a Colored–Negro–Black–Afro-American male and were South Georgia's First Negro Surgeon, I was triply prohibited from even wondering if at any time you weren't al-truistic. For me you were supposed to be several layers above being hu-man, and instead live in my mind for the remainder of my days, and then live in my children's minds for the rest of their days, and their children's minds for the rest of theirs and so on, as a legendary saint. But now I guess I've burst that bubble. In the process of exploring your life I've made you human, which for me, for all of us, I believe, is the best thing for you to be. So thank you, warts and all, for being who you were, for accomplishing all you accomplished against such tremen-dous odds, and in the process playing such a large role in who I am.

Thank you.

NOTES

PROLOGUE

5. Calculation of cost-of-living increase to construct building costing $250,000 in 1950, in terms of what it would cost in 1999: Courtesy of Professor Lawrence White, New York University Stern School of Business, January 11, 1999.

6. Willie Reid incident: recalled by numerous family members through the years and recorded in the oral history interview of Joseph H. Griffin, conducted by Barbara Richardson Cotton, Bainbridge, GA, October 20, 1979; incident also related in book *The Way It Was in the South: The Black Experience in Georgia*, by Donald L. Grant (Birch Lane Press, 1993), p. 333.

CHAPTER 1

13. Traits of industriousness and academic achievement encouraged in Jews: *Jews and the New American Scene*, by Seymour Martin Lipset and Earl Raab (Harvard University Press, 1995), p. 12.

19. Marvin Griffin's alleged corruption: *Atlanta Rising: The Invention of an International City 1946–1996*, by Frederick Allen (Longstreet Press Inc., 1996), p. 61.

CHAPTER 2

26. Background of Nathan Pearson: from numerous interviews with Mamie Pearson Jordan, telephone and in person, Kansas City, MO, June 1997.

CHAPTER 3

37. Henry Grady's role in building the new Atlanta and New South after the Civil War: *Booker T. Washington: The Making of a Black Leader, 1856–1901*, by Louis R. Harlan (Oxford University Press, 1972), pp. 165, 218–219; *Where Peachtree Meets Sweet Auburn: The Saga of Two Families and the Making of Atlanta*, by Gary M. Pomerantz (Scribner, 1996), pp. 59–60.

37. Garland Penn's role in the Cotton States and International Exposition and the formation of the National Medical Association during the exposition: "Address of Dr. I. Garland Penn (Stenographically Reported)," *Journal of the National Medical Association*, October–December 1910, Vol. II, No. 4, pp. 336–337.

38. Democratic Party poster in Pennsylvania in 1866: illustration in *Reconstruction: America's Unfinished Revolution 1863–1877*, by Eric Foner (Harper & Row, 1988; Perennial Library Edition, 1989).

38. Respective Reconstruction era philosophies of Democrats and Republicans: "The Birth of the New South," by Hugh Pearson, *Wall Street Journal*, June 24, 1996 (on the Reconstruction era exhibit at the Virginia Historical Society, Richmond, Virginia, June 1996).

39. Olmsted's observations of life in the antebellum South: *The Cotton Kingdom: A Traveler's Observations on Cotton and Slavery in the American Slave States, 1853–1861*, by Frederick Law Olmsted (1861; Da Capo Press edition, 1996), pp. 31–605.

40. "There is not a likely looking black girl in this state that is not . . .": *ibid.*, p. 240.

40. Mrs. Douglass's letter: *ibid.*, pp. 239–240.

41. Slave women desiring intimate relations with masters, in some cases having families with them: *Black Bourgeoisie: The Rise of the New Middle Class*, by E. Franklin Frazier (Free Press, 1957; paperback edition, 1965), pp. 136–137.

42. Physical punishment more likely than death for Negro male slave having sexual congress with Caucasian woman: "Dangerous Liaisons," by C. Vann Woodward, review of book entitled *White Women, Black Men: Illicit Sex in the Nineteenth Century South*, by Martha Hodes (Yale University Press, 1998), *New York Review of Books*, February 19, 1998, p. 16.

42. Characteristics of shiftlessness, lack of intellectual drive, and licentiousness in many Negroes, born of the slave experience: *W. E. B. Du Bois: Biography of a Race 1868–1919*, by David Levering Lewis (Henry Holt and Co., 1993), pp. 70, 196.

43. Death of Reconstruction and concomitant reenfranchisement of southern aristocracy: Pearson, "The Birth of the New South," *op. cit.*

43. More than one-fifth of adult Caucasian males in the South perishing in the Civil War: *America's Reconstruction: People and Politics After the Civil War*, by Eric Foner and Olivia Mahoney (Harper Perennial, 1995), p. 51.

44. Gruesome characteristics of lynchings and cause of death, "unknown perpetrators": Vann Woodward, "Dangerous Liaisons," *op. cit.*

44. James Weldon Johnson's initial encounter with Jim Crow on a Georgia train: *Along This Way: The Autobiography of James Weldon Johnson*, by James Weldon Johnson (Viking Penguin, 1933; Penguin Books edition, 1990), pp. 85–86.

46. "Harmony will come in proportion . . .": Harlan, *Booker T. Washington*, *op. cit.*, p. 160.

46. Booker T. Washington clandestinely protecting Negro lawyer: *ibid.*, pp. 171–175.

46. Promoters of Cotton States and International exhibition and Booker T. Washington traveling to Washington, D.C.: *ibid.*, pp. 204–207.

47. Washington successfully suggesting Penn as superintendent of Negro Building: *ibid.*, p. 208.

47. Handkerchief-headed "Auntie" on Negro Building: *ibid.*, p. 230.

47. How Washington was picked as a speaker at Cotton States Exposition, the circumstances surrounding his speech, its content and reactions to it: *ibid.*, pp. 209–228.

48. Total number of visitors to Cotton States Exposition: Pomerantz, *Where Peachtree Meets Sweet Auburn*, *op. cit.*, p. 60.

49. Dr. J. W. E. Bowen's speech at Cotton States Exposition: *Sixty Years of Medicine or The Life and Times of Dr. Miles V. Lynck: An Autobiography*, by Miles V. Lynck (Twentieth Century Press, 1951), pp. 45–47; "The Black American in Medicine," by Dr. W. Montague Cobb, *Journal of the National Medical Association*, 1981, Vol. 73, Supplement, pp. 1225–1226.

52. W. E. B. Du Bois initially praising Washington's Cotton States Exposition speech: Lewis, *W. E. B. Du Bois*, *op. cit.*, p. 175.

52. Founding of the NMA and its charter: Lynck, *op. cit.*, pp. 49–52. "Open Letter . . . ," by John A. Kenney, Sr., M.D., *Journal of the National Medical Association*, January–March 1910, Vol. II, No. 1, p. 48.

53. "As fast as merit shows up . . .": Harlan, *Booker T. Washington*, *op. cit.*, p. 201.

53. "The white race must dominate . . .": Pomerantz, *Where Peachtree Meets Sweet-Auburn*, *op. cit.*, p. 62.

53. "I want to give you niggers . . .": Harlan, *Booker T. Washington*, *op. cit.*, p. 231.

53. Alliance between Atlanta's leading Negroes and Caucasians in the early twentieth century and circumstances surrounding the Atlanta riot of 1906: "'Good Negro—Bad Negro': The Dynamics of Race and Class in Atlanta During the Era of

the 1906 Riot," by Gregory Dixon, *Georgia Historical Quarterly*, Fall 1997, Vol. LXXXI, No. 3, pp. 593–621.

56. Quote of William Fletcher Penn: *ibid.*, p. 613.

57. I. Garland Penn's account of the 1906 riot to members of the National Medical Association and admonition to uplift Negroes at the bottom: "Address of Dr. I. Garland Penn," *op. cit.*, p. 338.

57. Quote of Dr. Thomas Murrell and Dr. John A. Kenney, Sr.'s, response: "Syphilis and the American Negro—A Medico-Sociologic Study," by John A. Kenney, Sr., M.D., *Journal of the National Medical Association*, April–June 1910, Vol. II, No. 2, pp. 116–117.

58. First Negro physicians in America: "Progress and Portents for the Negro in Medicine," by Dr. W. Montague Cobb, *The Crisis*, April 1948, Vol. 55, No. 4, pp. 108–112.

59. Quote of Dr. Rush: *ibid.*, p. 108.

59. Number of Negro physicians in late nineteenth, early twentieth centuries: *ibid.*, p. 108.

60. Caucasian physician to population ratio: Calculation based on information in *Historical Statistics of the U.S.: Colonial Times to 1970, Bicentennial Edition, Part 1* (U.S. Department of Commerce, Bureau of the Census, 1975), pp. 9, 76.

60. Editorial in the *Washington Post*: "Twelve Million Negroes Do Not Sufficiently Support Doctors Now, says *Washington Post*," *Journal of the National Medical Association*, January–March 1910, Vol. II, No. 1, p. 46.

60. Negro medical schools in late nineteenth and early twentieth centuries: Cobb, "Progress and Portents," *op. cit.*, pp. 109–112; "Report on Medical Education," *Journal of the National Medical Association*, January–March 1910, Vol. II, No. 1, pp. 23–29.

60. Abraham Flexner sent to evaluate medical schools: Cobb, "The Black American in Medicine," *op. cit.*, pp. 1220–1221.

60. History of Negro medical schools as a whole: Cobb, "Progress and Portents," *op. cit.*, pp. 108–112.

61. History of Howard University: Cobb, "The Black American in Medicine," *op. cit.*, p. 1217.

61. Achievements of the Freedmen's Bureau: *op. cit.*, pp. 62–63.

61. Negroes in alley dwellings in Washington, D.C.: Cobb, "The Black American in Medicine," *op. cit.*, p. 1217.

62. Launching of Freedmen's Hospital: *ibid.*, pp. 1217–1218.

62. Founding of Meharry and role of George W. Hubbard: *ibid.*, p. 1219.

CHAPTER 4

66. Characteristics of early surgical operations at Freedmen's Hospital and role of Dr. Daniel Hale Williams: quote of Dr. William A. Warfield in a letter to Dr. John A. Kenney, 1941, in "Medical History," by W. Montague Cobb, *Journal of the National Medical Association*, September 1953, Vol. 45, No. 5, pp. 381–382.

66. General public's distrust of Negro surgeons, Williams's efforts to combat that, and all other characteristics of Williams: *ibid.*, pp. 382–384.

68. Biographical characteristics of Dr. John H. Hale, early surgery at Meharry: "Medical History," by W. Montague Cobb, *Journal of the National Medical Association*, January 1954, Vol. 46, No. 1, pp. 79–80.

69. Joseph Griffin's summer before matriculating at Meharry: *Non Verba Opera—Not Words but Works: The Biography of Joseph Howard Griffin, M.D.*, by Barbara R. Cotton (Florida A&M University Foundation, 1981), p. 23.

69. Courses taught at Georgia State Industrial: college catalogue from 1902.

70. Characteristics of D. C. Suggs: Cotton, *Non Verba Opera, op. cit.*, p. 22.

70. W. E. B. Du Bois's departure from Atlanta University: Lewis, *W. E. B. Du Bois, op. cit.*, p. 407.

71. Completion of first wing of Hubbard Hospital; characteristics and financing: "New Hospital Opened Today," *Journal of the National Medical Association,* January–March 1911, Vol. III, No. 1, pp. 105–107.

72. Consumption among Negroes, myths thereof, antispitting laws, anti-TB leagues formed, Negro medical care marshaled: "Health Problems of the Negroes," by John A. Kenney, Sr., M.D., *Journal of the National Medical Association,* April–June 1911, Vol. III. No. 2, pp. 127–135; "Annual Address of the President, Tennessee State Medical Association," *Journal of the National Medical Association,* July–September 1911, Vol. III, No. 3, pp. 224–225; "Remarks on the Health of Colored People," by J. Madison Taylor, M.D., *Journal of the National Medical Association,* July–September 1915, Vol. VII, No. 3, p. 162.

72. Sample questions that medical board examinees might face in second decade of twentieth century: from lists of questions featured periodically in issues of the *Journal of the National Medical Association* in section called "Post-Graduate Department," 1912 to 1915.

73. Number of patient beds at Freedmen's Hospital by 1911: *American Medical Directory,* 3rd edition (American Medical Association, 1912), p. 216.

73. Number of patient beds in Meharry's three teaching hospitals by 1911: *ibid.,* p. 1152.

73. Number of Meharry medical graduates versus Howard's: Cobb, "Progress and Portents," *op. cit.,* pp. 119–120.

73. Number of graduates in Joe Griffin's Meharry class: *ibid.*

73. Courses students at Meharry took in second decade of twentieth century: from Meharry ad featured in back of the *Journal of National Medical Association,* April–June 1913, Vol. V, No. 2.

74. Joe Griffin's lack of spending money while a medical student, working in hotel: transcripts of interview of Joseph H. Griffin by Barbara R. Cotton, October 20, 1979.

74. Characteristics of Hubbard Hospital by 1913 and patient admissions and operations performed: "George W. Hubbard Hospital," *Journal of the National Medical Association,* April–June 1913, Vol. V, No. 2, pp. 85–86.

74. Seventy Negro hospitals by 1913: "President's Address," by John A. Kenney, Sr., M.D., *Journal of the National Medical Association,* October–December 1913, Vol. V, No. 4, p. 218.

74. Dedication of John A. Andrew Memorial Hospital and story of its founding: "John A. Andrew Memorial Hospital," *Journal of the National Medical Association,* April–June 1913, Vol. V, No. 2, pp. 89–93.

75. "Too few are willing" and, by contrast, medical contributions of Caucasian physicians: Kenney, "President's Address," *op. cit.,* pp. 217–223.

75. Joe Griffin's class rank and comments about him in yearbook: Cotton, *Non Verba Opera, op. cit.,* p. 23.

CHAPTER 5

77. Jews not welcome in nineteenth-century Thomasville, but Bainbridge more hospitable: interview with Bertram Ehrlich, Atlanta, GA, June 26, 1997.

77. All passages describing Ehrlich and Kwilecki family history: *ibid.* and *I Remember Life in a Small Southern Town—Bainbridge, Georgia 1913–1985: The Reminis-*

cences of Bertram Ehrlich (Post Printing division of the *Bainbridge Post-Searchlight,* Inc., 1996).

78. Origins of Bainbridge: *Decatur County, Georgia: Past and Present, 1823–1991,* compiled by Decatur County Historical Society (W. H. Wolfe Associates, 1991), pp. 37–38.

79. Lack of railroad bridge limiting Bainbridge's growth: Ehrlich interview, *op. cit.*

80. Rapid Jewish assimilation with Caucasians of southwest Georgia: *I Remember Life, op cit.;* "A Garden of Irony and Diversity," by Lee W. Formwalt, in *The New Georgia Guide* (University of Georgia Press, 1996), pp. 528–529.

81. Origins of Griffin family: interview of Mary Griffin Richardson by Barbara R. Cotton, Jacksonville, FL, May 25, 1980; interview of Joseph H. Griffin by Barbara R. Cotton, Bainbridge, GA, October 20, 1979.

81. Origins of Caucasian settlements in Stewart County, Georgia, and characteristics of antebellum days in the county: "The View from Dowdell's Knob," by William W. Winn, in *The New Georgia Guide, op. cit.,* pp. 366–367; "Touring West Central Georgia," by Fred C. Fussell, in *The New Georgia Guide, op. cit.,* p. 416.

81. Antebellum Stewart County, Georgia, second-largest cotton producer in state: Winn, "The View from Dowdell's Knob," *op. cit.,* p. 367.

81. Robert Griffin's first land purchase and first Afro-American to own land in Stewart County: documentation in Office of Recorder of Deeds, Stewart County Courthouse, Lumpkin, Georgia, visited by author in July 1997; Cotton, *Non Verba Opera, op. cit.,* p. 13.

82. Only 8 percent of Negro farmers in Stewart County owning their own land: *Statistical Atlas of Southern Counties,* by Charles C. Johnson (University of North Carolina Chapel Hill Press, 1941), p. 11.

82. Former President Jimmy Carter recalling stories about "Uncle Bob": interview with Mary Louise Griffin Perry, Bainbridge, GA, August 4, 1997.

82. Details of Joseph Griffin's childhood and early education: Cotton, *Non Verba Opera, op. cit.,* pp. 13–23.

83. Lack of adequate spending on schooling for Negro youths in Stewart County: *ibid.,* pp. 17–18.

83. Characteristics of teachers teaching Negro youths in Stewart County: *ibid.,* pp. 18–20.

84. Meharry changing entrance requirements two years after Joe Griffin's arrival: *Journal of the National Medical Association,* October–December 1915, Vol. VII, No. 4, pp. 324–325.

84. Joe Griffin's class rank at Georgia State Industrial, Meharry, and postgraduate medical training: Cotton, *Non Verba Opera, op. cit.,* pp. 22–27; "Tributes to Meharrians: Dr. Joseph Howard Griffin," in *Meharry Today: A Publication of Meharry Medical College,* November 1975, Vol. 5, No. 1, p. 16.

84. Army days of Joe Griffin and search for a place to practice: interview of Joseph Howard Griffin by Barbara R. Cotton, October 20, 1979.

85. Julian Ehrlich encouraging Joseph Griffin to settle in Bainbridge: Ehrlich interview, June 26, 1997.

86. Residents of Bainbridge lynching Negro prisoner after watching play: Grant, *The Way It Was in the South, op. cit.,* p. 190.

86. The *Bainbridge Post-Searchlight* printing stories of Negro hardship in the North: "Negroes from South Failed to Receive the Wages Promised Them," *Bainbridge Post-Searchlight,* November 15, 1917; "Georgia Darkey Says 'T-N-T' Is 'Travel-Nigger-Travel,'" *Bainbridge Post-Searchlight,* July 18, 1918.

86. World War I "work or fight" laws outraging Negro citizens of Bainbridge: "Colored Citizens Hold Mass Meeting," *Bainbridge Post-Searchlight*, July 25, 1918; Grant, *The Way It Was in the South, op. cit.*, p. 307.

87. Liberty Bond ad in the *Bainbridge Post-Searchlight:* found in several issues of the newspaper including one dated April 11, 1918.

87. Decatur County Negro called "above average, law abiding . . .": "34 of Colored Selectmen of the County Feast in Public Square," *Bainbridge Post-Searchlight*, October 11, 1917.

87. Joe Griffin on dais in sendoff of troops and quote of T. H. Bynes: *ibid.*

88. Joe Griffin mistrusted at first as physician: interview of Joseph Howard Griffin by Barbara R. Cotton, Bainbridge, GA, March 23, 1978.

88. Death count from 1918–1919 influenza epidemic: "Influenza Epidemic of 1918–1919," *Encyclopaedia Britannica Online* (Encyclopaedia Britannica, 1994–1998).

88. Bainbridge reeling from epidemic: "Local and Personal," *Bainbridge Post-Searchlight*, October 24, 1918.

88. Flu treatment administered by Joe Griffin, and quote of Robert Griffin subsequent to Joe Griffin's anger about meager compensation for services: interview with Joseph Howard Griffin by Barbara R. Cotton, March 23, 1978.

88. 1918 influenza epidemic changing his reputation: *ibid.;* interviews with Susanne Mention, Josie Williams, and Ollie Harp, conducted by Barbara R. Cotton, Bainbridge, GA, March 21, 1980; Ehrlich interview, June 26, 1997.

89. Background of family of Elaine Johnson Griffin: interviews with Joseph Howard Griffin, Elaine Johnson Griffin, and Mary Louise Griffin Perry, conducted by Barbara R. Cotton, Bainbridge, GA, October 20, 1979.

89. Spontaneous celebration in Bainbridge because of end of World War I: "Big Celebration in Bainbridge Monday, Nov. 11," *Bainbridge Post-Searchlight*, November 14, 1918.

89. Daniel Mack sentenced to jail, then beaten to death: Grant, *The Way It Was in the South, op. cit.*, p. 307.

89. Wilbur Little incident: *ibid.*, pp. 307–308.

90. Negro veterans recognized in Bainbridge with separate celebration: "Colored People Hold Big Day," *Bainbridge Post-Searchlight*, April 17, 1919.

90. Background of Henry Lincoln Johnson and threat he became to Booker T. Washington: Grant, *The Way It Was in the South, op. cit.*, pp. 336–338.

90. G. R. Hutto's speech: "G. R. Hutto Heads Negro Pythians," *Bainbridge Post-Searchlight*, July 22, 1920.

91. Tuskegee in second tier of cities considered for first Negro VA hospital: testimony of the Reverend G. Lake Imes before U.S. Senate Subcommittee on Veterans Affairs, considering proposed Booker T. Washington VA Hospital, Washington, D.C., February 3, 1948, p. 132.

91. Racial trouble surrounding Tuskegee VA Hospital staffing: *Robert Russa Moton of Hampton and Tuskegee*, by William H. Hughes and Frederick Patterson (University of North Carolina Press, 1956), pp. 228–231.

92. Early days of Joe Griffin's medical practice: Cotton, *Non Verba Opera, op. cit.*, pp. 32–35.

93. "Doc, I got a nigger sow . . .": *ibid.*, p. 37.

94. Georgia leading nation in mob violence for 1918 and 1919: "South Leads in Thirty Years of Mob Violence," *Bainbridge Post-Searchlight*, May 19, 1919; "Lynching Record for 1919 Given Out," *Bainbridge Post-Searchlight*, January 8, 1920.

94. Rape or other assault on Caucasian women not even primary reason for Negro lynchings: "South Leads in Thirty Years of Mob Violence," *op. cit.*

94. Coffee County, Georgia, race-related slayings: "Negro Trio Slain by Coffee County Mob Near Douglas," *Bainbridge Post-Searchlight*, November 25, 1920.

95. Jim Roland incident: "Negro Shot Dead by Avenging Mob," *Bainbridge Post-Searchlight*, January 6, 1921; "White Man Shot; Negro Lynched," *Bainbridge Post-Searchlight*, January 13, 1921.

96. F. A. White incident: "Negro Preacher Is Whipped in Doerun," *Bainbridge Post-Searchlight*, December 9, 1920.

96. Minstrel show popularity: ad for forthcoming show at Callahan Theater, *Bainbridge Post-Searchlight*, May 13, 1920; "The Minstrel's Great Success," *Bainbridge Post-Searchlight*, May 20, 1920; "The Lasses White's All Star Minstrels," *Bainbridge Post-Searchlight*, September 22, 1921.

97. "Yankee" millionaires building hunting plantations outside of Thomasville: Ehrlich interview, June 26, 1997.

97. Florida real estate frenzy stretching to sites near Tallahassee: *I Remember Life*, *op. cit.*

97. Derailment of St. Louis Express: *ibid.*

97. Caucasian bootlegger hiring Negro youth: *ibid.*

98. History behind construction of Joe Griffin's first hospital: Cotton, *Non Verba Opera*, *op. cit.*, p. 35.

98. Joe Griffin's controversial operation on Negro woman and Dr. Alford's response: interviews with Joseph Howard Griffin, Elaine Johnson Griffin, and Mary Louise Griffin Perry, conducted by Barbara R. Cotton, Bainbridge, GA, October 20, 1979 (interview transcripts contain quote of nurse not found in *Non Verba Opera*); Cotton, *Non Verba Opera*, *op. cit.*, p. 36.

CHAPTER 6

100. Ralph McGill's column on Griffin Hospital and Clinic: "Ralph McGill: In the Deep Rural South," *Atlanta Journal-Constitution*, August 6, 1950.

101. McGill's political stance in the late 1940s constituting liberalism by southern standards: Allen, *Atlanta Rising*, *op. cit.*, pp. 43–44.

101. Quote of Elmer Wheeler's column on Griffin Hospital and Clinic: "Tributes to Meharrians: Dr. Joseph Howard Griffin," *op. cit.*, p. 16.

102. All background information on Crawford Richardson, Sr.: interview with Crawford Richardson, Jr., Jacksonville, FL, September 21, 1996.

102. Mary Griffin Richardson's recollections of living in Bainbridge as a teenager: interview of Mary Griffin Richardson by Barbara R. Cotton, Jacksonville, FL, May 25, 1980.

104. Klan making donation to Nelson Chapel and speaking to congregation: interview with Joseph Howard Griffin, conducted by Barbara R. Cotton, Bainbridge, GA, October 20, 1979 (with assistance of Mary Griffin Richardson).

107. All information on Edith Richardson Pearson's nursing school days and career as a nurse: from author's recollections of conversations with his mother.

107. Financing of Meharry's move to north side of Nashville: Cobb, "The Black American in Medicine," *op. cit.*, p. 1223.

107. Background of H. L. Pearson, Sr.: from numerous discussions between author and his father.

108. Average acceptance rate of Meharry Medical College by end of 1940s: "Report on Conference at Atlanta University on Problems of Medical Care for the Negro in the South," April 22–23, 1948, contained in Robert C. Mizell papers, housed in Special Collections Department, Robert C. Woodruff Library, Emory University, Atlanta.

109. Average acceptance rate for medical school applicants nationally by end of

1940s: "Choice of a Medical School," prepared by the Council on Medical Education and Hospitals of the American Medical Association, July 1951, p. 5.

109. Characteristics of H. L. Pearson, Sr., as teacher in Perry, GA: from numerous discussions author conducted with his father; from numerous interviews with Mamie Pearson Jordan, telephone and in person, Kansas City, MO, June 1997; from numerous discussions author has had with Lavester Pearson Rutland, Atlanta, GA.

109. Meharry training most of Negro medical doctors in the South: Cobb, "Progress and Portents, *op. cit.*, p. 116.

109. Howard catching up with Meharry in overall number of graduates: *ibid.*, p. 120.

110. By the end of the 1940s only 10 percent of Negro medical graduates were from predominantly Caucasian schools: *ibid.*, p. 109.

110. M.D.s awarded annually and ratios of M.D.s to population: *ibid.*, p. 109; "Report on Conference at Atlanta University on Problems of Medical Care for the Negro in the South," *op. cit.*

110. Meharry clinical teaching facilities in late 1940s, early 1950s: statement of Dr. Murray C. Brown, Director of Medical Education and Medical Director of Hubbard Hospital at Meharry Medical College, before U.S. Senate Subcommittee on Veterans Affairs, considering proposed Booker T. Washington VA Hospital, Washington, D.C., February 10, 1948, p. 143; telephone interview with Dr. H. L. Pearson, August 25, 1998; *American Medical Directory, 1955* (AMA Press, 1955), pp. 1090, 1877.

110. Rockefeller and Kellogg foundations reluctant to continue closing deficit at Meharry: from correspondence in a letter to Meharry alumni, written by President M. Don Clawson, dated June 4, 1948, contained in private papers of Dr. W. Montague Cobb, Moorland-Spingarn Research Center, Howard University, Washington, D.C.

110. Various proposals for dealing with financial crisis at Meharry: "The Meharry Story," by Louis J. Bernard, M.D., in *A Century of Black Surgeons*, Vol. 1, edited by Claude H. Organ, M.D., and Margaret M. Kosiba, R.N. (Transcript Press, 1987), pp. 135–136.

111. Meharry offering itself as regional southern medical school for Negroes: from correspondence in a letter to Meharry alumni, *op. cit.*

111. Meharry approved to receive financial support as Southern Regional School for Negroes: further statement of the Reverend G. Lake Imes before U.S. Senate Subcommittee on Veterans Affairs, considering proposed Booker T. Washington VA Hospital, Washington, D.C., February 10, 1948, p. 164; telephone interview with Dr. H. L. Pearson, August 25, 1998.

111. Meharry hiring Caucasian adjuncts from Vanderbilt: statement of Dr. Murray C. Brown, *op. cit.*, pp. 142–144; *Balm in Gilead: Journey of a Healer*, by Sara Lawrence-Lightfoot (Penguin Books, 1995), pp. 254–255.

111. Meharry often paying Vanderbilt adjuncts more than full-time Negro faculty: *ibid.*

111. Meharry and Howard faculty during segregation subjecting their students to more authoritarian treatment than at other schools: *ibid.* pp. 252–253; telephone interview with Dr. H. L. Pearson, August 25, 1998; interview with Dr. LaSalle Leffall, Howard University Hospital, Washington, D.C., July 11, 1998.

112. Meharry physicians' obsession with money: *ibid.*, pp. 255–256.

112. Marvin Griffin running gubernatorial campaign based on defiance of *Brown v. Board of Education:* contained in campaign literature found in private papers of Marvin Griffin, housed at Bainbridge Junior College, Bainbridge, GA.

113. Marvin Griffin and Harold West corresponding on the importance of Joseph Griffin's hospital: letter from West to Governor Griffin dated June 16, 1955, contained in private papers of Marvin Griffin, housed at Bainbridge Junior College, Bainbridge, GA.

113. H. L. Pearson, Sr., meeting Joseph Griffin for the first time and being advised against coming to Bainbridge: telephone interview with author, June 18, 1998.

113. David Griffin getting almost no breathing room from brother: interview with Elaine Richardson Smith, Jacksonville, FL, September 21, 1996; Ehrlich interview, June 26, 1997.

114. Dr. and Mrs. Pearson's wedding, honeymoon, journey to Lansing, MI: telephone interview with H. L. Pearson, Sr., June 18, 1998; numerous discussions between author and father through the years.

114. Elaine Richardson Smith's post–high school education and work at Griffin Hospital and Clinic: telephone interview with Elaine Richardson Smith, August 16, 1998.

114. Barbara R. Cotton's post–high school education and career: from numerous conversations with Ms. Cotton through the years.

114. Joseph Griffin's claim that he financed construction of a second hospital through investment in government bonds: Cotton, *Non Verba Opera, op. cit.*, p. 38.

115. Joe Griffin's allegedly acquiring real estate solely through wise investing of what money his patients could pay and working on homes in early morning: *ibid.*, pp. 34–35.

115. Segregated practices of Bainbridge Memorial Hospital and Riverside Hospital: interview with Dr. Frank Gibson, Bainbridge, GA, July 16, 1998.

115. Characteristics of Griffin Hospital and Clinic and Joseph Griffin as a physician: Cotton, *Non Verba Opera, op. cit.*, pp. 40–56.

117. John A. Andrew Clinical Society beginning postgraduate seminars in 1921: "John A. Andrew Memorial Hospital," by Eugene H. Dibble, Jr., M.D., and Ruth Ballard, *Journal of the National Medical Association*, March 1961, Vol. 53, No. 2, p. 109.

117. Joe Griffin serving as president of the John A. Andrew Clinical Society in 1937: Cotton, *Non Verba Opera, op. cit.*, p. 36.

117. Charles Drew's death: *One Blood: The Death and Resurrection of Charles R. Drew,* by Spencie Love (University of North Carolina Press, 1996), pp. 17–23.

117. Joe Griffin cofounding Southwestern Medical Association: Cotton, *Non Verba Opera, op. cit.*, p. 34.

117. *Pittsburgh Courier* article on Joe Griffin and his hospital: "Dr. Joseph Griffin: Giant of the Southland," by Trezzvant W. Anderson, *Pittsburgh Courier*, November 4, 1961.

117. Article on Joe Griffin and his hospital in *Our World*: "Georgia Pioneer," *Our World*, March 6, 1951.

119. Dr. F. Earl McClendon seeking money for equipping his hospital from Robert W. Woodruff: from letter to Robert W. Woodruff on behalf of Dr. McClendon, written by Robert C. Mizell, housed among Robert C. Mizell Papers in Special Collections Department, Robert W. Woodruff Library, Emory University, Atlanta.

119. Statistics on the health care situation for Negroes in Atlanta: *Report on Hospital Care and the Plight of the Negro*, produced by the Atlanta Urban League, 1948, housed among Robert C. Mizell Papers in Special Collections Department, Robert W. Woodruff Library, Emory University, Atlanta.

120. McClendon and Harris Hospital bed capacities by 1958: *American Medical Directory*, 20th ed., 1958 (American Medical Association, 1958), p. 472.

CHAPTER 7

122. Bertram Ehrlich and others in the 1950 minstrel show: "Minstrel Set for Monday and Tuesday," by B. A. Ehrlich, Publicity Chairman, *Bainbridge Post-Searchlight*, October 5, 1950.

125. Joseph Griffin listed by *Pittsburgh Courier* as a Top Ten Georgia Leader: Cotton, *Non Verba Opera, op. cit.*, p. 111.

125. Joseph Griffin in book *Distinguished Negro Georgians: Distinguished Negro Georgians,* by Cornelius Troupe (Royal Publishing Company, 1962).

125. All background information on Louis T. Wright: "Louis Tompkins Wright, 1891–1952," by W. Montague Cobb, M.D., in *Journal of the National Medical Association,* March 1953, Vol. 45, No. 2, pp. 130–148; "The Harlem Hospital Story," by Harold P. Freeman M.D., in *A Century of Black Surgeons,* Vol. 1, *op. cit.,* pp. 152–170; "Louis T. Wright," in *Contemporary Black Biography,* Volume 4, edited by Barbara C. Bigelow (Gale Research, Inc., 1993), p. 283; "Surgeons to the Poor," by Aubre de L. Maynard, M.D. (Appleton-Century-Crofts, 1978), p. 96; *The Harlem Hospital Story: 100 Years of Struggle Against Illness, Racism and Genocide,* by A. Peter Bailey (Native Son Publishers, 1991).

133. Only in ophthalmology and otolaryngology were there specialty boards in 1930: Bernard, "Meharry Story," *op. cit.,* p. 114.

133. Joseph Griffin's pending financial contribution to Meharry: based on letter from J. H. Griffin to Meharry president Lloyd C. Elam, M.D., dated May 12, 1970; based on photograph with caption entitled "Philanthropist—Dr. J. H. Griffin," featured in the *Philadelphia Afro-American,* June 17, 1972; based on telephone conversation with Mike Count, of the Trust Department, Nationsbank, Savannah, GA, January 11, 1999; calculation of current projected worth of pending donation based on estimate provided by Cathy Del Toro, Investor Relations Department, Coca-Cola Company, December 22, 1998.

CHAPTER 8

141. Joe Perry's background, experiences, and relations with his grandfather: interview with Joe Perry, Bainbridge, GA, July 21, 1997.

145. Mary Louise Griffin Perry's reminiscences: interview of Mary Louise Griffin Perry, Bainbridge, GA, July 21, 1997.

147. Comments of Barbara R. Cotton: conversation with Barbara R. Cotton, Tallahassee, FL, July 21, 1997.

148. Interview with Bill Austin, Joe Perry, and Mary Louise Griffin Perry: Bainbridge, GA, July 24, 1997.

153. Interview with Eunice Hinds-Adams: Bainbridge, GA, July 26, 1997.

157. Account of automobile incident in Blakely: interview with Mary Louise Griffin Perry, Bainbridge, GA, August 21, 1998.

159. Remembrances of "Ma" Griffin: discussion with Mary Agnes Gant, Bainbridge, GA, July 26, 1997.

162. Geographic explanation for economic backwardness of sub-Saharan Africa: first presented by economist Thomas Sowell of the Hoover Institute at Stanford University, Palo Alto, CA.

162. Background of Hosea Williams: *Pillar of Fire: American in the King Years,* by Taylor Branch (Simon and Schuster, 1998; First Touchstone Edition, 1999), pp. 124–126.

164. Interview with Hosea Williams: Atlanta, GA, February 14, 1998.

CHAPTER 9

169. Joe Griffin's landlord/tenant disputes: contained in documents on the case against him from the Office of Price Administration, 1943, and U.S. District Court, Middle District of Georgia, 1943; stored in Federal Archive Center, East Point, GA.

172. Joe Griffin's security deed practices: all cases are contained in deed record books stored at Decatur County Courthouse, Bainbridge, GA.

175. Joe Griffin's speech before students at Fort Valley State College: Cotton, *Non Verba Opera op. cit.,* pp. 92–96.

176. Insurance case against Joe Griffin and H. G. Pughsley: contained in documents on the case from U.S. District Court, Middle District of Georgia, dated 1952, stored at Federal Archives Center, East Point, GA.

177. Information on Dr. E. A. R. Lord: interview with Bertram Ehrlich, Atlanta, GA, June 26, 1997; documentation stored in Probate Court, Bainbridge, GA.

CHAPTER 10

180. History of abortion in the U.S.: *Doctors of Conscience: The Struggle to Provide Abortion Before and After Roe v. Wade,* by Carole Joffe (Beacon Press, 1995), pp. 27–52; *Abortion: A Reference Handbook,* 2nd ed., by Marie Costa (ABC-Clio, 1996), p. 10.

183. The lengths to which women would go to abort their unwanted pregnancies: Joffe, *Doctors of Conscience, op. cit.,* pp. 53–69; *The Healers,* by Anonymous M.D. (G. P. Putnam's Sons, 1967), pp. 175–186.

184. Abortion methods: Joffe, *Doctors of Conscience, op. cit.,* pp. 53–93; contained in court case documents related to 1956 abortion trial of Dr. Alpha O. Campbell, Leon County Courthouse, Tallahassee, FL.

186. Comments of Dr. Carl Gordon: interview with author, Albany, GA, October 9, 1997.

187. Illegal abortion deaths in 1940: "Induced Termination of Pregnancy Before and After *Roe v. Wade:* Trends in the Mortality and Morbidity of Women," by the Council on Scientific Affairs of the AMA, in *Journal of the American Medical Association,* December 9, 1992, Vol. 268, Issue 22, pp. 3231–3239.

188. Back-alley abortionists' methodology for bringing women to them: based on readings in Joffe, *Doctors of Conscience, op. cit.,* NOTE: Quote of prospective abortionist based on actual case reported in the aforementioned book; conversation with Dr. Carl Gordon.

189. Comments of Dr. Henry Bridges: interview with author, Bainbridge, GA, July 17, 1998.

189. Comments of Dr. Frank Gibson: interview with author, Bainbridge, GA, July 16, 1998.

189. Comments of Dr. LaSalle Leffall: interview with author, Howard University Hospital, Washington, D.C., July 11, 1998.

190. Comments of Barbara and William Cotton: conversation with author, July 21, 1997.

190. Comments of Dr. A. D. Brickler: interview with author, Tallahassee, FL, July 22, 1997.

190. Revelations about the abortions as reason H. L. Pearson didn't come to Bainbridge to practice medicine: telephone interview with Dr. H. L. Pearson, July 5, 1997.

190. Elaine Richardson Smith's revelation about watching an abortion at Griffin Hospital: telephone interview with Elaine Richardson Smith, August 16, 1998.

191. Ruby Jo Bryant Overart case: "Details Unfolded in Abortion Case," by Wiley Masters, *Albany Herald,* April 1, 1953; "Mrs. Conoly Gets Two to Four Year Sentence in Murder Case," by Wiley Masters, *Albany Herald,* April 2, 1953.

193. Dr. William Reese case: "Abortion Case Gets Under Way in Court Here," *Albany Herald,* April 27, 1953; "Juries Free Negro Doctor; Child Case Plea Is Made," *Albany Herald,* April 28, 1953.

193. Audrie Franich case: contained in court case documents related to 1956 abortion trial of Dr. Alpha O. Campbell, Leon County Courthouse, Tallahassee, FL.

194. Background of Dr. Alpha O. Campbell: *ibid.;* "The Rise and Fall of Alpha Omega Campbell," by Keith Thomas, *Tallahassee Democrat,* May 15, 1994.

195. M.O. for abortion patients who went to Dr. Campbell and experience of the

Pyles: contained in court case documents related to 1956 abortion trial of Dr. Alpha O. Campbell, *op. cit.*

196.   Joe Griffin's accolades: Cotton, *Non Verba Opera, op. cit.* p. 111.

198.   Details of Lois Brown case: "Coed Testifies at Trial of Bainbridge Negro Doctor," by Mary F. Donalson, *Albany Herald*, November 13, 1968; "Bainbridge Negro Doctor Guilty on Abortion Charge," by Mary F. Donalson, *Albany Herald*, November 13, 1968; "Bainbridge Negro Doctor Fined, Put on Probation," *Albany Herald*, May 13, 1969.

198.   Details of Melissa Cain case: based on affidavit from Ms. Cain, dated November 19, 1968, contained in documents related to the abortion trial of Dr. J. H. Griffin, housed in Decatur County Courthouse, Bainbridge, GA.

CHAPTER 11

200.   Account of Paul Kwilecki: based on interview with author, Bainbridge, GA, May 1, 1998.

CHAPTER 12

206.   Surveillance of Griffin Hospital and Clinic: details contained in documents related to the abortion trial of Dr. J. H. Griffin, housed in Decatur County Courthouse, Bainbridge, GA.

206.   Details of patients' illnesses: contained in motion to admit to bail filed on behalf of Dr. J. H. Griffin, November 9, 1967, housed in Decatur County Courthouse, Bainbridge, GA.

206.   Statistics on Decatur County demographics: *ibid.*

207.   All details on trial of Dr. Griffin and outcome: "Bainbridge Negro Physician Is Indicted," by Mary F. Donalson, *Albany Herald*, November 9, 1967; "Indicted Physician Hospitalized," *Albany Herald*, November 10, 1967; "Attorneys for Dr. Griffin Seek Continuance of Case," *Albany Herald*, November 14, 1967; "Doctor's Trial Gets Under Way in Bainbridge," *Albany Herald*, November 12, 1968; Donalson, "Coed Testifies at Trial of Bainbridge Negro Doctor," *op. cit.*; Donalson "Bainbridge Negro Doctor Guilty on Abortion Charge,"*op. cit.*; "Doctor Acquitted in Decatur Trial," by Mary F. Donalson, *Albany Herald*, November 15, 1968; "Murder Trial Gets Under Way in Bainbridge," *Albany Herald*, November 20, 1968; "Negro Physician: Witnesses Snarl Griffin Case," by Mary F. Donalson, *Albany Herald*, November 21, 1968; "Bainbridge Jury Acquits Doctor of Murder Charge," *Albany Herald*, November 22, 1968; "Remaining Cases Against Negro Doctor Are Dropped," *Albany Herald*, December 3, 1968; "Bainbridge Negro Doctor Fined, Put on Probation," *op. cit.*

207.   Donald L. Hollowell called in, Hollowell's background and relationship to Dr. Griffin, and background of C. B. King: interview with Donald Hollowell, Atlanta, GA, October 7, 1997; narrative of *The Sacred Call: A Tribute to Donald L. Hollowell, Civil Rights Champion,* by Louise Hollowell and Martin C. Lehfeldt (Four-G Publishers, 1997).

210.   Interview of Dr. Louis Sullivan, and his background: Atlanta, GA, July 22, 1997; *African American Medical Pioneers,* by Charles H. Epps, M.D., David G. Johnson, M.D., and Audrey L. Vaughan, M.D. (Betz Publishing, 1994), pp. 113–115.

212.   LaSalle Leffall's background: *ibid.*, pp. 81–84.

212.   W. Montague Cobb's comments about Dr. Leffall: *Nine Negro Doctors*, by Robert C. Hayden and Jacqueline Parks (Addison-Wesley, 1976), pp. 174–175.

212.   Dr. Leffall's reminiscences of Dr. Griffin: interview with Dr. Leffall, Howard University Hospital, Washington, D.C., July 11, 1998.

EPILOGUE

222. Discussion with Julian Braswell: Bainbridge, GA, August 21, 1998.

224. Interview with Cheney Griffin: Bainbridge, GA, February 24, 1998.

225. Cheney allegedly giving new meaning to the term "spoils system": "Marvin Griffin and the Politics of the Stump," by Robert W. Dubay in *Georgia Governors in the Age of Change: From Ellis Arrnall to George Busbee*, edited by Harold P. Henderson and Gary L. Roberts (University of Georgia Press, 1988), p. 105.

226. Discussion with Mary Louise Griffin Perry: Bainbridge, GA, August 21, 1998.

ACKNOWLEDGMENTS

First, I'd like to thank my aunt Dr. Barbara Richardson Cotton for laying the groundwork for this book. Without her initial research and writing and the several interviews she conducted with Dr. Joseph Howard Griffin for her 1981 book *Non Verba Opera: Not Words, but Works* this book would not have been possible, since I lacked the foresight and knowledge to embark on an investigation of how our uncle was able to become all that he became. It is obvious that she wrote her book to satisfy him. Most of us simply cannot be completely candid about ourselves, which is why autobiographies and cooperative biographies often are not the best sources of information on a person. But that doesn't mean they aren't useful at all. The perspective of the person being written about is crucial to a complete picture of that individual. And as I combed through speeches delivered by my great-uncle, I regretted that I couldn't include in the narrative of this book all of his insights regarding the predicament of Afro-Americans. Despite the questionable nature of much of what he did, it is obvious that, with regard to all the positive contributions he made in his life, as one of my interviewees, Mrs. Eunice Hinds-Adams stated, he was a man way ahead of his time, and what he believed about Afro-American preparedness for the future is a lesson that still bears repeating.

Next, I must thank Dr. Griffin's daughter, my cousin Mrs. Mary Louise Griffin Perry, for lending her assistance to the extent she could, but, more important, for not blocking what I was attempting to do, as she could have. It was not my intention to hurt her in any way by writing this book. However, I have always felt that fealty to the truth was of the utmost importance and that loyalty to family must take a backseat, since, as the narrative makes clear, I'm convinced that too often families refuse to step back and attempt any objective analysis of their place in society. Yet this is no argument against attempting honesty and candor in a project such as this, since I feel it is our duty to posterity to describe our lives as truthfully as possible. Next, I must thank my father, Dr. Huey L. Pearson, for planting the seed that caused this book to be written. Though, ultimately, it grew into something he didn't originally have in mind, I probably would have never embarked on writing it without his desire for posterity to hear his story. I thank my aunt Mrs. Mamie Pearson Jordan for her valuable insight into the life of my paternal grandfather, and thank her husband, Mr. Louis Jordan, for the same, and for their hospitality on my visit to Kansas City to hear part of what they had to say. I thank my aunt Mrs. Lavester Pearson Rutland for the insight she provided about my father's side of the family, and for her hospitality during my many trips to Atlanta. I thank my aunt Mrs. Elaine Richardson Smith, who was also crucial to the success of this book. Without the material she sent me and her candor, the book would have lacked a nuanced analysis that her recollections of what it was like working with my great-uncle made possible. Next, I would like to thank Joseph Griffin's grandson, my cousin Joseph Howard Griffin Perry. Without his aid in setting up interviews and his recollections of his grandfather, this book would have come out lacking too much. I would also like to thank my uncle Mr. Crawford C. Richardson, Jr., for valuable insight into the life of my maternal grandfather and thank our cousin Mr. Harold Norris for the same. And I cannot leave out either my cousin Mrs. Mary Agnes Gant for her hospitality, warmth, and humor during many of my visits to Bainbridge, or my aunt Barbara's husband, Mr. William Cotton, for a couple of his insights.

Next I would like to thank Mr. Bertram Ehrlich for volunteering his time and candor before all other nonrelatives. Others who must be singled out are the following people: Mrs. Eunice Hinds-Adams, Mr. Bill Austin, and especially Mr. Hosea Williams and Mr. Paul Kwilecki. Without those two, who were farsighted enough to understand what I was trying to do, this book wouldn't have been anywhere near as perceptive as I hope readers found it. Others who must be singled out include Dr. LaSalle Leffall; Dr. Louis Sullivan; Mr. Donald Hollowell; Dr. Carl Gordon; Dr. A. D. Brickler; Ms. Susan Goodman; Mr. Samuel Griffin; Mr. Cheney Griffin; Dr. Henry Bridges; Dr. Frank Gibson; Mr. Bruce Kirbo; Mr. David Garrow; the staff of the Decatur County (Georgia) Courthouse; the Leon County (Florida) Courthouse; the library staffs of the New York

Academy of Medicine, Bainbridge Junior College, the Special Collections Department at Robert W. Woodruff Library of Emory University, the Moreland-Spingarn Research Center at Howard University, the Alonzo F. Herndon Library in Atlanta; the medical library staff of Harlem Hospital; the Schomburg Center for Research in Black Culture of the New York Public Library System; and the staff at the Federal Archives Center in East Point, Georgia.

Next, I must thank my literary agent, Eric Siminoff of Janklow and Nesbit, for piloting this project through the process of obtaining a book contract, and Adam Bellow and Mitch Horowitz of the Free Press for having the foresight to sign it up. I'd like to thank Elizabeth Maguire and Chad Conway for continuing through with helping prepare the book for publication after Adam Bellow and Mitch Horowitz departed the Free Press and thank Ann T. Keene for copyediting the manuscript. I'd like to thank the Daniel and Joanna S. Rose Fund and the New York Council for the Arts for additional financial support for this project.

I'd also like to thank four people who read portions of this book and/or the jacket copy prior to publication and gave me their opinions: my sister Carol Pearson, Ms. Tonya Douglas, Ms. Jennifer Leigh, and Mr. Carlton Bush.

Most important, I must thank the lovely woman in my life, Nancy Ross, for the tremendous support she provided me during the researching and writing of this book, and for the patience and sacrifices she made caring for our family during my many trips away from home. And I must also thank my children, Jordan, Francesca, and Nathaniel, for being patient during my many absences from home and for providing me with so much delight during the ups and downs of this project. Thank you all.

9/02 7